EXPLORE
PREPARE
SUCCEED

UNIVERSITY OF NORTH CAROLINA - WILMINGTON

Edited By
ERIKA HANSON

Kendall Hunt
publishing company

Cover image © Shutterstock.com

Kendall Hunt
publishing company

www.kendallhunt.com
Send all inquiries to:
4050 Westmark Drive
Dubuque, IA 52004-1840

Published in the United States of America

Reader Organization

- Brown, P. C., Roediger, H. L., & McDaniel, M. A. (2014). *Make it stick: The science of successful learning*. Cambridge, MA: Harvard University Press. (Ch. 1 Learning is misunderstood: p. 1-22).

- Medina, J. (2008). *Brain rules: 12 principles for surviving and thriving at work, home, and school.* Seattle, WA: Pear Press. (Rule 8 Stress: p. 169-196)

Chapter 1

What will you be asked to do in this course?

REFLECTION AND LEARNING FROM EXPERIENCE

Dannelle D. Stevens and Joanne E. Cooper

My journal has become a symbol of independence. It allows me the luxury of time to myself. The journal requirement for this class gave me permission to stop and spend some time on my thoughts. My family would consider journal writing self-absorbed, selfish and a waste of time. I had to over-come and reframe this mindset that has influenced me throughout my life. It was a slow process for me to change my attitude about the importance and utility of the journaling activity. I found that writing in my journal gave me justification to spend time focusing, venting or thinking metacognitively about different aspects of the semester. The professor said it well when she said, "writing is thinking."

Laura, returning graduate student

BEFORE COMPLETING CLASS ASSIGNMENTS IN HER JOURNAL, Laura viewed journal keeping as "self-absorbent." She has modified her prior assumption and now knows the power of journal writing. She connects writing, learning, and reflection. The theoretical foundation for journal writing lies in learning models that place reflection as a centerpiece in learning. Because of the connection between reflection, writing, and learning, we use the work of three well-known learning theorists: John Dewey, David Kolb, and Donald Schön, who all emphasize that reflection is a fundamental component in human learning and development.

Reflection is more than merely thinking or musing (Boud, 2001; Dewey, 1933). Reflection is a complex and intentional intellectual activity that generates learning from experience (Boyd & Fales, 1983). What kind of learning results from reflection? Dewey (1933), a prominent 20th-century educational philosopher, argues that reflective thinking builds the foundation for the furtherance of democratic principles. Kolb (1984) and Schön (1983) assert that reflection helps adults cope with and learn from ill-structured, complex problems in social settings and the work-place. If the potential results of reflective thinking are that adults develop positive democratic attitudes and practices and are more able to address problems in their social and professional lives, then as educators it is important for us to find ways to foster reflection. Journals promote reflection on and learning from experience (Boud, 2001; English & Gillen, 2001; Fulwiler, 1987; Moon, 1999a, 1999b, 2006).

This chapter addresses the following key questions:

- What are the three leading theoretical perspectives on reflection and learning from experience?
- How do these theoretical perspectives link to journal writing?

The purpose of this chapter is to describe and explain how three well-known and respected theorists use reflection in their explorations of human learning and how those theories support the use of journal-writing activities in classroom learning and in professional life.

Three Leading Theoretical Perspectives on Reflection and Learning From Experience

John Dewey (1859–1952): Experience, Reflection, and Learning

As the father of the 20th-century progressive movement in education and an eminent philosopher, John Dewey's work is particularly helpful in defining and describing the relationships among experience, reflection, and learning. Because faculty expect students to learn, especially the knowledge within their respective disciplines, reflection on course readings and field experiences is essential. Across a variety of disciplines, journals are a well-established way to record, reflect, and continue to learn from experience. John Dewey has defined what experiences are educative, how learning proceeds, and what role reflection plays in learning.

Dewey (1933) states that an *experience* is an interaction between the individual and the environment. An experience first includes more than participation in activities; experience could be reading a book, taking lecture notes, or talking with others. Secondly, an experience contains what Dewey referred to as *continuity,* a continuous flow of knowledge from previous experiences. Dewey writes:

> What [a person] has learned in the way of knowledge and skill in one situation becomes an instrument of understanding and dealing effectively with the situations that follow. The process goes on as long as life and learning continue. (1938, p. 44)

Learning, therefore, is a continuous and cumulative process. Prior learning becomes the fodder for further understanding and insight.

In his 1933 work, *How We Think,* Dewey distinguishes between four different modes of thinking: imagination, belief, stream of consciousness, and reflection. Dewey acknowledges that imagination, belief, and stream of consciousness are certainly part of our thinking activities, yet they do not necessarily contribute to learning and even less to lifelong learning. Reflection, however, plays a different role. Dewey defines reflection as the:

> . . . active, persistent and careful consideration of any belief or supposed form of knowledge in light of the grounds that support it and the further conclusions to which it tends. (1933, p. 9)

Reflection is active. When we reflect we examine prior beliefs and assumptions and their implications. Reflection is an intentional action. A "demand for a solution of a perplexity is the steadying, guiding factor in the entire process of reflection" (Dewey, 1933, p. 14). Dewey adds

> The function of reflective thought is, therefore, to transform a situation in which there is experienced obscurity, doubt, conflict, disturbance of some sort into a situation that is clear, coherent, settled, harmonious. (1933, p. 100)

Reflection starts with discomfort during an experience and leads a person to a balanced state. It takes time and focus to reach clarity of thought.

Dewey writes that reflection "gives an individual an increased power of control" (Dewey, 1933, p. 21). It "emancipates us from merely impulsive and merely routine activity. . . . It converts action that is merely appetitive, blind and impulsive into intelligent action" (1933, p. 17). It is not enough just to have an experience. Reflection directs that experience to learning and deeper insights. Many of the journal writers we have interviewed highly value the role of the journal in their thinking and learning. Barbara, professor and college president emerita, describes her journal as a place

> . . . where I can be most fully conscious. I trust that process. My journal is where I am consciously conscious of what it means to be a human being on this earth. It is where I listen to myself. (personal communication, November 19, 2006)

Reflective thinking takes time and requires one to engage in several different "phases" or "aspects" of reflective thought:

1. *Perplexity:* responding to suggestions and ideas that appear when confronted with a problem
2. *Elaboration:* referring to past experiences that are similar
3. *Hypotheses:* developing several potential hypotheses
4. *Comparing hypotheses:* finding some coherence within these hypotheses
5. *Taking action:* experiencing "mastery, satisfaction, enjoyment" when selecting and then acting on these hypotheses (Dewey, 1933, pp. 106–115)

Dewey asserts that these are not steps but aspects of reflective activity. An individual may stop at some point and find it necessary to go back and, for example, collect more experiences.

A key point is that informed action follows this reflective thinking process and leads to more ideas and therefore generates more experience on which to reflect. "Reflective thinking impels to inquiry" (Dewey, 1933, p. 7). Journal writing is particularly helpful in this recursive process of examining and generating ideas to address problems or confusions (Boud & Walker, 1998; English & Gillen, 2001; Kerka, 2002).

In fact, to Dewey, reflective thinking fosters the development of three attitudes that further the "habit of thinking in a reflective way." These three attitudes are:

- Openmindedness (freedom from prejudice)
- Wholeheartedness or absorbed interest
- Responsibility in facing consequences (Dewey, 1933, p. 33)

These dispositions are the foundation for education that gives people "a personal interest in social relationships and control and the habits of mind that secures social changes without introducing disorder" (Dewey, 1944, p. 99).

As in Laura and Barbara's reflections, journal writing gives journal keepers the tools to examine and learn from the life events that swirl around them. Research in a variety of disciplines underscores the powerful role reflective journal writing can play in the adult life. Durgahee (1997) found that when nursing students kept a journal, they continually reflected on the social and personal meanings of interactions in clinical settings. Rodriquez and Sjostrom (1997) helped their student teachers examine their preconceived notions about students of color through a series of journal-keeping activities followed by class discussions. Faculty who assign journals in their classrooms believe that journals help students develop ways to understand their motives, thoughts, and learning, as well as to grapple with many personal dilemmas (Stevens, Cooper, & Lasater, 2006).

Faculty and administrators who keep a journal at work often cite addressing problems as one of its key benefits. They use the journal not only to document and organize the continuous work flow but also to converse with themselves about problems and issues in the workplace (Cooper & Stevens, 2006). Cooper and Dunlap (1991) found that administrators used their journals to examine and reexamine the complex problems in their work settings and to develop deeper understandings. Through written documentation of observations, responses, and insights, adults create fuel for current reflections and for even deeper and broader connections and informed actions in the future.

Dewey's work has been cited in numerous studies as the theoretical ground for reflective journal writing (English & Gillen, 2001; Kerka, 2002). Two other theorists who use reflection in their work, David Kolb (1984) and Donald Schön (1983, 1987), also add to our understanding of the role of reflection in human learning. Kolb describes the elements in the cycle of learning from experience; Schön focuses on the role of reflection in professional practice settings such as education and medicine.

David Kolb (1939–): Reflection and an Experiential Learning Model

David Kolb's (1984) theory of experiential learning elaborates the process by which adults learn from their experience. "The significance of his work may be that he sets experience in a context in learning. He sees it as a reflective process that develops concepts from the medium of experience" (Moon, 1999a, p. 24). Kolb's model (1984) (Figure 2.1) illustrates the four stages of learning from experience: concrete experience, reflective observation, abstract conceptualization, and active experimentation.

The first phase in the Kolb cycle—concrete, "real world" experience—means direct, practical experience that results in "knowledge by acquaintance" as opposed to "knowledge about" something. Concrete experience precedes reflective observation of that experience. The next phase, reflective observation, involves focusing on what that experience means and its connotations in light of past learning. In the third phase, abstract conceptualization, learners relate their reflective observations to what they already know: extant theories, preconceived notions, and embedded assumptions. During active experimentation, the last phase before the cycle begins again, the learner applies new concepts and theories to the real world.

For Kolb (1984), learning is a cycle that perpetuates more learning. "The learner moves 'from actor to observer' from 'specific involvement to general analytic detachment,' creating a new form of experience on which to reflect. The quality of reflection is crucial in ensuring that the learner does progress in [his or her] learning" (Moon, 1999b, p. 25). Reflection is the engine that moves the learning cycle along its path to further learning, action, and more reflection. Without it, the learner is "stuck" in the experience without gaining any new understanding.

Kolb did not address journal writing per se as a reflective tool. Yet the journal offers a unique opportunity to chronicle and examine more closely and carefully our concrete experiences, and then to ask the hard questions about how these experiences relate to what is already known. When students or faculty keep a journal, they are capturing a concrete experience in a written form. During writing, journal writers can readily examine their concrete experiences, and even step back and reflect on how those observations might relate to other experiences. To extend the learning further, during abstract conceptualization the writing can be reread and analyzed for underlying assumptions and beliefs that contribute to positive outcomes (Boud, 2001; Brook-field, 1995; Hatcher & Bringle, 1997). According to Kolb's theory, then, journal writers can actively experiment with the ideas that motivate their actions and thus approach new experiences with fresh insights and the possibility for new learning.

Faculty who require students to complete service learning projects often have students record their observations in a log or a journal that is used for class discussion and reflection (Eyler, 2002; Hatcher & Bringle, 1997). "Service learning extends the classroom into the community, and students frequently encounter unfamiliar situations that challenge and contradict their perspectives" (Hatcher & Bringle, 1997, p. 154). Using Kolb's model and a written "values clarification" activity, Hatcher and Bringle helped students express and analyze their perspectives during a service learning assignment.

When students are involved in a service learning activity at a homeless shelter, for example, an instructor might assign the students to list the words or phrases that describe their senses, feelings, and actions in this site. These are their reflective observations. Then, after this brainstorming activity, they might write about their overall impressions and thoughts about the homeless as well as identify the contradictions and challenges to their prior assumptions. These activities encourage students to unlock and examine their abstract conceptualizations that were closely held assumptions about the homeless. Using these journal entries in small-group or whole-class discussion informs the students' future active experimentation on these ideas at the homeless shelter service site.

Many examples of the use of journals in field settings appear in the nursing education literature. Research on preservice nurses who journal during their initial service learning and clinical experience has shown that their written observations of concrete experience are a critical underpinning for reflective observations of all the experience and knowledge they bring to the clinical setting (Craft, 2005;

Durgahee, 1998; Eyler, 2002). To move students to a deeper examination of course content, as well as to persuade students to grapple with their preexisting beliefs and unexamined assumptions, faculty often make comments in the margins of student journals. By asking questions and linking student journal reflections to course material, faculty can begin a written conversation with the student (Durgahee, 2002; Shuttloffel, 2005; Stevens, Cooper, & Lasater, 2006).

In summary, these service learning and clinical setting examples highlight the fact that merely exposing students to a new off-campus experience is not enough. For students to uproot and dissect their prior knowledge and preconceived notions, to foster integration of new insights, and to boost the overall effects of clinical experience, service learning, and community projects, faculty must guide their students through a reflective activity. A journal is an appropriate location for documenting experience, generating reflections, and examining assumptions. Boyd and Fales further argue that reflective learning is the

> . . . core difference between whether a person repeats the same experience several times, becoming highly proficient at one behavior, or learns from experience in such a way that he or she is cognitively or effectively changed. Such a change involves essentially changing his or her meaning structures. (1983, p. 100)

Kolb's work elaborates a cycle of learning that leads to informed future action. Another theorist, Donald Schön, describes the power of two different kinds of reflection to develop expertise in professional practice fields such as education and medicine.

D. A. Schön (1930–1997): Reflection and Professional Practice

Schön (1983, 1987) was interested in how and when professionals use reflection to build professional knowledge and expertise. Schön's work appeals to professionals who teach professionals because he distinguishes between the static knowledge found in textbooks and the dynamic, adaptive knowledge that the expert uses in clinical and professional settings. To bridge this gap, preservice professionals need guided practice. Given the dynamic, complex, and unstructured settings in which professionals work, developing reflective capacity is essential.

Schön's initial work (1983) was geared toward those who educate professionals. He asserts that in the past, professional practice programs have delineated the profession's "espoused theories" to novices. Yet these theories may make sense in the textbooks but may not actually be applied in daily practice. The theories that guide daily decision making, the "theories-in-use," are contextually specific, idiosyncratic, and often not mentioned in textbooks of professional practice. Over and over again the theories-in-use are tested and developed to become proven, sometimes even unconscious, ways of performing. One of Schön's central concerns is how to help novices learn the theories used by experts in real life settings.

Schön describes two processes that contribute to the development of expertise: reflection-in-action and reflection-on-action. Professionals reflect while they are engaged in an experience (reflection-in-action) and after an experience (reflection-on-action). In this process of reflection, novice professionals develop the theories-in-use that underlie competent, expert decision making.

Research indicates that the nursing and education fields have frequently used reflective journal writing to help professionals develop theories-in-use (Boud &

Walker, 1998; Brookfield, 1995; Craft, 2005; Durgahee, 1998). Gil-Garcia and Cintron (2002) analyzed the journals of 35 teachers and administrators over 2 years for their value as a reflective tool. The predominant topics of reflective journaling were analysis of teaching actions, introspection of the teaching or administrating decisions, and testing of ways to adapt and modify lessons. The participants in the study concluded that their journals were beneficial. As one participant noted, "I will continue to keep a journal where I can review my classroom activities and my students' reactions because that helps me keep in touch with what I am doing and keep an eye on improving my teaching" (Gil-Garcia & Cintron, 2002, p. 7).

For most professionals, the journal is a reflection-on-action zone allowing them to slow down the constant array of demands, scrutinize their actions, and determine whether their present activities contribute in the long run to their goals and desires. Thus the journal can become a place where professionals can develop the ability to identify tacit, unspoken knowledge that is not typically taught. Many professional preparation programs have relied on Schön's work to guide their use of journal-writing activities.

How These Theoretical Perspectives Link to Journal Writing

Through the reflective activity of journal writing, the writer records, examines, and learns from experience. Reflection is a critical and central construct in Dewey, Kolb, and Schön's theories. Analysis and comparison of their theories leads to the following themes.

- Reflection occurs in a cycle of action–reflection–action.
- Reflection contributes to the development of valued human capabilities.

How Does Reflection Occur? The Action–Reflection–Action Cycle

Reflection occurs in a cycle of action, reflection, and action. Dewey, Kolb, and Schön included reflection in at least one step in their theories on learning from experience. For all three, reflection is not isolated from experience; it is part of a cycle of learning and experiencing. Dewey described "aspects" of reflection. Kolb described "phases." Schön divided reflection into two parts: reflection "in" and "on" action. All include experience followed by reflection and the generation of hypotheses or experimental conclusions that are applied to further experience. For each, learning from experience requires shuttling back and forth from observations, to examination and reflection on those observations, and then acting on those conclusions. The more people reflect on action, the better they get at reflecting and the more they can learn about themselves (Boyd & Fales, 1983; Fulwiler, 1987; Rainer, 1978; Valli, 1993).

Journal writing promotes a cycle of reflection, experience, reflection, and ultimately learning through observation of the self in action. When faculty ask students to summarize and respond to a class reading in their journals, several things happen. First, students have to review, select, and organize what they have read and then put their reactions into their own words. This should be an engaging and active learning activity. In one of our surveys of student response to journal writing, we found that 94% of students felt that journal writing helped them to track their learning, and 98% considered writing a reflection on all their journal entries at the end of the term to be a valuable activity as well (Stevens & Cooper, 2007). Because the entries are dated, journal writers can track the development of their thinking and insights over time. Journal entries can be reread, reviewed, and reexamined at different times. Reflecting on past journal entries affirms that one can learn from experience and can allow the journal writer to witness a developing self.

Why Is Reflection Worthwhile?
Development of Valued Human Capabilities

Through the development of reflective capacity and the habit of reflective thinking the student or professional achieves certain broader, more lasting outcomes as well. Dewey (1933) asserts that reflection is the foundation for democracy through developing the capacity for openmindedness, wholeheartedness, and responsibility. Kolb's (1984) theory shows how important it is to assess our basic beliefs that may blind us to new knowledge. Finally, Schön's model (1987) leads the professional to becoming an expert.

Journal writing over time can lead to the development of these valued outcomes. Written reflections are more than a mirror of experience. Because perceptions and insights based on reflections can be distorted by prior knowledge and beliefs, writing these reflections down and reviewing them allows the journal writer to scrutinize assumptions and beliefs and glean a deeper understanding of the assumptions that underlie their decision making. Learning how to learn, how to examine assumptions, how to abstract key ideas from experience, and how to feed those ideas back into our next experience are valued human activities that may lead to those qualities that Dewey propounds: openness, absorbed interest, and responsibility. Journal-writing activities document the thinking and observations of writers, allow writers to go back and review their thinking, acknowledge their own misconceptions, and adjust their thinking accordingly.

Conclusion

Journal writing can be justified from a variety of theoretical perspectives. This chapter introduces three theories that can be used to justify journal keeping as a reflective activity. Three classic theorists, Dewey, Kolb, and Schön, use reflection as the engine that drives their theories of human learning. Journal writing has a place in each one of these theories because it reinforces and boosts learning whether it is in the context of social settings, service learning sites, or professional practice programs. In the next chapter we explore another set of theories that interface well with journal writing, those associated with adult development, transformational learning, and personal development.

Table 2.1 summarizes this chapter's key themes and shows how these themes are manifested in classrooms and in professional life. In the last column on the right, we have added some specific assignments that demonstrate how this theme might be realized in classroom journal-writing assignments.

Discussion Questions

Before you begin the reading - What do you already know about journaling or writing reflections? How has journaling or writing reflections impacted your learning in the past?

Choose one of the theorists mentioned (Kolb, Dewey, Schön) and summarize the impact they believe reflection has on learning.

What differences and similarities do you see between your experience/knowledge of reflecting and those of the theorist you chose?

How might you incorporate reflection regularly in your life? How might you benefit?

WHAT IS CRITICAL THINKING?

Stephen D. Brookfield

As a reader and a working classroom teacher I always appreciate a chapter, or even a book, that starts by telling me what I'm going to be reading in the next few pages. That way, if it's of no interest to me I can skip it and spend my time doing something more useful or pleasurable (hopefully both). So let me begin this introduction by saying that in this chapter I want to introduce what I understand as the basic process of critical thinking. This entails (1) identifying the assumptions that frame our thinking and determine our actions, (2) checking out the degree to which these assumptions are accurate and valid, (3) looking at our ideas and decisions (intellectual, organizational, and personal) from several different perspectives, and (4) on the basis of all this, taking informed actions. I also propose a basic typology of different kinds of assumptions that critical thinking unearths and scrutinizes—paradigmatic, prescriptive, and causal.

I'm also using this chapter to make some strong claims about critical thinking. I argue that if you can't think critically your survival is in peril because you risk living a life that—without your being aware of it—hurts you and serves the interests of those who wish you harm. If you can't think critically you have no chance of recognizing, let alone pushing back on, those times you are being manipulated. And if you can't think critically you will behave in ways that have less chance of achieving the results you want. So critical thinking is not just an academic process that leads to good scores on SATs, elegantly argued essays, or experimental hypotheses that can stand the toughest scrutiny. It is a way of living that helps you stay intact when any number of organizations (corporate, political, educational, and cultural) are trying to get you to think and act in ways that serve their purposes.

How Critical Thinking Saved My Life

As a way of leading into these ideas I want to begin on a personal note by showing how critical thinking saved my life. A few years ago I was at rock bottom emotionally. I was one of the 20 million Americans diagnosed with clinical depression and anxiety, convinced most days that I was on the verge of death and feeling worthless and ashamed about my inability to control my state of mind. I spent a great deal of energy hiding my depression as best I could from family, friends, and colleagues, and steadfastly refused to seek medical help. Since, objectively, I had nothing to be depressed about (I had a job I loved and a loving family) my response to my depression was to tell myself to snap out of it. I believed the way to beat depression was to reason my way through it, to tell myself that since there was no earthly reason I should be depressed, I ought to just stop being that way. My depression's persistence and debilitating effect were heightened dramatically because I wasn't thinking critically about it. Once I started to do this, things improved dramatically. So, I begin this chapter with a bold statement; the ability to think critically about one's assumptions, beliefs, and actions is a survival necessity.

I've written about this period of depression in much greater detail elsewhere (Brookfield, 2011) and this may be entirely too much information about me for you to digest so early! If that's the case, then skip this introductory section and go to the next section, Hunting Assumptions. If you're still with me I want to focus on just one point—what was getting in the way of my dealing with my depression was my inability to think critically about it. What I mean by that is that I refused to consider the possibility that any of my assumptions regarding my depression were wrong. For example, I assumed that the right way to deal with depression was to think your way out of it. I assumed that depression was a sign of weakness, unless external circumstances (such as divorce, being fired, or the death of a loved one) warranted it. Because I assumed I was weak, I assumed I needed to hide my condition from peers and colleagues. More fundamentally, I assumed that if I was a real man I would be able just to stare this condition down and force myself out of it by an act of will. I assumed it was up to me to "dig deep" (as the sports cliché has it) and dredge up the mental strength to beat it.

Some of the assumptions I've just outlined were on the surface and were reasonably easy to identify. These mostly had to do with how I understand cause and effect. For example, I reasoned that depression was caused by external circumstances and therefore, since my circumstances were good, it was a mistake to be depressed. The assumption that by engaging in intentional self-talk ("come on now, don't be ridiculous, it's all in your head, you are in great shape, there's no reason at all to feel the way you do") I could move beyond depression was also causal. Causal assumptions can always be stated as cause and effect linkages, as in "if I do A, then B will happen." Hence, they are both explanatory and predictive. They explain why the past happened by establishing the causes of particular events. They predict the future by positing what will be the consequences and effects of certain decisions.

Some of the assumptions about depression I reviewed were more about how good professionals (which is how I thought of myself) are supposed to behave. These were prescriptive assumptions. Prescriptive assumptions are assumptions we hold about what are desirable ways of thinking or acting. They can usually be recognized by their inclusion of the word *should,* as in "a good professional should be able to respond to cultural diversity," or "a good marriage is one in which partners can be totally honest with each other." Prescriptive assumptions state what a good friendship or relationship looks like, what should be the characteristics of a truly democratic decision, or how social resources should be allocated. I held a prescriptive assumption that a normal, fully functioning person copes well with life and doesn't get depressed. I believed that good professionals don't let irrational feelings of depression, worthlessness, or shame dominate their lives.

The third type of assumptions I held about depression was harder for me to uncover and challenge. These assumptions lay deeper within my mental structures and were not immediately apparent to me. They were so much a part of my outlook, and so central to my self-identity, that when they were pointed out to me as being assumptions I was tempted to reply, "that's not an assumption, that's reality." Specifically, I assumed that a fully functioning man is logical, clear-headed, and determined, a sort of steely-jawed, no nonsense mental equivalent of an early Clint Eastwood character, or Howard Roark in Ayn Rand's *The Fountainhead.* Although I would have strenuously denied it at the time, I had assumed that the ideology of patriarchy—the belief that men are governed by reason, women by emotion, and therefore that men's powers of rationality equip them to be natural leaders—was correct. As I say, this was not an assumption I held consciously. It was much more subtle than that; it had wormed its way into my consciousness, so to speak. I call this kind of assumption a paradigmatic assumption.

Paradigmatic assumptions are the deeply held assumptions that frame the whole way we look at the world. When we discover paradigmatic assumptions it often comes as a shock. In the case of depression I had no real awareness of just how strongly I had successfully internalized the assumptions of patriarchy. Patriarchy views men as natural leaders and decision makers because they are guided by reason and logic, unlike women who are regarded as being guided by irrational emotion. Patriarchy says that a "real" man has no need for drugs to fight depression and, moreover, that a real man doesn't suffer from depression in the first place. Because men are deemed to be naturally strong and in command they assume that if they simply tell themselves not to be depressed that will take care of the problem.

I had been well socialized over five decades into accepting the ideology of patriarchy, and it was so much a part of me that it was very difficult for me to see just how powerfully that ideology was shaping my behavior. But I'm convinced that one reason I didn't seek help until after years of misery was because I believed that if I was a "proper man," a "real man," I wouldn't need a psychiatrist, or drugs, to help me deal with depression. All I would need was manly inner fortitude. "I'm a man, I'm supposed to be ruled by reason, I should be able to keep my feelings under control" was the inner voice that rumbled beneath my more conscious conversations. To take drugs to deal with a problem was something that would be OK if I was a woman, but was surely a sign of weakness for a man. So month after month, year after year, I refused to consider any suggestion of medication. This refusal was underscored by the fact that the only people I knew who were taking medication for mental problems were all women. There was no male I was aware of under meds for depression.

One thing I learned about overcoming shame was that for me, a man, it required a process of ideological detoxification. I had to understand just how deeply and powerfully the ideology of patriarchy had been implanted in me over my five decades on the planet. And I had to understand, too, that stopping it from determining how I thought about, and responded to, my own depression would be a long haul. Even today, despite having written books on critical theory (Brookfield, 2004) and radicalizing learning (Brookfield and Holst, 2010)—both of which explore how to resist ideological manipulation—I still feel there's an unseemly lack of manliness, or grit, in my suffering from and disclosing my depression.

A second paradigmatic assumption I had to uncover had to do with the etiology of depression. I assumed that people feel depressed because something bad has happened to them. So the fact that depression had settled on me seemingly out of the blue was completely puzzling. Yes, 9/11 had happened a few months before, and yes, I had nursed my mother during her last weeks of cancer a year earlier, and yes, some test results I had received had been worrying—but none of those seemed to account for the overwhelming anxiety and depression that gripped me. The paradigmatic assumption that depression was rationally caused, and therefore treated by the application of reason, took me years to unearth, challenge, and discard. I had always considered myself a sentimental person, given to emotional reactions to people, compassion, sport, music, and film, and had no idea of just how deeply the epistemology of European rationality was assimilated within me. Challenging and changing my unquestioning belief in rationality with the assumption that depression was the result of chemical imbalances in the brain was enormously difficult. I was so fixated on my inability to reason myself out of feeling depressed that I was unable to consider any other way of understanding how depression was caused.

Once this second paradigmatic assumption was challenged then many of my causal and prescriptive assumptions started to totter. Having managed to reframe my assumptions about the etiology of depression, it became much easier to keep the debilitating effects of shame under control. If depression is linked to chemical imbalances in the brain, I could tell myself, then part of its treatment has to be pharmaceutical. Suddenly, drugs didn't seem a sign of weakness, an indication that I was a pathetic excuse as a human being. After all, my psychiatrist told me, you're fine with taking drugs for bodily imbalances such as high cholesterol, high blood pressure, acid reflux—why should taking drugs to redress chemical imbalances in the brain be any different? Instead of assuming that depression was always caused by the existence of depressing external circumstances that a real man should be able to transcend, I started to see it as a medical condition like asthma, diabetes, or high blood pressure. Once I started to view depression as caused by a chemical imbalance in my brain and not by the external circumstances of life, I opened myself up to the possibility that it might be appropriate to treat my condition with pharmaceuticals.

All this is by way of illustration of how critical thinking saved my life. Because I identified and challenged several assumptions I held about the nature, cause, and treatment of depression I was able to seek psychiatric help and eventually settle on a combination of medications that kept me emotionally stable. Instead of being plagued by permanent feelings of shame and worthlessness, and feeling suicidal on some days, I returned to my old self. That's not to say I don't have days when I feel down, get fed up with things, or feel anxious about situations. But because I was able to think critically about it, depression doesn't rule my life as it did. Had I not been able to think critically about it, the depression would still be overwhelming me.

Hunting Assumptions

The core process described in the example I've just given in the opening section of this chapter—as it is in all critical thinking—is hunting assumptions. Trying to discover what our assumptions are, and then trying to judge when, and how far, these are accurate, is something that happens every time critical thinking occurs. You cannot think critically without hunting assumptions; that is, without trying to uncover assumptions and then trying to assess their accuracy and validity, their fit with life.

Assumptions are guides to truth embedded in our mental outlooks. They are the daily rules that frame how we make decisions and take actions. Everyday communications are subject to a continuous and ever-present set of assumptions. We make assumptions about the meaning behind the words we, and others, use, about the meaning of certain gestures, expressions, or pauses, or about how to respond to a comment. Assumptions inform our judgments about whether or not someone is telling the truth, or how to recognize when we are being manipulated.

As we move through each hour of each day our actions are always based in assumptions, most of which have been confirmed by repeated experience. I brush my teeth assuming that doing so will prevent tooth decay and cut down on the expense and pain of dental procedures. I choose my food for the day based on assumptions about how healthy, or how pleasurable, eating those foods will be. I set the thermostat and choose clothes based on assumptions I'm making drawn from the weather report. As I drive to an appointment I fill the gas tank, lock the back door, follow traffic lights, and rely on street signs on the assumption that doing all these things will get me where I want to go in the speediest and safest way possible. All the assumptions I've mentioned are held because experience has shown them to be accurate. When I want to get to Fridley, Minnesota, I follow the AAA map and the interstate road signs, and set the GPS, because doing this in the past for other destinations has been successful. So I assume that it will be equally successful this time around.

Assumptions as instinctive guides to truth operate at much deeper levels than that of daily routine, however. In the example of depression, a host of assumptions were present about what it meant to be a man. Some of these were highly personal and context specific, but others were linked to dominant ideologies such as patriarchy and what critical theorists call the instrumentalization of reason (Brookfield, 2004). This is a fearsome sounding piece of academic jargon that actually is pretty easy to understand. Instrumentalized reasoning is described by Horkheimer and Adorno (1972) and Marcuse (1964) as the kind of thinking that is most valued in contemporary life. Basically, you reason instrumentally whenever you try to fix a problem without ever questioning whether or not the problem is the one that needs fixing. You reason instrumentally when you tinker with a system—for example, how to assess whether students are learning correctly—so as to improve it, to make it more effective. You don't ask whose interests are served by solving the problem, because you're so focused on being a good fix-it kind of person.

When people think critically they question the fundamental assumptions behind how problems are defined. They ask the big questions of life—what constitutes learning? How do we organize organizations and communities to encourage compassion or fairness? What is the fundamental purpose of teaching? What does it mean to work authentically? Needless to say, in an instrumentalized culture asking these questions is usually seen as either Utopian, impractical, or idealistic, something we grow out of and come to regard as an annoying waste of time.

Assumptions that spring from dominant ideologies are particularly hard to uncover, precisely because these ideologies are everywhere, so common as to be thought blindingly obvious and therefore not worthy of being the object of sustained questioning. These are the paradigmatic assumptions described earlier. Ideologies are the sets of beliefs and practices that are accepted by the majority as commonsense ways of organizing the world. Some of them operate at macro-levels, such as the assumption that majority vote democracy is the decision-making system that most fairly meets the most important needs of the majority. Others operate at micro-levels, such as the assumption that a secret vote gives the most accurate result, or that an action supported by a majority vote has the greatest legitimacy and is therefore the one that should be followed.

Along with democracy, free-market capitalism is another ideology that exercises enormous influence. On a macro-level capitalism holds that the less you regulate economic activity, the more you encourage individual entrepreneurship. Capitalism further assumes that individual economic enterprise and political liberty are inextricably intertwined, so that if you want to safeguard a free democracy you must defend capitalism. Consequently, socialism, communism, even social democracy are viewed as inherently undemocratic. After all, if capitalism is viewed as the economic arrangement that best guarantees individual freedom, then any noncapitalist alternatives must be regarded as threatening freedom to various degrees.

Capitalism and democracy are two dominant ideologies that are highly public. We learn them in school, from the media, in our families, at our workplaces, and through the organizations of civil society such as the church or local political associations. Much harder to identify but equally influential are ideologies that are submerged, such as White supremacy, patriarchy, or heterosexism. These ideologies all hold that leadership is best exercised by Whites and males and heterosexuals, because these are deemed to be smarter, more stable, and more accomplished. Civil rights legislation has ensured that these beliefs are rarely spoken. But ideology is learned not just through the spoken or written word, but also through behavior (what critical theorists call practices). When we go through life seeing leadership positions filled by Whites, particularly White men, and when no one remarks on this fact, we are learning dominant ideology. When a person of color, or a woman, or an "out" Gay or Lesbian attains a position of prominence or influence, and this fact is highlighted as an example of democracy and liberty in action, dominant ideology is in action. After all, when a heterosexual White male attains the some position, his race, gender, or sexuality is rarely mentioned. This is because Whiteness, maleness, and heterosexuality are the leadership norms that we observe everywhere and that we internalize without being aware of it. Paradoxically, an event that seems to disrupt and challenge dominant ideology—such as the election of a biracial president, or the appointment of an African American woman as secretary of state—actually confirms it, at least in the short term. The very fact that these are exceptions, and celebrated as such, actually confirms the enduring influence of the norm.

So Exactly What Is Critical Thinking?

Let's begin answering this question by dispensing a few misconceptions. Here's what critical thinking is *not*. It's *not* something that only people with a college degree can do. It's not the same as being logical, solving problems, or being creative—though aspects of some or all of these are sometimes present when we think critically. It's *not* something you do only if you've studied philosophy. It's *not* necessarily the same thing as being critical of something, as in when we tear apart a film, or criticize a partner's, friend's, or colleague's behavior, for their shortcomings. It's *not* something that only happens when you reach a certain age. It's *not* something that can only be pursued when you have the time to sit and reflect on an idea or a situation. And, finally, it's *not* correlated to IQ, personality, or other measures of intelligence. So whether or not you've been to college, how you score on intelligence tests, whether you're an extrovert or introvert, how busy or leisurely your life is, or what subjects you did best in at school are all irrelevant when considering how well you do critical thinking.

So what is it? Well, my best way of describing it is to say that critical thinking happens when we do four things . . .

Hunting Assumptions

Critical thinking happens first when we try to discover the assumptions that influence the way we think and act. Pretty much every action we take is based on assumptions that we have accepted, sometimes unthinkingly, as accurate. Critical thinking involves deliberately trying to find out what these assumptions are.

Checking Assumptions

When we become aware of the assumptions that are guiding our actions and ways of thinking, we begin to check out whether those assumptions are as accurate as we think they are. This is the second element of critical thinking—trying to assess whether or not our assumptions are valid and reliable guides for action. Here we're engaged in a process of appraisal—trying to see when assumptions make sense, and when they don't, what assumptions cover lots of situations and what assumptions are specific to very particular events. Key to this process is identifying and assessing what we regard as convincing evidence for our assumptions. Sometimes this evidence is experiential (the things that have happened to us), sometimes it's authoritative (what people we trust have told us is the truth), and sometimes it's derived from disciplined research and inquiry we've conducted.

Seeing Things from Different Viewpoints

One of the best ways to decide whether or not an assumption is accurate—or under what conditions it does or doesn't make sense—is to try and see our assumptions and actions from multiple, and different, points of view. In the different roles I play in life—partner, parent, teacher, scholar, bandleader—I usually act assuming that people around me are reading into my actions the same meanings I intend them to pick up. Experience has taught me that this broad—some would say meta—assumption is often seriously flawed. Often my words and actions have been understood in ways that are completely different from the ways I intended them to be understood. So one way to find out how accurate our assumptions are is to try and see ourselves as others see us.

Taking Informed Action

The whole point of critical thinking is to take informed action. The reason I'll do the first three things I've just described is so that I don't waste energy acting in ways that I think are good for me, and that I believe will have the effects I want, only to find out that the opposite is true. Life is too short, and too dangerous, to waste a lot of time acting in uncritical ways. Let me emphasize this point again. The main reason we need to think critically is so we can take informed actions. In shorthand terms, we think critically not just to survive, but also to live and love well. And a life in which our actions are based on what we feel are accurate understandings of our situations is likely to be experienced as much more satisfactory than a life in which our actions are haphazard and arbitrary.

But what exactly is an informed action? Well, it's an action that is based on thought and analysis, which means there is some evidence we take seriously as supporting such an action. To use a trite example, as a bandleader I sequence the sets our band plays based on the evidence of previous audience's reactions. The more I do this, the more I realize that audiences are different. Songs and jokes that go down well when we play the last set at a dive bar may bomb when we play a bowling alley full of families. So an informed action is one that is supported by evidence we find convincing. If someone asks us why we're acting the way we are, we can explain our choices and decisions in ways that allow our questioner to see that they're based on evidence.

Of course, the evidence we're basing our actions on can be nonsensical. For example, plenty of people act on evidence solely because of the source of that evidence. "If so and so says it's true," this reasoning goes, "then it must be true because I trust their insight." I'm no different. I often listen to music, read literature, or watch TV shows or films solely because someone whose taste and opinions I trust tells me they're good. This is how what has been called groupthink (Janis, 1982), automaton conformity (Fromm, 1941), or hegemony (Gramsci, 1971) develops. These three concepts all describe the easy way we fall unthinkingly into assuming that certain things are obviously true, a matter of common sense. The trouble with habitually relying on people with authority or credibility to tell us what to think is that sometimes these people are, at worst, evil and manipulative, at best, prejudiced or unreliable. After all, people have been willing to commit genocide because someone they believe to be superior in some way has convinced them of the filthy ideology that a person's race, ethnicity, creed, or culture means that person is less than fully human.

So to act based on evidence is itself no guarantee that critical thinking is happening. We also need to know that our actions are having the effects we wish them to have. In this sense an informed action is one that plays out the way we want it to—it has the results we want it to have. When the set list I have constructed for a particular club brings down the house, I usually conclude it's because I've scanned my previous experiences playing this, or similar bars, and chosen a sequence of songs that will have this result.

Why Should We Think Critically?

Up to now, I've presented critical thinking as the habit of making sure our assumptions are accurate and that our actions have the results we want them to have. Understood this way, critical thinking is uncontroversial, something that seems so obviously good that no reasonable person could object to it. This conception of critical thinking appears neutral, simply a question of checking and citing evidence. And it's this conception—drawn largely from the tradition of analytic philosophy— that is the most widespread one in American elementary, secondary, and higher education. When my two children went through the St. Paul, Minnesota, public school system, their annual report cards assessed their ability to think critically. Teachers explained this to me as assessing whether or not my kids could give reasons for their opinions and quote the evidence for their conclusions. Nothing controversial or contentious there.

However, as soon as you understand critical thinking to be linked to action you enter the realm of values, because you have to ask the questions, "Action for what?"

and "Whose actions do we want to support?" Sometimes actions serve the ends of the actor, and if the actor is trying to hoodwink, manipulate, harm, or brutalize another, then those actions surely are questionable. After all, a skilled advertiser can think critically about which emotions to tap into and examine research on how to do this, all with the purpose of selling a product and improving stockholder dividends. Political spin-doctors think critically about how best to disguise the errors of their clients and how to present these as successes. Demagogues and racists examine the evidence of how best to whip up racial hatred and use potent narratives and symbols to play on people's insecurities to keep a racist system intact.

At other times the actions we think are in our best interests are actually harmful to us, even when we're not aware of that fact. This is how I connect the concept of hegemony (drawn from critical theory) to critical thinking. Hegemony is in place when people behave in ways that they think are good for them, not realizing that they are being harmed and colluding in their own misery. People suffering from anorexia assume that by not eating they make themselves more beautiful and less unsightly, closer to the idealized body images they see in advertising. People who assume that good workers need to be available 24/7 to serve the ends of their employers think ill health and exhaustion are natural. I know of what I speak here. Three times at work I have collapsed—once in my office, once at an airport on the way to give a speech, and once in my car driving home from a workshop I had given—each time to be rushed to the emergency room, hospitalized overnight, only to find out that there was nothing wrong with me other than exhaustion. All the time I was exhausted, I was congratulating myself on how well I was fulfilling my vocation as an educator. The more burned out I felt, the more professional and committed I told myself I was being. Instead of fighting against an insane situation I was a willing victim, feeling perversely proud of myself the more tired I became.

So part of critical thinking is making sure that the actions that flow from our assumptions are justifiable according to some notion of goodness or desirability. This is where things start to get complicated, and where questions of power arise. What if you and I disagree about the right response to a situation? How do we decide which is the better, more critical response? For example, if I think capitalism rewards those who already have and secures permanent inequity, and you think it ensures that the spirit of individual entrepreneurship stays vigorous and therefore is essential for the functioning of a healthy democracy, how do we assess who is thinking more correctly? Each of us can cite evidence, scan experience, and produce credible, authoritative individuals who support our respective point of view. But ultimately, each of us has arrived at our position from a mixture of analyzing our experiences, thinking in the most critical way we can about them, and then allying our analysis with our vision of what the world looks like when it's working properly.

Critical thinking can't be analyzed as a discrete process of mental actions that can be separated from our object of analysis, from exactly *what* it is that we're thinking critically about. If critical thinking is understood only as a process of analyzing information so we can take actions that produce desired results, then some of the most vicious acts of human behavior could be defined as critical thinking. Serial killers presumably analyze how best to take steps to avoid detection by examining their assumptions about how to stalk victims, hide evidence, and dispose of bodies. Religious cult leaders think critically about how to disassociate new recruits from their past lives and allegiances, and how then to create an identification with the new leader. Spousal abusers can think critically about how to beat up a partner in a way that hides bruises and overt signs of injury, while making partners feel that they deserved the abuse and that the abuser was doing it for their own good.

Josef Goebbels' use of propaganda is an example of critical thinking if we restrict our understanding of it solely to the mental process of how it happens. After all, he worked from paradigmatic and prescriptive assumptions about Jewish impurity, and the need for genocide to rid Germany of Jewish people and culture, that he felt were philosophically justified and empirically correct. He then developed carefully analyzed causal assumptions to decide that the best way to do this was to use propaganda—in particular moving and still visual images of Jews and the Führer—to bolster the official Nazi line that it was Jews' presence that was sabotaging Germany and preventing it from being the world power it was destined to be. This was also the thinking behind the Nazi adoption of Sorel's *Big Lie* theory—the notion that if a lie is repeated frequently and vociferously enough it becomes accepted as truth. Goebbels' critical thinking was successful in the terms set for it—to create a cultural atmosphere where extreme anti-Semitism became accepted as so obviously true that untold numbers of ordinary Germans became complicit in the mechanics of genocide.

This is one of the limits we should acknowledge about critical thinking. It can't be considered separately from values and commitments, whether they be moral or political. Neither can it account for spirituality. One can think critically about one's own spiritual belief or religious commitments, or about the practice of religious tenets, but you can't think your way to enlightenment, Satori, rapture, or salvation. Those states of being are realized through other means than the process of rational analysis.

What Are the Different Kinds of Assumptions We Think Critically About?

I've already partially answered this question in the discussion up to this point. But let me return to it and say a little more about the three kinds of assumptions people need to be alert to—paradigmatic, prescriptive, and causal.

Paradigmatic assumptions are the hardest of all assumptions to uncover. They are the structuring assumptions we use to order the world into fundamental categories. Usually we don't even recognize them as assumptions, even after they've been pointed out to us. Instead we insist that they're objectively valid renderings of reality, the facts as we know them to be true. Some paradigmatic assumptions I have held at different stages of my life as a teacher are that adults are self-directed learners, that critical thinking is an intellectual function only characteristic of adult life, that good adult educational processes are inherently democratic, and that education always has a political dimension. Paradigmatic assumptions are examined critically only after a great deal of resistance to doing this, and it takes a considerable amount of contrary evidence and disconfirming experiences to change them. But when they are challenged and changed, the consequences for our lives are explosive. The example I gave earlier of my assumptions about the causes and treatment of depression were paradigmatic in that they underlay everything I thought about how best to understand and deal with depression. Either they were obviously true to me, or they were so embedded in my consciousness (patriarchy) that I didn't even realize how much sway they held over my decisions.

Prescriptive assumptions are assumptions about what we think ought to be happening in a particular situation. They are the assumptions that are surfaced as we examine how we think we, or others, should behave, what good learning and educational processes should look like, and what obligations students and teachers owe to each other. Inevitably they are grounded in, and extensions of, our paradigmatic assumptions. For example, if you believe that adults are self-directed learners then you assume that the best teaching is that which encourages students to take control over designing, conducting, and evaluating their own learning. If you believe that depression is only caused by external circumstances, then you believe that if your external circumstances are fine, you shouldn't be depressed. You also then believe that the best way to respond to depression is to tell yourself you have no reason to be depressed.

Causal assumptions are assumptions about how different parts of the world work and about the conditions under which these can be changed. Of all the assumptions we hold, causal ones are the easiest to uncover. In workshops and classes I have taught on critical thinking over the past 30 years these assumptions are the ones that are by far the most common. At a rough estimate, I'd say that maybe 80% of assumptions covered in any one conversation, class, course, or workshop will be causal ones.

Causal assumptions are usually stated in two ways, the first of which is when those assumptions govern future behavior. This kind of causal assumption is usually expressed predictively, such as "if I do a, then b will happen". For example, my first year of teaching I was told "start off strict, show the kids who's boss, then you can ease off." I often tell beginning teachers "model everything you want students to do before asking them to do it." I also tell colleagues in courses I'm teaching, "We need to demonstrate what respectful disagreement looks like to students before asking them to do it." When bringing up a contentious issue such as racism I always tell myself I need to talk about my own racism before asking anyone else to start looking at theirs. These are all predictive causal assumptions; I'm assuming that if I follow them certain consequences will occur.

The second way causal assumptions are stated is retroactively, or historically. This is where we very explicitly draw on past experience and use that as a guide for future conduct. For example, I'm a guitarist, writer, and singer in a punk-rockabilly band, The 99ers (http://the99ersband.com) that regularly plays shows in bars, clubs, and festivals. When I construct a set list (the order of songs we're going to play live) for the evening I work on a number of causal assumptions, all of which are derived from noticing audiences' reactions to previous shows. I often start with a cover song, one the audience might recognize and like, to get their attention. We follow that with two quick tempo songs that segue straight into each other so as to create a feeling of energy. We then switch who is the lead singer on the next song to keep the audience's interest, follow that with another cover so they hear something they like and recognize, and on and on. All the assumptions I base a set list on (start with a cover because people will recognize and like it and therefore pay attention to it, follow with a fast two-song block to keep their attention and create energy, switch vocalists to give variety, follow with another cover to regain any wandering attention) are causal. They are also all retroactive, developed after playing many different kinds of venues and seeking what consistently works best.

Here's another example drawn this time from teaching. When I teach content-heavy courses on critical theory, in which students have to read material translated from German, French, and Italian that in English is dense, jargon-ridden, and almost impenetrable at times, I often disclose to students how hard critical theory is for me to understand and how much I struggle when I read it. I'll tell them I often read and reread a paragraph for 15 minutes and that at the end of that time I have absolutely no idea of what I've just read. I do this quite deliberately because I assume many of them will have the same response to the reading that I'm describing, and I want them to know that this is normal and predictable and that it doesn't mean they're not smart or academic enough for the course. I want them to know this work is sometimes a struggle. My assumption is that if they know that I also struggle with this material then they won't be so quick to give up when they hit a rough spot. This assumption has been confirmed for me by thousands of anonymous student evaluations over the past 30 years where students specifically mention how reassuring it was for them to hear me say how I also struggled with the material.

But although this assumption is accurate for me and over the years has apparently worked to ease my students' anxieties regarding their own struggles the first time they encounter critical theory, it only works because students know that at some level they trust I *know* this stuff, I know what I'm talking about. They tell me I know my stuff for two reasons. First, because when I use examples drawn from everyday life and explain ideas in everyday language it really helps them understand an idea that otherwise seems elusive. I assume the fact that I can do this shows I really understand the material inside and out. I also assume that my ability to give appropriate everyday examples that are a bridge between a difficult idea expressed opaquely and the students' own experiences and language means students trust in my teaching expertise. Second, they point to the articles and books I've published (such as *The Power of Critical Theory*) that have won international awards and that, to them, clearly signify I know what I'm talking about.

This is all by way of saying that my assumption is conditional; it works because certain conditions are in place (principally the fact that students trust in my basic command of the subject). If this condition did not exist, if I had published nothing on critical theory and found it very difficult to give meaningful everyday examples that illustrated difficult and opaque concepts, then telling students I really struggled to understand the material and often spent 15 minutes reading a paragraph and being no clearer at the end of it than at the beginning would create a very different result. Students might wonder why they were being taught by an incompetent, they may find out whether someone else was teaching another section or the same course, or they might just decide to drop out and take the course in a future semester when they could study with a different professor. This leads us to another important element in understanding critical thinking, particularly when it focuses on hunting and researching assumptions—contextuality.

Assumptions Are Rarely Right or Wrong—They Are Contextually Appropriate

Contextually appropriate—sounds like a $50 academic term designed to impress people at academic receptions or the dean's sherry party! I use this two-word term as a shorthand way of describing a situation that takes a little longer to explain. Most of the causal assumptions that critical thinking uncovers are not always right or always wrong in some absolute or universal sense. It is not even that they are right at some times and wrong at others. No, most causal assumptions are more or less appropriate depending on the situation that exists at any particular time. For example, starting off a 99ers gig by playing a cover song to draw in the audience only works if the audience is of an age to recognize the song or if the genre of the song is one that matches the audience's taste or if the way we play the song is either recognizable or good! A badly played cover song that people know can actually drive an audience away.

This is all by way of saying that an important element of critical thinking is doing our best to understand the conditions that are in place when we are deciding which assumptions are more or less accurate. The only chance we have of making an informed judgment about the accuracy of any particular assumption is if we have the fullest possible information about the conditions surrounding its use. Often we assume that an assumption we follow has a much broader range of accuracy than is actually the case. Let me give an example of an assumption that anyone in a leadership role has probably followed at some time:

ASSUMPTION—*Giving praise for work well done motivates the person receiving the praise to work hard in the future*

This is an assumption you hear a lot in leadership workshops. It is grounded in the theory of behavioral reinforcement, the notion that you shape behavior best by rewarding the behaviors you like to see, rather than punishing the behaviors you wish to eliminate. It has always seemed an assumption to me that had a wide range of generality so I've followed it when I've been in a lot of leadership roles—as a parent trying to shape the behavior of my own young children, as a teacher trying to encourage students to undertake the risky business of thinking critically and to ask critical questions of me, and as a leader in multiple contexts (football team captain, band leader, department head, community organizer) trying to make sure people who were under my direction felt acknowledged and appreciated.

But this assumption that I have a lot of confidence in, and that I've followed many times over the years, is rendered either irrelevant or actually harmful in the following situations:

- If the praise isn't recognized as praise—to some in leadership positions not tearing a subordinate's work to pieces and publicly humiliating them is equivalent to giving praise. To the subordinate, however, this may be interpreted as one of those lucky days in which the leader forgot to notice what you were doing.
- If the praise given is *too* public—for people who grow up in collectivist cultures, where individual identity is inextricably bound up with membership of the collective, being singled out for praise is excruciatingly embarrassing. If this is the case then receiving individual public praise for doing something well will make you resolve not to do that in the future.
- If the praise is not passed on by the team leader—sometimes a leader gives praise to a team leader and asks that it be passed on to individual members. Unless the team leader follows through and tells each person how well he has done, team members are none the wiser and there'll be no desire to repeat the behavior in the future.
- If the praise is contradicted by other actions—if a leader tells team members how much she liked it when they made an independent decision but then punishes that action the next time it happens, the initial praise is forgotten. If a team leader praises members for trying something new and taking risks but penalizes them for making mistakes when doing so, this kills the likelihood of risk-full experimentation in the future.

Summary

At the end of this opening chapter I hope you have understood the following:

1. Critical thinking is a process of hunting assumptions—discovering what assumptions we and others hold, and then checking to see how much sense those assumptions make.
2. One way we can assess the accuracy of assumptions is by trying to look at them from multiple viewpoints.
3. We do critical thinking so we can take informed actions—actions that are grounded in evidence, can be explained to others, and stand a good chance of achieving the results we desire.
4. Critical thinking can't be understood just as a process of mental analysis; it is always done for some wider purpose. So we always need to be clear what values inform critical thinking, why it's being done, and how such thinking will improve a situation.
5. The most difficult assumptions to identify and question are those embedded in dominant ideologies such as democracy, capitalism, White supremacy, patriarchy, and heterosexism.
6. Assumptions are not all the same. Three important types of assumptions are paradigmatic assumptions (assumptions that frame how we view the world), prescriptive assumptions (assumptions about how we think the world should work and how people should behave), and causal assumptions (assumptions we have about why things happen the way they do).
7. Assumptions are rarely right are wrong; they are best thought of as more or less contextually appropriate. How accurate an assumption is will depend on the conditions that are in place when that assumption is followed.

Discussion Questions

Before you begin the reading—What are some assumptions you have about college? College classes? College students? College instructors? College roommates?

Choosing one of the above elements of college life, provide examples of paradigmatic, prescriptive and causal assumptions on this topic.

Thinking about your experience during the first week of fall semester, how accurate are your assumptions?

How might your peers, instructors or roommates view this topic? In what ways might their perception mirror your own and in what ways might it differ?

Whose assumptions are correct?

WE HAVE TO TALK: A STEP-BY-STEP CHECKLIST FOR DIFFICULT CONVERSATIONS

Judy Ringer

Think of a conversation you've been putting off. Got it? Great. Then let's go.

There are dozens of books on the topic of difficult, crucial, challenging, fierce, important (you get the idea) conversations. (In fact, I list several excellent resources at the end of this article). Those times when you know you should talk to someone, but you don't. Maybe you've tried and it went badly. Or maybe you fear that talking will only make the situation worse. Still, you feel stuck, and you'd like to free up that stuck energy for more useful purposes.

What you have here is a brief synopsis of best practice strategies: a checklist of action items to think about before going into the conversation; some useful concepts to practice during the conversation; and some tips and suggestions to help you stay focused and flowing in general, including possible conversation openings.

You'll notice one key theme throughout: you have more power than you think.

Working on Yourself: How to Prepare for the Conversation

Before going into the conversation, ask yourself some questions:

1. What is your purpose for having the conversation? What do you hope to accomplish? What would be an ideal outcome? Watch for hidden purposes. You may think you have honorable goals, like educating an employee or increasing connection with your teen, only to notice that your language is excessively critical or condescending. You think you want to support, but you end up punishing. Some purposes are more useful than others. Work on yourself so that you enter the conversation with a supportive purpose.

2. What assumptions are you making about this person's intentions? You may feel intimidated, belittled, ignored, disrespected, or marginalized, but be cautious about assuming that this was the speaker's intention. Impact does not necessarily equal intent.

3. What "buttons" of yours are being pushed? Are you more emotional than the situation warrants? Take a look at your "backstory," as they say in the movies. What personal history is being triggered? You may still have the conversation, but you'll go into it knowing that some of the heightened emotional state has to do with you.

"We Have to Talk: A Step-By-Step Checklist for Difficult Conversations" by Judy Ringer, Power & Presence Training, 2016, http://www.judyringer.com/resources/articles/we-have-to-talk-a-stepbystep-checklist-for-difficult-conversations.php. Reprinted by permission of Judy Ringer.

4. How is your attitude toward the conversation influencing your perception of it? If you think this is going to be horribly difficult, it probably will be. If you truly believe that whatever happens, some good will come of it, that will likely be the case. Try to adjust your attitude for maximum effectiveness.
5. Who is the opponent? What might he be thinking about this situation? Is he aware of the problem? If so, how do you think he perceives it? What are his needs and fears? What solution do you think he would suggest? Begin to reframe the opponent as partner.
6. What are your needs and fears? Are there any common concerns? Could there be?
7. How have you contributed to the problem? How has the other person?

Steps to a Successful Outcome

The majority of the work in any conflict conversation is work you do on yourself. No matter how well the conversation begins, you'll need to stay in charge of yourself, your purpose and your emotional energy. Breathe, center, and continue to notice when you become off center–and choose to return again. This is where your power lies. By choosing the calm, centered state, you'll help your opponent/partner to be more centered, too. Centering is not a step; centering is how you are as you take the steps. (For more on Centering, see the Resource section at the end of the article.)

Step #1: Inquiry

Cultivate an attitude of discovery and curiosity. Pretend you don't know anything (you really don't), and try to learn as much as possible about your opponent/partner and his point of view. Pretend you're entertaining a visitor from another planet, and find out how things look on that planet, how certain events affect the other person, and what the values and priorities are there.

If your partner really was from another planet, you'd be watching his body language and listening for unspoken energy as well. Do that here. What does he really want? What is he not saying?

Let your partner talk until he is finished. Don't interrupt except to acknowledge. Whatever you hear, don't take it personally. It's not really about you. Try to learn as much as you can in this phase of the conversation. You'll get your turn, but don't rush things.

Step #2: Acknowledgment

Acknowledgment means showing that you've heard and understood. Try to understand the other person so well you can make his argument for him. Then do it. Explain back to him what you think he's really going for. Guess at his hopes and honor his position. He will not change unless he sees that you see where he stands. Then he might. No guarantees.

Acknowledge whatever you can, including your own defensiveness if it comes up. It's fine; it just is. You can decide later how to address it. For example, in an argument with a friend, I said: "I notice I'm becoming defensive, and I think it's because your voice just got louder and sounded angry. I just want to talk about this topic. I'm not trying to persuade you in either direction." The acknowledgment helped him (and me) to re-center.

Acknowledgment can be difficult if we associate it with agreement. Keep them separate. My saying, "this sounds really important to you," doesn't mean I'm going to go along with your decision.

Step #3: Advocacy

When you sense your opponent/partner has expressed all his energy on the topic, it's your turn. What can you see from your perspective that he's missed? Help clarify your position without minimizing his. For example: "From what you've told me, I can see how you came to the conclusion that I'm not a team player. And I think I am. When I introduce problems with a project, I'm thinking about its long-term success. I don't mean to be a critic, though perhaps I sound like one. Maybe we can talk about how to address these issues so that my intention is clear."

Step #4: Problem-Solving

Now you're ready to begin building solutions. Brainstorming and continued inquiry are useful here. Ask your opponent/partner what he thinks might work. Whatever he says, find something you like and build on it. If the conversation becomes adversarial, go back to inquiry. Asking for the other's point of view usually creates safety and encourages him to engage. If you've been successful in centering, adjusting your attitude, and engaging with inquiry and useful purpose, building sustainable solutions will be easy.

Practice, Practice, Practice

The art of conversation is like any art–with continued practice you will acquire skill and ease.

Here are some additional tips and suggestions:

- A successful outcome will depend on two things: how you are and what you say. How you are (centered, supportive, curious, problem-solving) will greatly influence what you say.
- Acknowledge emotional energy–yours and your partner's–and direct it toward a useful purpose.
- Know and return to your purpose at difficult moments.
- Don't take verbal attacks personally. Help your opponent/partner come back to center.
- Don't assume your opponent/partner can see things from your point of view.
- Practice the conversation with a friend before holding the real one.
- Mentally practice the conversation. See various possibilities and visualize yourself handling them with ease. Envision the outcome you are hoping for.

How Do I Begin?

In my workshops, a common question is how do I begin the conversation? Here are a few conversation openers I've picked up over the years and used many times!

- I have something I'd like to discuss with you that I think will help us work together more effectively.
- I'd like to talk about _____ with you, but first I'd like to get your point of view.
- I need your help with what just happened. Do you have a few minutes to talk?
- I need your help with something. Can we talk about it (soon)? If the person says, "Sure, let me get back to you," follow up with him.
- I think we have different perceptions about _____. I'd like to hear your thinking on this.
- I'd like to talk about _____. I think we may have different ideas about how to _____.
- I'd like to see if we might reach a better understanding about _____. I really want to hear your feelings about this and share my perspective as well.

Write a possible opening for your conversation here:

Discussion Questions

Provide an example of a difficult conversation you had recently. What about this conversation was difficult?

How could you apply the advice given by Ringer (2016) to create a more positive outcome?

What types of difficult conversations can you anticipate having in college? How will you prepare to engage in these conversations productively and positively?

Considering the categories of assumptions presented in the previous reading on critical thinking, identify some of the assumptions that you brought into this difficult conversation? How would you categorize these assumptions; paradigmatic, prescriptive or causal?

Chapter 2
Who are you?

POPULATING THE SELF

Kenneth J. Gergen

The very din of imaginal voices in adulthood—as they sound in thought and memory, in poetry, drama, novels, and movies, in speech, dreams, fantasy, and prayer . . . can be valued not just as subordinate to social reality, but as a reality as intrinsic to human existence as the literally social.

—Mary Watkins, *Invisible Guests*

Consider the moments:

- Over lunch with friends you discuss Northern Ireland. Although you have never spoken a word on the subject, you find yourself heatedly defending British policies.
- You work as an executive in the investments department of a bank. In the evenings you smoke marijuana and listen to the Grateful Dead.
- You sit in a café and wonder what it would be like to have an intimate relationship with various strangers walking past.
- You are a lawyer in a prestigious midtown firm. On the weekends you work on a novel about romance with a terrorist.
- You go to a Moroccan restaurant and afterward take in the latest show at a country-and-western bar.

In each case individuals harbor a sense of coherent identity or self-sameness, only to find themselves suddenly propelled by alternative impulses. They seem securely to be one sort of person, but yet another comes bursting to the surface—in a suddenly voiced opinion, a fantasy, a turn of interests, or a private activity. Such experiences with variation and self-contradiction may be viewed as preliminary effects of social saturation. They may signal a *populating of the self,* the acquisition of multiple and disparate potentials for being. It is this process of self-population that begins to undermine the traditional commitments to both romanticist and modernist forms of being. It is of pivotal importance in setting the stage for the postmodern turn. Let us explore.

Gergen, K. J. (1991). "The Process of Social Saturation" in *The Saturated Self: Dilemmas of Identity in Contemporary Life*. Copyright © 1991 by Basic Books, a Member of the Perseus Books Group. Reprinted by permission of Basic Books, a Member of the Perseus Books Group.

The technologies of social saturation expose us to an enormous range of persons, new forms of relationship, unique circumstances and opportunities, and special intensities of feeling. One can scarcely remain unaffected by such exposure. As child-development specialists now agree, the process of socialization is lifelong. We continue to incorporate information from the environment throughout our lives. When exposed to other persons, we change in two major ways. We increase our capacities for *knowing that* and for *knowing how*. In the first case, through exposure to others we learn myriad details about their words, actions, dress, mannerisms, and so on. We ingest enormous amounts of information about patterns of interchange. Thus, for example, from an hour on a city street, we are informed of the clothing styles of blacks, whites, upper class, lower class, and more. We may learn the ways of Japanese businessmen, bag ladies, Sikhs, Hare Krishnas, or flute players from Chile. We see how relationships are carried out between mothers and daughters, business executives, teenage friends, and construction workers. An hour in a business office may expose us to the political views of a Texas oilman, a Chicago lawyer, and a gay activist from San Francisco. Radio commentators espouse views on boxing, pollution, and child abuse; pop music may advocate machoism, racial bigotry, and suicide. Paperback books cause hearts to race over the unjustly treated, those who strive against impossible odds, those who are brave or brilliant. And this is to say nothing of television input. Via television, myriad figures are allowed into the home who would never otherwise trespass. Millions watch as talk-show guests—murderers, rapists, women prisoners, child abusers, members of the KKK, mental patients, and others often discredited—attempt to make their lives intelligible. There are few six-year-olds who cannot furnish at least a rudimentary account of life in an African village, the concerns of divorcing parents, or drug-pushing in the ghetto. Hourly our storehouse of social knowledge expands in range and sophistication.

This massive increase in knowledge of the social world lays the ground-work for a second kind of learning, a *knowing how*. We learn how to place such knowledge into action, to shape it for social consumption, to act so that social life can proceed effectively. And the possibilities for placing this supply of information into effective action are constantly expanding. The Japanese businessman glimpsed on the street today, and on the television tomorrow, may be well confronted in one's office the following week. On these occasions the rudiments of appropriate behavior are already in place. If a mate announces that he or she is thinking about divorce, the other's reaction is not likely to be dumb dismay. The drama has so often been played out on television and movie screens that one is already prepared with multiple options. If one wins a wonderful prize, suffers a humiliating loss, faces temptation to cheat, or learns of a sudden death in the family, the reactions are hardly random. One more or less knows how it goes, is more or less ready for action. Having seen it all before, one approaches a state of ennui.

In an important sense, as social saturation proceeds we become pastiches, imitative assemblages of each other. In memory we carry others' patterns of being with us. If the conditions are favorable, we can place these patterns into action. Each of us becomes the other, a representative, or a replacement. To put it more broadly, as the century has progressed selves have become increasingly populated with the character of others.[31] We are not one, or a few, but like Walt Whitman, we "contain multitudes." We appear to each other as single identities, unified, of whole cloth.

However, with social saturation, each of us comes to harbor a vast population of hidden potentials—to be a blues singer, a gypsy, an aristocrat, a criminal. All the selves lie latent, and under the right conditions may spring to life.

The populating of the self not only opens relationships to new ranges of possibility, but one's subjective life also becomes more fully laminated. Each of the selves we acquire from others can contribute to inner dialogues, private discussions we have with ourselves about all manner of persons, events, and issues. These internal voices, these vestiges of relationships both real and imagined, have been given different names: *invisible guests* by Mary Watkins, *social imagery* by Eric Klinger, and *social ghosts* by Mary Gergen, who found in her research that virtually all the young people she sampled could discuss many such experiences with ease.[32] Most of these ghosts were close friends, often from earlier periods of their lives. Family members were also frequent, with the father's voice predominating, but grandparents, uncles, aunts, and other relatives figured prominently. Relevant to the earlier discussion of relations with media figures, almost a quarter of the ghosts mentioned were individuals with whom the young people had never had any direct interchange. Most were entertainers: rock stars, actors and actresses, singers, and the like. Others were religious figures such as Jesus and Mary, fictitious characters such as James Bond and Sherlock Holmes, and celebrities such as Chris Evert, Joe Montana, Barbara Walters, and the president.

The respondents also spoke of the many ways the social ghosts functioned in their lives. It was not simply that they were there for conversation or contemplation; they also served as models for action. They set standards for behavior; they were admired and were emulated. As one wrote, "Connie Chung was constantly being used as a role model for me and I found myself responding to a question about what I planned to do after graduation by saying that I wanted to go into journalism just because I had been thinking of her." Or, as another wrote of her grandmother, "She showed me how to be tolerant of all people and to show respect to everyone regardless of their state in life." Ghosts also voiced opinions on various matters. Most frequently they were used to bolster one's beliefs. At times such opinions were extremely important. As one wrote of the memory of an early friend, "She is the last link I have to Christianity at this point in my life when I am trying to determine my religious inclinations." Still other respondents spoke of the way their ghosts supported their self-esteem: "I think my father and I know that he would be proud of what I have accomplished." Many mentioned the sense of emotional support furnished by their ghosts: "My grandmother seems to be watching me and showing that she loves me even if I am not doing so well."

In closely related work, the psychologists Hazel Markus and Paula Nurius speak of *possible selves,* the multiple conceptions people harbor of what they might become, would like to become, or are afraid to become.[33] In each case, these possible selves function as private surrogates for others to whom one has been exposed—either directly or via the media. The family relations specialists Paul Rosenblatt and Sara Wright speak similarly of the *shadow realities* that exist in close relationships.[34] In addition to the reality that a couple shares together, each will harbor alternative interpretations of their lives together—interpretations that might appear unacceptable and threatening if revealed to the partner. These shadow realities are typically generated and supported by persons outside the relationship—possibly members of the extended family, but also figures from the media. Finally, the British psychologist Michael Billig and his colleagues have studied the values, goals, and ideals to which people are committed in their everyday lives.[35] They found the typical condition of the individual to be internal conflict: for each belief there exists a strong countertendency. People feel their prejudices are justified, yet it is wrong to be intolerant; that there should be equality but hierarchies are also good; and that we are all basically the same, but we must hold on to our individuality. For every value, goal, or ideal, one holds to the converse as well. Billig proposes that the capacity for contradiction is essential to the practical demands of life in contemporary society.

This virtual cacophony of potentials is of no small consequence for either romanticist or modernist visions of the self. For as new and disparate voices are added to one's being, committed identity becomes an increasingly arduous achievement. How difficult for the romantic to keep firm grasp on the helm of an idealistic undertaking when a chorus of internal voices sing the praises of realism, skepticism, hedonism, and nihilism. And can the committed realist, who believes in the powers of rationality and observation, remain arrogant in the face of inner urges toward emotional indulgence, moral sentiment, spiritual sensitivity, or aesthetic fulfillment? Thus, as social saturation adds incrementally to the population of self, each impulse toward well-formed identity is cast into increasing doubt; each is found absurd, shallow, limited, or flawed by the onlooking audience of the interior.

Multiphrenia

> *Modern man is afflicted with a permanent identity crisis, a condition conducive to considerable nervousness.*
>
> —*Peter Berger, Brigitte Berger, and Hansfried Kellner, The Homeless Mind*

It is sunny Saturday morning and he finishes breakfast in high spirits. It is a rare day in which he is free to do as he pleases. With relish he contemplates his options. The back door needs fixing, which calls for a trip to the hardware store. This would allow a much-needed haircut; and while in town he could get a birthday card for his brother, leave off his shoes for repair, and pick up shirts at the cleaners. But, he ponders, he really should get some exercise; is there time for jogging in the afternoon? That reminds him of a championship game he wanted to see at the same time. To be taken more seriously was his ex-wife's repeated request for a luncheon talk. And shouldn't he also settle his vacation plans before all the best locations are taken? Slowly his optimism gives way to a sense of defeat. The free day has become a chaos of competing opportunities and necessities.

If such a scene is vaguely familiar, it attests only further to the pervasive effects of social saturation and the populating of the self. More important, one detects amid the hurly-burly of contemporary life a new constellation of feelings or sensibilities, a new pattern of self-consciousness. This syndrome may be termed *multiphrenia*, generally referring to the splitting of the individual into a multiplicity of self-investments. This condition is partly an outcome of self-population, but partly a result of the populated self's efforts to exploit the potentials of the technologies of relationship. In this sense, there is a cyclical spiraling toward a state of multiphrenia. As one's potentials are expanded by the technologies, so one increasingly employs the technologies for self-expression; yet, as the technologies are further utilized, so do they add to the repertoire of potentials. It would be a mistake to view this multiphrenic condition as a form of illness, for it is often suffused with a sense of expansiveness and adventure. Someday there may indeed be nothing to distinguish multiphrenia from simply "normal living."

However, before we pass into this oceanic state, let us pause to consider some prominent features of the condition.[36] Three of these are especially noteworthy.

Vertigo of the Valued

> *Because of the constant change and feeling "off balance," it is essential for men and women to develop . . . coping skills. First, understand that you will never "catch up" and be on top of things and accept this as all right. . . . Put a high priority on spending time relaxing and enjoying life, in spite of all that needs to be done.*
>
> —*Bruce A. Baldwin, Stress and Technology*

With the technology of social saturation, two of the major factors traditionally impeding relationships—namely time and space—are both removed. The past can be continuously renewed—via voice, video, and visits, for example—and distance poses no substantial barriers to ongoing interchange. Yet this same freedom ironically leads to a form of enslavement. For each person, passion, or potential incorporated into oneself exacts a penalty—a penalty both of *being* and of *being with*. In the former case, as others are incorporated into the self, their tastes, goals, and values also insinuate themselves into one's being. Through continued interchange, one acquires, for example, a yen for Thai cooking, the desire for retirement security, or an investment in wildlife preservation. Through others one comes to value whole-grain breads, novels from Chile, or community politics. Yet as Buddhists have long been aware, to desire is simultaneously to become a slave of the desirable. To "want" reduces one's choice to "want not." Thus, as others are incorporated into the self, and their desires become one's own, there is an expansion of goals—of "musts," wants, and needs. Attention is necessitated, effort is exerted, frustrations are encountered. Each new desire places its demands and reduces one's liberties.

There is also the penalty of being with. As relationships develop, their participants acquire local definitions—friend, lover, teacher, supporter, and so on. To sustain the relationship requires an honoring of the definitions—both of self and other. If two persons become close friends, for example, each acquires certain rights, duties, and privileges. Most relationships of any significance carry with them a range of obligations—for communication, joint activities, preparing for the other's pleasure, rendering appropriate congratulations, and so on. Thus, as relations accumulate and expand over time, there is a steadily increasing range of phone calls to make and answer, greeting cards to address, visits or activities to arrange, meals to prepare, preparations to be made, clothes to buy, makeup to apply . . . And with each new opportunity—for skiing together in the Alps, touring Australia, camping in the Adirondacks, or snorkling in the Bahamas—there are "opportunity costs." One must unearth information, buy equipment, reserve hotels, arrange travel, work long hours to clear one's desk, locate babysitters, dogsitters, home-sitters . . . Liberation becomes a swirling vertigo of demands.

In the professional world this expansion of "musts" is strikingly evident. In the university of the 1950s, for example, one's departmental colleagues were often vital to one's work. One could walk but a short distance for advice, information, support, and so on. Departments were often closeknit and highly interdependent; travels to other departments or professional meetings were notable events. Today, however, the energetic academic will be linked by post, long-distance phone, fax, and electronic mail to like-minded scholars around the globe. The number of interactions possible in a day is limited only by the constraints of time. The technologies have also stimulated the development of hundreds of new organizations, international conferences, and professional meetings. A colleague recently informed me that if funds were available he could spend his entire sabbatical traveling from one professional gathering to another. A similar condition pervades the business world. One's scope of business opportunities is no longer so limited by geography; the technologies of the age enable projects to be pursued around the world. (Colgate Tartar Control toothpaste is now sold in over forty countries.) In effect, the potential for new connection and new opportunities is practically unlimited. Daily life has become a sea of drowning demands, and there is no shore in sight.

The Expansion of Inadequacy

Now You Can Read the Best Business Books of 1989 in Just 15 Minutes Each!

—Advertisement, US Air Magazine

Information anxiety is produced by the ever-widening gap between what we understand and what we think we should understand.

—Richard Saul Wurman, Information Anxiety

It is not simply the expansion of self through relationships that hounds one with the continued sense of "ought." There is also the seeping of self-doubt into everyday consciousness, a subtle feeling of inadequacy that smothers one's activities with an uneasy sense of impending emptiness. In important respects this sense of inadequacy is a by-product of the populating of self and the presence of social ghosts. For as we incorporate others into ourselves, so does the range of proprieties expand—that is, the range of what we feel a "good," "proper," or "exemplary" person should be. Many of us carry with us the "ghost of a father," reminding us of the values of honesty and hard work, or a mother challenging us to be nurturing and understanding. We may also absorb from a friend the values of maintaining a healthy body, from a lover the goal of self-sacrifice, from a teacher the ideal of worldly knowledge, and so on. Normal development leaves most people with a rich range of "goals for a good life," and with sufficient resources to achieve a sense of personal well-being by fulfilling these goals.

But now consider the effects of social saturation. The range of one's friends and associates expands exponentially; one's past life continues to be vivid; and the mass media expose one to an enormous array of new criteria for self-evaluation. A friend from California reminds one to relax and enjoy life; in Ohio an associate is getting ahead by working eleven hours a day. A relative from Boston stresses the importance of cultural sophistication, while a Washington colleague belittles one's lack of political savvy. A relative's return from Paris reminds one to pay more attention to personal appearance, while a ruddy companion from Colorado suggests that one grows soft.

Meanwhile newspapers, magazines, and television provide a barrage of new criteria of self-evaluation. Is one sufficiently adventurous, clean, well traveled, well read, low in cholesterol, slim, skilled in cooking, friendly, odor-free, coiffed, frugal, burglarproof, family-oriented? The list is unending. More than once I have heard the lament of a subscriber to the Sunday *New York Times*. Each page of this weighty tome will be read by millions. Thus each page remaining undevoured by day's end will leave one precariously disadvantaged—a potential idiot in a thousand unpredictable circumstances.

Yet the threat of inadequacy is hardly limited to the immediate confrontation with mates and media. Because many of these criteria for self-evaluation are incorporated into the self—existing within the cadre of social ghosts—they are free to speak at any moment. The problem with values is that they are sufficient unto themselves. To value justice, for example, is to say nothing of the value of love; investing in duty will blind one to the value of spontaneity. No one value in itself recognizes the importance of any alternative value. And so it is with the chorus of social ghosts. Each voice of value stands to discredit all that does not meet its standard. All the voices at odds with one's current conduct thus stand as internal critics, scolding, ridiculing, and robbing action of its potential for fulfillment. One settles in front of the television for enjoyment, and the chorus begins: "twelve-year-old," "couch potato," "lazy," "irresponsible". . . One sits down with a good book, and again, "sedentary," "antisocial," "inefficient," "fantasist". . . Join friends for a game of tennis and "skin cancer," "shirker of household duties," "underexercised," "overly competitive" come up. Work late and it is "workaholic," "heart attack–prone," "overly ambitious," "irresponsible family member." Each moment is enveloped in the guilt born of all that was possible but now foreclosed.

Rationality in Recession

> *A group of agents acting rationally in the light of their expectations could arrive at so many outcomes that none has adequate reasons for action.*
>
> —Martin Hollis, *The Cunning of Reason*

LATIN DEBTS: LACK OF CONSENSUS

Washington Awash in Arguments,

Dry on Agreements

> —Headlines, *International Herald Tribune*

A third dimension of multiphrenia is closely related to the others. The focus here is on the rationality of everyday decision making—instances in which one tries to be a "reasonable person." Why, one asks, is it important for one's children to attend college? The rational reply is that a college education increases one's job opportunities, earnings, and likely sense of personal fulfillment. Why should I stop smoking? one asks, and the answer is clear that smoking causes cancer, so to smoke is simply to invite a short life. Yet these "obvious" lines of reasoning are obvious only so long as one's identity remains fixed within a particular group.

The rationality of these replies depends altogether on the sharing of opinions—of each incorporating the views of others. To achieve identity in other cultural enclaves turns these "good reasons" into "rationalizations," "false consciousness," or "ignorance." Within some subcultures a college education is a one-way ticket to bourgeois conventionality—a white-collar job, picket fence in the suburbs, and chronic boredom. For many, smoking is an integral part of a risky life-style; it furnishes a sense of intensity, offbeatness, rugged individualism. In the same way, saving money for old age is "sensible" in one family, and "oblivious to the erosions of inflation" in another. For most Westerners, marrying for love is the only reasonable (if not conceivable) thing to do. But many Japanese will point to statistics demonstrating greater longevity and happiness in arranged marriages. Rationality is a vital by-product of social participation.

Yet as the range of our relationships is expanded, the validity of each localized rationality is threatened. What is rational in one relationship is questionable or absurd from the standpoint of another. The "obvious choice" while talking with a colleague lapses into absurdity when speaking with a spouse, and into irrelevance when an old friend calls that evening. Further, because each relationship increases one's capacities for discernment, one carries with oneself a multiplicity of competing expectations, values, and beliefs about "the obvious solution." Thus, if the options are carefully evaluated, every decision becomes a leap into gray vapors. Hamlet's bifurcated decision becomes all too simple, for it is no longer being or nonbeing that is in question, but to which of multifarious beings one can be committed. T. S. Eliot began to sense the problem when Prufrock found "time yet for a hundred indecisions/And for a hundred visions and revisions,/Before taking of a toast and tea."[37]

The otherwise simple task of casting a presidential vote provides a useful illustration. As one relates (either directly or vicariously) to various men and women, in various walks of life, and various sectors of the nation or abroad, one's capacities for discernment are multiplied. Where one might have once employed a handful of rational standards, or seen the issues in only limited ways, one can now employ a variety of criteria and see many sides of many issues. One may thus favor candidate *A* because he strives for cuts in the defense budget, but also worry about the loss of military capability in an unsteady world climate. Candidate *B*'s plans for stimulating the growth of private enterprise may be rational from one standpoint, but the resulting tax changes seem unduly to penalize the middle-class family. At the same time, there is good reason to believe that *A*'s cuts in defense spending will favor *B*'s aims for a stimulated economy, and that *B*'s shifts in the tax structure will make *A*'s reductions in the military budget unnecessary. To use one criterion, candidate *A* is desirable because of his seeming intelligence, but from another, his complex ideas seem both cumbersome and remote from reality. Candidate *B* has a pleasing personality, useful for him to garner popular support for his programs, but in another sense his pleasant ways suggest he cannot take a firm stand. And so on.

Increasing the criteria of rationality does not, then, move one to a clear and univocal judgment of the candidates. Rather, the degree of complexity is increased until a rationally coherent stand is impossible. In effect, as social saturation steadily expands the population of the self, a choice of candidates approaches the arbitrary.

A toss of a coin becomes equivalent to the diligently sought solution. We approach a condition in which the very idea of "rational choice" becomes meaningless.

So we find a profound sea change taking place in the character of social life during the twentieth century. Through an array of newly emerging technologies the world of relationships becomes increasingly saturated. We engage in greater numbers of relationships, in a greater variety of forms, and with greater intensities than ever before. With the multiplication of relationships also comes a transformation in the social capacities of the individual—both in knowing how and knowing that. The relatively coherent and unified sense of self inherent in a traditional culture gives way to manifold and competing potentials. A multiphrenic condition emerges in which one swims in ever-shifting, concatenating, and contentious currents of being. One bears the burden of an increasing array of oughts, of self-doubts and irrationalities. The possibility for committed romanticism or strong and single-minded modernism recedes, and the way is opened for the postmodern being.

Discussion Questions

In your own words, what is social saturation and how does this concept affect your sense of identity?

Identify the three dimensions of multiphrenia. What is their relationship to social saturation?

Create a visual/graphic illustration of your identity including key concepts from this reading.

"WHAT'S THE RUSH?": GUYLAND AS A NEW STAGE OF DEVELOPMENT

Michael Kimmel

When do you become an adult? How do you know? What are the markers of adulthood today? Is it when you can legally drink? Get married? Drive a car? Vote? Serve in the military?

Demographers typically cite five life-stage events to mark the transition to adulthood: leaving home, completing one's education, starting work, getting married, and becoming a parent. Of course, not all adults would actually check off all those markers, but they represent a pattern, a collection of indicators. In 1950, when social scientists first identified these markers of adulthood, they all clicked in at almost exactly the same time.

My parents' story is typical. They got married in 1948, after my father returned from the wartime Navy, and both he and my mother began their careers. At first, like so many of their generation, they lived in the bottom floor of my grandparents' home, saving their money to flee the city and buy a house in the New York suburbs—part of the great wave of suburban migration of the 1950s. My mother, and her five closest lifelong friends, all had their first children within two years of their weddings, and their second child three years later—all within five years of graduating from college.

Flash forward to my generation. A few years ago, I went to my twenty-fifth college reunion. Some of the women in my graduating class had college-age children; indeed, one or two already had a child at my alma mater. At the time, my wife and I were just deciding about whether or not to start a family. As I looked around, my former classmates were arranged across the spectrum—some with toddlers in strollers and others with adolescents in full pubescent rebellion. One former class-mate had just become a grandmother! In one short generation, our class had extended child-bearing from a period within a year or two of graduation to a full generation.

We also took our time completing our education, getting married, settling into our careers, and leaving home. More than half went to graduate or professional schools; many of my classmates were in their late twenties to early thirties when they completed their education (I was 30). Many had interrupted their educations (as I had) to test out a possible career path. Some waited until their late twenties or early thirties to get married; others married right after college and divorced within a few years of their weddings.

The pendulum is swinging in the same direction for the next generation. The U.S. census shows a steady and dramatic decline in the percentage of young adults, under 30, who have completed these demographic markers. In 2000, 46 percent of women and 31 percent of men had reached those markers by age 30. In 1960, just forty years earlier, 77 percent of women and 65 percent of men had reached them.

The passage between adolescence and adulthood has morphed from a transitional moment to a separate life stage. Adolescence starts earlier and earlier, and adulthood starts later and later. This stage of life—call it "the odyssey years" as does *New York Times* columnist David Brooks, or "adultolescence," or "young adulthood"—now encompasses up to two full decades, beginning at puberty and ending around one's 30th birthday. Everyone knows that 30 is the new 20. But it's equally true these days that 12 is the new 20.

A New Life Stage

We often fret how our children "grow up so fast" as we watch our precocious preteens doing things we would not even have considered until we were at least 16. On the other hand, "When will he ever grow up?" is the refrain of many older parents whose 26-year-old is also doing the same things he was doing at 16—including living at home! Both are true. Kids are growing up faster than ever, and they're staying un-grownup longer than ever, too. The "seasons of a man's life," those supposedly naturally evolving developmental stages, have undergone a dramatic climate change. In the effort to avoid an early frost, this generation is prolonging its Indian summer—sometimes for decades.

In many respects this is understandable. After all, to a guy, growing up is no bargain: It means being a sober, responsible, breadwinning husband and father. It means mortgage payments, car payments, health insurance for the kids, accountability for your actions. Just think about how manhood is portrayed on network television, where shows like *Everybody Loves Raymond* and *According to Jim* feature grown men being infantilized by their wives, unable to do the simplest things for themselves, clueless about their kids' lives, and begging for sex—or reduced to negotiating for it in exchange for housework. "Where's the fun in that?" they ask, and rightly so. Adulthood is seen as the negation of fun. It sucks. Who can blame them for not wanting to jump right in with both feet? If that's your idea of adulthood, of marriage, and of family life, it makes sense that you'd want to postpone it for as long as possible, or at least take the time to figure out a way to avoid the pitfalls so that your own life doesn't turn out that way. Here's Ted, 25, a Northwestern graduate who is working "in a soulless office" in Chicago's Loop:

> At least I got time. I mean, I'm only 25, and I'm gonna live to what, 90? So, like, why hurry on the marriage and kids thing? And besides, this gives me lots more time to meet the perfect woman, and figure out the perfect career. What's the rush?

In some ways, these young people grew up too fast. As children they were overscheduled and overobserved, every utterance and gesture parsed endlessly for clues to their developmental progress. They've coped with divorces; navigated their ways through the treacherous middle-school waters of mean girls and bullies, cliques and teams; thrown themselves into extracurricular activities and sports in order to write brilliant college application essays. They often feel that they've spent their entire childhoods being little grownups—being polite, listening attentively, and prepping for college since elementary school.

"I feel like my whole life has been one long exercise in delayed gratification," says Matt, a graduate student in psychology at the University of Wisconsin:

> I mean, in high school, I had to get good grades, study hard, and do a bunch of extra-curricular things so I could get into a good college. Okay, I did that. Went to Brown. Then, in college, I had to work really hard and get good grades so I could get into a good graduate school. Okay, I did that. I'm here at Wisconsin. Now, though, I have to work really hard, publish my research, so I can get a good tenure track job some-where. And then I'll have to work really hard for six years just to get tenure. I mean, by the time I can exhale and have a little fun, I'll be in my mid–30s—and that's too old to have fun anymore!

Matt is paving the way for his career, but he can't wait to regress; adulthood is a burden.

"My grandfather died at 66," Matt says, "and he was already working and sup-porting a family at age 23. I expect to live to my nineties—so what's the rush? I got 30 more years than he had!"

What happened? What happened to the clearly defined path from adolescence to adulthood? What has made it expand so dramatically? The answers to these questions lead us back to some significant changes in American society—economic and demographic shifts that have had a profound impact on young people today. Before we get inside Guyland, it is important to understand the historical trajectory, set the cultural context, and map the terrain in which guys now become men. Not because these changes are either good or bad: They're neither—and both. Rather because without understanding the economic, social, and cultural context, we cannot adequately understand the pressures and the realities that face young men as they try to become adults in America today.

A Brief History of Adolescence

Once, Americans understood that a boy became a man when he completed school, got a job, and began to raise a family. In the nineteenth century, the passage from boyhood to manhood took place, for most boys, in their early teens, when they left school for the farm or factory. It wasn't that far from the truth for a Jewish boy to declare, at his bar mitzvah, that "today I am a man."

Just over a century ago, in 1904, the famous psychologist G. Stanley Hall published his massive tome, *Adolescence,* demarcating a psychological stage between child-hood puerility and adult virility. Coinciding roughly with the biological changes of puberty, and coincident with its time period (roughly 12 to 15), adolescence was described as a time of transition, a time when the boy (or girl, of course, though Hall conveniently overlooked them himself) develops his adult identity, tests himself, and finds out who he really is. He enters the stage a boy, but he leaves a full-fledged man, able to negotiate his way through the thicket of adult life issues: job, family, responsibility.

Hall saw adolescence as a "storm," a perilous time of dramatic and rapid transfor-mation. Shielded from the demands of work, boys could engage with the question of identity. But at the turn of the century, and even as late as the 1920s and 1930s, boys still entered the workplace, and adulthood, at 16. It was only when high-school graduation rates began to rise, throughout the first half of the twentieth century, that the adolescent years began to expand. By the time America entered World War II, the high-school graduation rate was at an all-time high, and a new word, "teenager," had entered the American vocabulary. Critics worried that this "sudden and dramatic prolongation of adolescence" meant that over half of those who had "passed the terminal age of adolescence" were not acting as adults—physically, socially, or economically.

And Americans have been worrying about teenagers ever since. Some worried about teen sexuality, especially after the publication of the two volumes of the Kinsey Reports on American sexual behavior. Some worried about "juvenile delinquency," another new term from the era—lonely disaffected boys who sought approval from their peers by increasingly dangerous stunts and petty crime. "Let's Face It" read the cover of *Newsweek* in 1956, "Our Teenagers Are Out of Control." Many youths, the magazine reported, "got their fun" by "torturing helpless old men and horsewhipping girls they waylaid in public parks."

Perhaps the most influential thinker on this new stage of development was psychologist Erik Erikson. His path-breaking books, *Childhood and Society* (1950) and *Identity: Youth and Crisis* (1968), identified the seven life-stages of individual psychological development that became a mantra in developmental psychology classes for decades. By labeling adolescence as a "moratorium," a sort of prolonged time-out between childhood and adulthood, Erikson tamed and sanitized Hall's fears that adolescence was a maelstrom, a chaos of uncontrolled passions.

This moratorium was a time for regrouping, reassessing oneself before undertaking the final quest for adult identity, "a vital regenerator in the process of social evolution," as Erikson put it. Rather than rushing headlong into work and family lives, as children did in earlier societies, adolescence slows down the process to allow young people to accomplish certain identity tasks. The venerable institutions that once structured a young person's socialization—family, church, school—could no longer provide those identity needs, and thus, though plagued by doubts, adolescents were beginning to take those tentative steps toward autonomy by themselves, before facing the responsibilities of adulthood that loomed ominously ahead. In a sense, Erikson did for adolescence what Dr. Spock did for babies: reassured parents that the everyday crises their children were experiencing were simply a normal and healthy part of growing up, and that there was little they could do to screw it up.

Sociologist James Coleman had a somewhat less sanguine view. In *The Adolescent Society* (1961), he argued that the gradual recession of education, religion, and family as the primary institutions of socialization left a vacuum, and high-schoolers had largely become the agents of their own socialization. Anti-intellectualism abounded, sports reigned supreme, and everyone simply wanted to be popular! Hardly tremulous individualists, Coleman saw adolescents as frighteningly dependent on peer culture, and boys, especially, as desperate to prove their masculinity in the eyes of other boys. This certainly seems to be the case today, as guys continue to turn to one another for the validation of manhood that was once provided by the community of adults.

Biology and Science Weigh In

One reason why adolescence starts so much earlier today is that puberty, the collection of physiological markers of adolescence, now occurs four to five years earlier than it did about a century ago. Improvements in nutrition, sanitation, and healthcare have lowered the average age of puberty about one year for every twenty-five years of development. Each generation enters puberty about a year earlier than its predecessor. In the years just before the Civil War, the average age for the onset of puberty was 16 for girls, and 18 for boys; today it is about 12 for girls, and 14 for boys. Anyone who has actually spent more than five minutes in the company of contemporary 12-year-old girls and 14-year-old boys knows that these pubescent children are already well into their adolescence.

But just as adolescence reaches us earlier and earlier, what we now know about the brain suggests that it stretches longer and longer. Biologically, though puberty begins earlier, full physiological maturation still doesn't take place until well into our twenties. By 18, neuropsychological development is far from complete; the brain continues to grow and develop into the early twenties. (In a bit of a stretch, one biologist suggests that this immature brain lacks the "wiring" for placing long-term benefits over shorter-term gains, which explains how we are "hardwired" for high-risk behaviors like drug taking, smoking, and drinking when we're young.)

Markers of Adulthood: Marriage and Family

The five classic demographic markers—education, marriage, parenthood, career, and residential independence—have not simply shifted over the past generation. They've scattered across a time span that now stretches to more than a decade for a large swath of American youth. Take marriage and family. In 1950, the average age of marriage was 20.3 for women and 22.8 for men. Close to half of all women were married by age 20. By 1975, the median age had climbed about a year for both. But today it is 27.4 for men and 25.8 for women. And young people are having their first child four years later than they did in 1970.

Many of these changes have been pushed along, in part, by changes in women's lives, which have not only dramatically affected young women but young men as well. The entry of overwhelming numbers of middle-class women into the workplace is largely responsible for the postponement of marriage and child-rearing for both sexes. Today, with women appearing to be every bit as professionally competent, career-oriented, and ambitious as men, and equally capable of earning a living wage, there is no longer the same sense of urgency for men to move toward "getting a good job" to eventually provide for the material needs of a wife and children.

In much the same way, the sexual revolution of the 1960s, coupled with the invention of the birth control pill, has had a profound impact on the lives of young women, which again, in turn, has changed the lives of young men. Before the sexual revolution, young adulthood certainly didn't promise the smorgasbord of sexual experiences that it does today. Premarital sex, while certainly in existence, was nowhere near as ubiquitous. In fact, given the injunctions against it, particularly for women, it might not be too off the mark to suggest that many young people got married *in order to* have sex.

In this sense, ironically, women's newfound freedom invites men to delay adulthood even longer. With no family to support, no responsibilities to anyone other than themselves, and young women who appear to be as sexually active and playful as they could possibly ever fantasize, they're free to postpone adulthood almost indefinitely. They now assume, rightly, that since they'll live into their eighties, they have all the time in the world to commit to a career and marriage. They keep all their options open, even into their thirties (and sometimes their forties), and see their early jobs and relationships more as placeholders than as stepping-stones to adult life. There is no reason to get a real job if you don't actually need one. No reason for marriage, or even a serious relationship, if sex is really all you want. Why *should* they grow up, they wonder?

In part, this might be because parenthood and family life are no longer as appealing as they may have been in the past. Today's young people come from much less stable and settled family lives; they're far more likely to have been raised in a single-parent home and, if not, are living in a culture where divorce is the norm for half of the population. "I'm in no rush to get married, and even less in a rush to have a kid," says Jeff, a UC, San Diego, senior. "I watched my own parents get a divorce, and it became pretty clear that they got married and started having kids—namely, me—before they were ready. I'm not going to make that mistake."

Their reticence is the result of both high expectations for their own relationships and fears that their love lives will resemble their parents'. Afraid to commit, yet desperate to connect, they form close friendships with members of the opposite sex, but often make sure that sex is just about hooking up at the moment, and not about building a relationship.

"Serial Jobogamy"

They feel similarly about their careers. Middle-class kids know that their career is supposed to be more than a job; it is supposed to be financially rewarding, emotionally rich and satisfying, and offer them a sense of accomplishment and inner satisfaction. Work, for them, is an "identity quest." And while there is certainly nothing wrong with wanting a satisfying and financially rewarding professional life, many have absolutely no idea of what's available, what they want to do, or how they might begin. They have utterly unrealistic expectations about the range of jobs they might find satisfying, and no real understanding of the level of commitment and diligence involved in developing those careers. They all seem to want to write for television, become famous actors, or immediately become dot-com entrepreneurs. Whatever they do, they want to make an impact—starting on Day 1. One employment recruiter calls them "the Entitlement Generation" since they have such "shockingly high expectations for salary, job flexibility, and duties but little willingness to take on grunt work or remain loyal to a company."

While their parents fret, and wonder "when is he going to get a good job?" the truth is he'd be lucky to find a job at all. In 2000, 72.2 percent of Americans aged 20 to 24 were employed; four years later, it was 67.9 percent, barely two-thirds. The career expectations of a generation raised to feel special, their self-esteem protected at every turn, spiral upward at the same time that their economic forecast looks increasingly bleak. The secure economic foundation on which previous generations have come of age has eroded. For both the traditional blue-collar and white-collar guys, globalization has changed everything. Working-class guys face a decline in manufacturing jobs, a decline in union protection, and an increase only in the least secure dead-end service sector jobs, with neither pension nor health benefits. Middle-class guys watch their fathers get "outsourced," "downsized," "reallocated"—and they know those are just nice words for the difficult task of finding a new job at mid-life in a less certain job market than ever.

Both groups know that corporations are no longer loyal to their employees—just consider all those companies that picked up and moved out of towns they had helped to build, watching indifferently as entire communities unraveled. They've watched as corporate executives lined their pockets with the pension funds of their own employees. They've seen that despite all the promises, there's been no "trickle down" of the bloating at the top. All the tax breaks for the wealthy and wealthier have only strapped the middle class even further to their credit card debts. So why should they be loyal to the company? Or to the economy? Or to some vision of the future? They have come to believe that the only way to get rich in this culture is not by working hard, saving and sacrificing, but by winning the lottery.

Unlike virtually every single previous generation of Americans, the income trajectory for the current generation of young people is downward. Between 1949 and 1973, during that postwar economic boom, men's earnings doubled and the income gap narrowed. But since the early 1970s, annual earnings for men aged 25 to 34 with full-time jobs has steadily declined, dropping 17 percent from 1971 to 2002. Of male workers with only a high-school diploma, the average wage decline from 1975 to 2002 was 11 percent. Only half of all Americans in their mid-twenties earn enough to support a family. Two-thirds of this current generation "are not living up to their parents' standard of living," commented Andrew Sum, the Director of the Center for Labor Market Studies at Northeastern University.

The gap between college-educated and noncollege-educated has increased as well. In the late 1970s, male college graduates earned about 33 percent more than high-school graduates; by the end of the 1980s, that gap had increased to 53 percent "When I graduated from high school, my classmates who didn't want to go to college could go to the Goodyear plant and buy a house and support a wife and family," Steven Hamilton of the Cornell University Youth and Work Program told *Time* magazine. "That doesn't happen anymore."

Nor do they have much protection. Once they're 18 or 19, young people are only covered as dependents on their parents' medical and healthcare plans if they go to college. All government healthcare covers children only through their eighteenth year. (They lose healthcare under these programs on their nineteenth birthday.) And many young people work at low-wage, temporary, low- or no-benefit jobs, or remain dependent on their parents.

There is no mistaking the economic signs: This generation of young people is downwardly mobile. Gen X'ers and Gen Y'ers will earn less than their parents did at every single age. Young adults, those 18 to 26 years old are the lowest ranked in earned income of all age groups. Their household income is the second lowest (right above 65 and older). "On most socioeconomic measures, the young were the worst-off age group in 1997—and the gap has widened since," notes Tom Smith, the director of the General Social Survey, that has tracked Americans' life experiences since 1972.

The only economic sector in which jobs are being created is entry-level service and sales. In *Generation X,* author Douglas Coupland calls it "McJob"—"low-paying, low-prestige, low-dignity, no future job in the service sector." Young people, along with immigrants, minorities, and the elderly, are the bulk of workers in the new service economy. Half of all workers in restaurants, grocery stores, and department stores are under 24. As one journalist recently put it, "hundreds of thousands of young people are spending hours making decaf lattes, folding jeans, grilling burgers, or unpacking boxes of books and records for minimum wage." And their poverty rates are twice the national average.

Since these jobs are so plentiful, many young people don't feel the need to commit to a career right out of college. And because so many of the entry-level "real" jobs pay almost as badly, and are almost as mind-numbing, they are even less motivated to do so. The young have been raised in a culture that promises instant gratification; the idea of working hard for future rewards just doesn't resonate with them. They don't have their eyes on the prize; it's really more like their "eyes on the fries," as a recent documentary film put it. The increased instability of their long-term employment prospects, coupled with their sense that jobs must be emotionally and financially fulfilling, leads to a volatile career trajectory. Many experience the "two-month itch" and switch jobs as casually as they change romantic partners. They take "stop-gap jobs," engaging in what I like to call "serial jobogamy." Listen to Jon, a 1992 Rutgers grad, who told a journalist about his career cluelessness:

> I had absolutely no idea what I wanted to do right out of college. I fell blindly into a couple of dead-end jobs, which were just there for me to make money and figure out what I wanted to do. When I had no idea what I wanted to do, I couldn't even picture myself doing anything because I was so clueless about what was out there. I had so little direction. I was hanging on to these completely dead-end jobs thinking that maybe something would turn up. I was unhappy about the situation, and the only thing that made it better was that all of my friends out of college were in the same boat. We would all come home and complain about our jobs together. We were all still drunks back then.

Many young adults feel they are just treading water, waiting for the right job, the right person, the right situation, to reveal itself. "I'm just sitting around waiting for my life to begin, while it's all just slippin' away," sings Bruce Springsteen on "Better Days."

Most guys do grow out of this phase, eventually. They get tired of living four-to-a-room, tired of dead-end jobs that leave them broke and exhausted, tired of answering to their parents if they live at home, and they begin to reconsider career paths that they once dismissed as being "too boring." Some go on to graduate school; others accept those entry-level jobs that, they hope, will lead to something better. But in our increasingly competitive economy, where the cost of living is rising and the availability of well-paying jobs is shrinking, they're facing a tougher time of it than ever. When their first real job requires that they work late every night, yet only pays enough to cover the rent if they share a two-bedroom apartment with four other people, it's no wonder guys are reluctant to grow up.

Education for What?

Young people today are the most highly educated group of young people in our history. At the turn of the last century, only a small fraction of male teens attended secondary schools. Most lived with their families and made considerable financial contributions to the family income. In fact, for many working-class families, the family's most prosperous years were the years their children were living at home with them.

Now, the vast majority of teens attend secondary school. In 2000, over 88 percent of all people 25 to 29 had completed high school and nearly 30 percent (29.1 percent, to be precise) had a BA—up from 17 percent only thirty years ago.

Although more are going to college, it's taking them longer to finish. Four years after high school, 15 percent of the high-school graduating class of 1972 had obtained their degree. Ten years later, the percentage had been cut to less than 7 percent, and today it's closer to 4 percent four years out.

They also leave college with huge debts. Two-thirds of all college graduates owe more than $10,000 when they graduate; the average debt is nearly $20,000, and 5 percent owe more than $100,000. Recent college graduates owe 85 percent more in student loans alone than graduates a decade ago according to the Center for Economic and Policy Research. (The amount you are allowed to borrow has steadily increased as well, enabling more students to stay in school, yet increasing their repayment burdens when they leave.) And this doesn't begin to touch the credit card debt amassed by this age group, which has more than doubled between 1992 and 2001. Bombarded daily with promotional offers from credit card companies, many rack up debt like I used to collect baseball cards.

The twentieth century has seen these kids move from being productive citizens to being dependent on their families, the educational system, and the state. Less than one-third of this age group are employed enough to make them potentially financially independent. Those who live with their parents make virtually no contribution to family income. The opposite is true, and for a lot longer time. More than one-third of youth aged 18 to 34 receive cash from their parents, and nearly half receive what sociologists call "time-help" from their parents in any given year—that is significant contributions of time helping kids with their daily lives, from cooking, to cleaning, to doing laundry—averaging about $3,410 in cash and about 367 hours of help.

No wonder two-thirds of all young people 18 to 24 live with their parents or other relatives, and one-fifth of all 25-year-old Americans still live at home. And no wonder that 40 percent of all college graduates return to live with their parents for at least some period of time in that age span. Forget the empty nest syndrome—for one in five American families it's still a "full nest."

One reality that makes this possible is that we live in a culture of privilege. Many parents today can afford to a greater extent than ever before to let their children take advantage of this situation. They have large homes, larger disposable incomes, and are more receptive to the idea of kids coming back to the nest. This is not necessarily a bad trend, but it certainly helps explain why young people are taking so much longer to reach adulthood.

What the Experts Say—and Don't Say

Others have surely noticed that something is happening, that there is a difference from the way previous generations passed from adolescence to adulthood. A front-page story in *USA Today* in September 2004 was followed a few months later by a cover story in *Time* calling them "twixters"—neither kids nor adults, but betwixt and between. But the subsequent letters the magazine published offer a glimpse into our national confusion. The twixters themselves wrote eloquently about their situations. One moved back home after college because she couldn't find a job that paid enough to live on her own—only to find that ". . . the majority of my high school class had done the same thing." But, she insisted, ". . . we are not lazy. We want to work and make our way in the world." Another pointed out that her generation is ". . . overwhelmed by indecision. We have the necessary tools, but now have too many options and not enough options at the same time. We are stuck."

By contrast to the twixters themselves adult letter writers were uniformly unsympathetic. They blamed the kids, as if the disastrous economy, sky-high housing costs, and high aspirations with no ways to fulfill them were somehow the fault of job seekers, not job-suppliers—namely the adults themselves. "If only their parents had cut the golden apron strings and left them to their own devices, they would have learned to be more independent," wrote one. "There's not a single thing wrong with the young adults who live off their parents that a stint in the U.S. Marine Corps couldn't fix," wrote another. "Why do we need to come up with a new label for kids who stay home with their parents while figuring out what to do?" asked another, before reminding us that "we've had a name for that for years: moocher."

Ironically, all of the twixter letters were from women, and all of the adult respondents were male. And though *Time* did not comment on this interesting gender difference, it is an important element in our conversation: It is fathers—far more than mothers—who deeply resent the return of their college-graduate children. Mothers may, for a time, mourn the absence of their children, as if their world has suddenly lost its center of gravity and spins aimlessly off its axis. Fathers, by contrast, often celebrate their new freedom from child-care responsibilities: They buy new golf clubs, load up on Viagra, and talk about this being, finally, their "turn." Mothers may be ambivalent about the "full nest" syndrome, but their husbands seem to be universally unhappy about it.

Developmental psychologists and sociologists have also tried to map this newly emerging stage of life. Sociologist James Cote, at the University of Western Ontario, calls the period "youthhood," while Terri Apter, a social psychologist in Cambridge, England, calls them "thresholders," who suffer from the neglect and scorn from parents who mistake their need for support and guidance as irresponsibility and immaturity.

Perhaps the most ambitious effort to map this post-adolescent *terra incognita* has been psychologist Jeffrey Arnett's studies of what he calls "emerging adulthood." Like Erickson a half-century ago, Arnett sees emerging adulthood as a time for the gradual unfolding of a life plan, a "time for serious self-reflection, for thinking about what kind of life you want to live and what your Plan should be for your life." It's a period of increased independence—including independence from the preordained roles that they inherited from their elders. They are moving deliberately if unevenly toward intimate relationships, a steady and stable career path, and family lives, and along the way they are developing closer friendships with their parents, since the old issues of adolescent rebellion have been resolved by time and experience.

In an ideal world, this might be a dream trajectory. Yet Arnett's view of this stage of life is so sanguine, so sanitized, it's hardly recognizable. It's hard to square such serious self-reflection with the bacchanalian atmosphere of a college weekend; increasing autonomy and a decreasing reliance on peer groups with the fraternity initiations, athletic hazing, and various forms of sexual predation that often fill exposes of campus life.

Perhaps the chief characteristic of this stage of life is its indeterminacy. There's a massive mismatch between the ambitions of this group and their accomplishments.

They graduate from college filled with ideas about changing the world, making their contribution, and making lots of money, and they enter a job market at the bottom, where work is utterly unfulfilling, boring, and badly paid. "It concerns me that of the many gifted people I went to school with, so few of them are actually doing what they really want to do," said one. This was a generation that was told from the get-go that each of them was special, in which their self-esteem was so inflated they became light-headed, in which they were rewarded for every normal developmental milestone as if they were Mozart.

Extremely other-directed, they perform to please grownups—parents, teachers—but exhibit little capacity for self-reflection or internal motivation. They have high self-esteem, but often little self-awareness. Many suspect that their self-esteem, so disconnected from actual achievement, is a bit of a fraud. Many lack a moral compass to help negotiate their way in the world.

For these young people, the world is unstable and uncertain. They drink more than they think they should, take more drugs, and probably get involved in more hookups and bad relationships than they think they should. And they also get more down on themselves, because at this stage they also think they should know better. Their suicide rate is the highest for any age group except men over 70.

They're also more disconnected from society. They have less confidence in social, economic, and political institutions. They are less likely to read a newspaper, attend church, belong to a religion or a union, vote for a president, or identify with a political party than any other age group, according to the General Social Survey. They're more cynical or negative about other people and less trusting. They are less likely to believe that people are basically trustworthy, helpful, fair, or that human beings are naturally good.

Adulthood Is an Attitude

If the demographic markers of adulthood are now scattered across a decade or more, young people today are turning to more attitudinal indicators of when they become adults. Arnett found that the traditional demographic markers held little sway in determining whether or not a student felt like an adult. On the other hand, psychological criteria received much higher endorsements. "Accept responsibility for the consequences of your actions" led the list. Being able to "decide on personal beliefs and values independently of parents or other influences" was next, tied with being "less self-oriented, develop[ing] greater consideration for others."

So, today people become adults when they *feel* like adults. They experience a "situational maturity." Sometimes they want to be treated like adults, sometimes they want to be treated like children. (And their parents invariably guess wrong!) "You don't get lectures about what life is like after college," comments a guy named Brandon to journalist Alexandra Robbins in her book, *Quarterlife Crisis.* "You don't have a textbook that tells you what you need to do to find success." "People have to invent their own road map," commented another.

And they don't experience a calamitous break with their childhoods, since there is no one time when all five transitional indicators are achieved. By spreading them out, adulthood becomes a gradual process, a series of smaller decisions. One looks back suddenly and realizes one is actually an adult. The General Social Survey found that most people believe the transition to adulthood should be completed by age 26, a number that seems to rise every year.

One young man recently wrote to me that, a year after graduating from college and moving across the country, his father had come to visit him. And the father stayed at the son's apartment. "I'm starting to feel like a real adult," he wrote. "I mean, when you live in a different city from your parents and when they visit, they stay with you, well . . . you're an adult!"

Gender: The Missing Conversation

One reason Jeffrey Arnett and his colleagues can be so sanguine about emerging adulthood is because there is nary a word about gender in their work. But how can one possibly discuss the age group 16 to 26 and not talk about gender? It's the most gendered stage of a person's development. Sociologists James Cote and Anton Allahar call it "gender intensification"—the assertion of "exaggerated notions associated with the different roles that still hold many men and women in separate spheres of endeavor." This stage is when the struggle to prove manhood becomes even more intense, in part because it's no longer as easy to differentiate between men and women as it was in the past. The traditional markers of manhood—being the head of a household, having a steady job, and providing for the material needs of a family—are obsolete. The days when "girls were girls and men were men," are long gone. What once marked manhood today marks adulthood—for both sexes. So what does it mean to be a man? That's something most guys are still trying to figure out.

Today's young men are coming of age in an era with no road maps, no blueprints, and no primers to tell them what a man is or how to become one. And that's why none of the terms given to this stage of development—"emerging adulthood," "transition to adulthood," "twixters," "thresholders"—has any resonance whatever with the young men I have spoken to on college campuses and in workplaces around the country. Almost all of them call themselves—and call each other—"guys." It's a generic catch-all term that demarcates this age group, setting it apart from "kids" and "grownups."

Understanding exactly what guys are up against is vital and urgent—for the young men, for those who love them, and for our society. Young men need more than the often volatile combination of anomie and entitlement that can come to characterize Guyland. They need guidance. They need the adults who orbit their world—their parents, teachers, counselors, bosses, coaches, administrators—to understand what is happening in their lives, the pressure they feel to live up to unattainable ideals of masculinity, and the feelings of doubt, anxiety, and shame that often accompany that quest. And they need—and deserve—a larger public conversation about the world they inhabit, to enable them to better navigate its more hazardous shoals.

Even *with* a map, it is a difficult passage to chart. After all, part of the definition of masculinity is to act as if one knows exactly where one is going. If men have a difficult time asking for directions when they get lost driving their cars, imagine what it feels like to feel lost and adrift on the highway of life! One must act as if one knows where one is going, even if it isn't true. And it's this posture, and the underlying sense that one is a fraud, that leaves young men most vulnerable to manipulation by the media and by their peers. It's as if they're saying, "If I just follow along and don't ask any questions, everyone will assume I have it all together—and I won't be exposed."

Guyland thus becomes the arena in which young men so relentlessly seem to act out, seem to take the greatest risks, and do some of the stupidest things. Directionless and often clueless, they rely increasingly on their peers to usher them into adulthood and validate their masculinity. And their peers often have some interesting plans for what they will have to endure to prove that they are real men.

They feel incomplete and insecure, terrified that they will fail as grownups, that they will be exposed as fraudulent men. "Every man's armor is borrowed and ten sizes too big and beneath it, he's naked and insecure and hoping you won't see," is how journalist Norah Vincent put it in her cross-dressing memoir, *Self-Made Man*. Caught between being "real boys" and real men, they have all the entitlement and none of the power. No wonder that, to guys, boyhood is a safe and secure retreat— it's a regression with a mission.

Guyland is a volatile stage, when one has access to all the tools of adulthood with few of the moral and familial constraints that urge sober conformity. These "almost men" struggle to live up to a definition of masculinity they feel they had no part in creating, and yet from which they feel powerless to escape. Individually, a guy often feels that if there is a playbook everyone else has read it—except him. That playbook is called "The Guy Code."

Discussion Questions

Before you begin the reading—What do you believe are the markers of adulthood?

How do your markers compare to those of 1950? What do you believe explains the similarities or differences?

IDENTITIES AND SOCIAL LOCATIONS

WHO AM I? WHO ARE MY PEOPLE?

Gwyn Kirk and Margo Okazawa-Rey

Born and educated in Great Britain, Gwyn Kirk (1945–) is a political sociologist, peace activist, and multimedia producer. Margo Okazawa-Rey (1949–) is a Japanese-born educator and social worker active in numerous public policy organizations and grassroots educational efforts. Both women work in the United States as writers, lecturers, lobbyists, and teachers. The following essay, excerpted from a chapter of their textbook, Women's Lives: Multicultural Perspectives *(2004), provides a perceptive analysis of the complex factors that shape our identities.*

Our identity is a specific marker of how we define ourselves at any particular moment in life. Discovering and claiming our unique identity is a process of growth, change, and renewal throughout our lifetime. As a specific marker, identity may seem tangible and fixed at any given point. Over the life span, however, identity is more fluid. For example, an able-bodied woman who suddenly finds herself confined to a wheelchair after an automobile accident, an assimilated Jewish woman who begins the journey of recovering her Jewish heritage, an immigrant woman from a traditional Guatemalan family "coming out" as a lesbian in the United States, or a young, middle-class college student, away from her sheltered home environment for the first time and becoming politicized by an environmental justice organization on campus, will probably find herself redefining who she is, what she values, and what "home" and "community" are. [. . .]

Identity formation is the result of a complex interplay among a range of factors: individual decisions and choices, particular life events, community recognition and expectations, societal categorization, classification and socialization, and key national or international events. It is an ongoing process that involves several key questions:

Who am I? Who do I want to be?
Who do others think I am and want me to be?
Who and what do societal and community institutions, such as schools, religious
    institutions, the media, and the law, say I am?
Where/what/who are my "home" and "community"?
Which social group(s) do I want to affiliate with?
Who decides the answers to these questions, and on what basis?

Answers to these questions form the core of our existence. In this chapter, we examine the complex issue of identity and its importance in women's lives.

The *American Heritage Dictionary* (1993) defines *identity* as

the collective aspect of the set of characteristics by which a thing is definitely known or recognizable;

a set of behavioral or personal characteristics by which an individual is recognizable as a member of a group;

the distinct personality of an individual regarded as a persisting entity; individuality.

The same dictionary defines *to identify* as "to associate or affiliate (oneself) closely with a person or group; to establish an identification with another or others."

These definitions point to the connections between us as individuals and how we are perceived by other people and classified by societal institutions. They also involve a sense of individual agency and choice regarding affiliations with others. Gender, race, ethnicity, class, nationality, sexual orientation, age, religion, disability, and language are all significant social categories by which people are recognized by others. Indeed, on the basis of these categories alone, others often think they know who we are and how we should behave. Personal decisions about our affiliations and loyalties to specific groups are also shaped by these categories. For example, in many communities of color, women struggle over the question of race versus gender. Is race a more important factor than gender in shaping their lives? If a Latina speaks out publicly about sexism within the Latino community, is she betraying her people? This separation of categories, mirrored by our segregated social lives, tends to set up false dichotomies in which people often feel that they have to choose one aspect of their identity over another. It also presents difficulties for mixed-race or bisexual people, who do not fit neatly into such narrow categories.

In order to understand the complexity and richness of women's experiences, we must examine them from the micro, meso, macro, and global levels of social relations. [. . .]

Critically analyzing the issue of identity at all of these levels of analysis will allow us to see that identity is much more than an individual decision or choice about who we are in the world. Rather, it is a set of complex and often contradictory and conflicting psychological, physical, geographical, political, cultural, historical, and spiritual factors, as shown in the readings that follow.

Being Myself: The Micro Level

At the micro level, individuals usually feel the most comfortable as themselves. Here one can say, for example, "I am a woman, heterosexual, middle class, with a movement disability; but I am also much more than those categories." At this level we define ourselves and structure our daily activities according to our own preferences. At the micro level we can best feel and experience the process of identity formation, which includes naming specific forces and events that shape our identities. At this level we also seem to have more control of the process, although there are always interconnections between events and experiences at this level and the other levels.

Critical life events, such as entering kindergarten, losing a parent through death, separation, or divorce, or the onset of puberty, may all serve as catalysts for a shift in how we think about ourselves. A five-year-old Vietnamese American child from a traditional home and community may experience the first challenge to her sense of identity when her kindergarten teacher admonishes her to speak only in English. A White, middle-class professional woman who thinks of herself as "a person" and a "competent attorney" may begin to see the significance of gender and "the glass ceiling" for women when she witnesses younger, less experienced male colleagues in her law office passing her by for promotions. A woman who has been raped who attends her first meeting of a campus group organizing against date rape feels the power of connection with other rape survivors and their allies. An eighty-year-old woman, whose partner of fifty years has just died, must face the reality of having lost her life-time companion, friend, and lover. Such experiences shape each person's ongoing formulation of self, whether or not the process is conscious, deliberate, reflective, or even voluntary.

Identity formation is a lifelong endeavor that includes discovery of the new; recovery of the old, forgotten, or appropriated; and synthesis of the new and old [. . .]. At especially important junctures during the process, individuals mark an identity change in tangible ways. An African American woman may change her name from the anglicized Susan to Aisha, with roots in African culture. A Chinese Vietnamese immigrant woman, on the other hand, may adopt an anglicized name, exchanging Nu Lu for Yvonne Lu as part of becoming a US citizen. Another way of marking and effecting a shift in identity is by altering your physical appearance: changing your wardrobe or makeup; cutting your hair very short, wearing it natural rather than permed or pressed, dyeing it purple, or letting the gray show after years of using hair coloring. More permanent changes might include having a tattoo, having your body pierced, having a face lift or tummy tuck, or, for Asian American women, having eye surgery to "Europeanize" their eyes. Transsexuals – female to male and male to female – have surgery to make their physical appearance congruent with their internal sense of self. Other markers of a change in identity include redecorating your home, setting up home for the first time, or physically relocating to another neighborhood, another city, or another part of the country in search of a new home.

For many people, home is where we grow up until we become independent, by going to college, for example, or getting married; where our parents, siblings, and maybe grandparents are; where our needs for safety, security, and material comfort are met. In reality, what we think of as home is often a complicated and contradictory place where some things we need are present and others are not. Some people's homes are comfortable and secure in a material sense but are also places of emotional or physical violence and cruelty. Some children grow up in homes that provide emotional comfort and a sense of belonging, but as they grow older and their values diverge from those of their parents, home becomes a source of discomfort and alienation.

Regardless of such experiences – perhaps because of them – most people continue to seek places of comfort and solace and others with whom they feel they belong and with whom they share common values and interests. Home may be a geographic, social, emotional, and spiritual space where we hope to find safety, security, familiarity, continuity, acceptance, and understanding, and where we can feel and be our best, whole selves. Home may be in several places at once or in different places at different times of our lives. Some women may have a difficult time finding a home, a place that feels comfortable and familiar, even if they know what it is. Finally, this search may involve not only searching outside ourselves but also piecing together in some coherent way the scattered parts of our identities – an inward as well as an outward journey.

Community Recognition, Expectations, and Interactions: The Meso Level

It is at the meso level – at school, in the workplace, or on the street – that people most frequently ask "Who are you?" or "Where are you from?" in an attempt to categorize us and determine their relationship to us. Moreover, it is here that people experience the complexities, conflicts, and contradictions of multiple identities, which we consider later.

The single most visible signifier of identity is physical appearance. How we look to others affects their perceptions, judgments, and treatment of us. Questions such as "Where do you come from?" and questioning behaviors, such as feeling the texture of your hair or asking if you speak a particular language, are commonly used to interrogate people whose physical appearances especially, but also behaviors, do not match the characteristics designated as belonging to established categories. At root, we are being asked, "Are you one of us or not?" These questioners usually expect singular and simplistic answers, assuming that everyone will fit existing social categories, which are conceived of as undifferentiated and unambiguous. Among people with disabilities, for example, people wanting to identify each other may expect to hear details of another's disability rather than the fact that the person being questioned also identifies equally strongly as, say, a woman who is White, working class, and bisexual.

Community, like home, may be geographic and emotional, or both, and provides a way for people to express group affiliations. "Where are you from?" is a commonplace question in the United States among strangers, a way to break the ice and start a conversation, expecting answers like "I'm from Tallahassee, Florida," or "I'm from the Bronx." Community might also be an organized group like Alcoholics Anonymous, a religious group, or a political organization like the African American civil rights organization, the National Association for the Advancement of Colored People (NAACP). Community may be something much more abstract, as in "the women's community" or "the queer community," where there is presumed to be an identifiable group. In these examples there is an assumption of shared values, interests, culture, or language sometimes thought of as essential qualities that define group membership and belonging. This can lead to essentialism, where complex identities get reduced to specific qualities deemed to be essential for membership of a particular group: being Jewish or gay, for example.

At the community level, individual identities and needs meet group standards, expectations, obligations, responsibilities, and demands. You compare yourself with others and are subtly compared. Others size up your clothing, accent, personal style, and knowledge of the group's history and culture. You may be challenged directly, "You say you're Latina. How come you don't speak Spanish?" "You say you're working class. What are you doing in a professional job?" These experiences may both affirm our identities and create or highlight inconsistencies, incongruities, and contradictions in who we believe we are, how we are viewed by others, our role and status in the community, and our sense of belonging.

Some individuals experience marginality if they can move in two or more worlds and, in part, be accepted as insiders (Stonequist 1961). Examples include bisexuals, mixed-race people, and immigrants, who all live in at least two cultures. Margaret, a White, working-class woman, for instance, leaves her friends behind after high school graduation as she goes off to an elite university. Though excited and eager to be in a new setting, she often feels alienated at college because her culture, upbringing, and level of economic security differ from those of the many upper-middle-class and upper-class students. During the winter break she returns to her hometown, where she discovers a gulf between herself and her old friends who remained at home and took full-time jobs. She notices that she is now speaking a slightly different language from them and that her interests and preoccupations are different from theirs. Margaret has a foot in both worlds. She has become sufficiently acculturated at college to begin to know that community as an insider, and she has retained her old community of friends, but she is not entirely at ease or wholly accepted by either community. Her identity is complex, composed of several parts. [. . .]

Social Categories, Classifications, and Structural Inequality: Macro and Global Levels

Classifying and labeling human beings, often according to real or assumed physical, biological, or genetic differences, is a way to distinguish who is included and who is excluded from a group, to ascribe particular characteristics, to prescribe social roles, and to assign status, power, and privilege. People are to know their places. Thus social categories such as gender, race, and class are used to establish and maintain a particular kind of social order. The classifications and their specific features, meanings, and significance are socially constructed through history, politics, and culture. The specific meanings and significance were often imputed to justify the conquest, colonization, domination, and exploitation of entire groups of people, and although the specifics may have changed over time, this system of categorizing and classifying remains intact. For example, Native American people were described as brutal, uncivilized, and ungovernable savages in the writings of early colonizers on this continent. This justified the near-genocide of Native Americans by White settlers and the US military and public officials, as well as the breaking of treaties between the US government and Native American tribes (Zinn 1995). Today, Native Americans are no longer called savages but are often thought of as a vanishing species, or a nonexistent people, already wiped out, thereby rationalizing their neglect by the dominant culture and erasing their long-standing and continuing resistance. [. . .]

Colonization, Immigration, and the US Landscape of Race and Class

Global-level factors affecting people's identities include colonization and immigration. Popular folklore would have us believe that the United States has welcomed "the tired, huddled masses yearning to breathe free" (Young et al. 1997). This ideology that the United States is "a land of immigrants" obscures several important issues excluded from much mainstream debate about immigration. Not all Americans came to this country voluntarily. Native American peoples and Mexicans were already here on this continent, but the former experienced near-genocide and the latter were made foreigners in their own land. African peoples were captured, enslaved, and forcibly imported to this country to be laborers. All were brutally exploited and violated – physically, psychologically, culturally, and spiritually – to serve the interests of those in power. The relationships between these groups and this nation and their experiences in the United States are fundamentally different from the experiences of those who chose to immigrate here, though this is not to negate the hardships the latter may have faced. These differences profoundly shaped the social, cultural, political, and economic realities faced by these groups throughout history and continue to do so today.

Robert Blauner (1972) makes a useful analytical distinction between colonized minorities, whose original presence in this nation was involuntary, and all of whom are people of color, and immigrant minorities, whose presence was voluntary. According to Blauner, colonized minorities faced insurmountable structural inequalities, based primarily on race, that have prevented their full participation in social, economic, political, and cultural arenas of US life. Early in the history of this country, for example, the Naturalization Law of 1790 (which was repealed as recently as 1952) prohibited peoples of color from becoming US citizens, and the Slave Codes restricted every aspect of life for enslaved African peoples. These laws made race into an indelible line that separated "insiders" from "outsiders." White people were designated insiders and granted many privileges while all others were confined to systematic disadvantage. [. . .]

Studies of US immigration "reveal discrimination and unequal positioning of different ethnic groups" (Yans-McLaughlin 1990, p. 6), challenging the myth of equal opportunity for all. According to political scientist Lawrence Fuchs (1990), "Freedom and opportunity for poor immigrant Whites in the seventeenth and eighteenth centuries were connected fundamentally with the spread of slavery" (p. 294). It was then that European immigrants, such as Irish, Polish, and Italian people began to learn to be White (Roediger 1991). Thus the common belief among descendants of European immigrants that the successful assimilation of their foremothers and forefathers against great odds is evidence that everyone can pull themselves up by the bootstraps if they work hard enough does not take into account the racialization of immigration that favored White people.

On coming to the United States, immigrants are drawn into the racial landscape of this country. In media debates and official statistics, this is still dominated by a Black/White polarization in which everyone is assumed to fit into one of these two groups. Demographically, the situation is much more complex and diverse, but people of color, who comprise the more inclusive group, are still set off against White people, the dominant group. Immigrants identify themselves according to nationality – for example, as Cambodian or Guatemalan. Once in the United States they learn the significance of racial divisions in this country and may adopt the term *people of color* as an aspect of their identity here. [. . .]

This emphasis on race tends to mask differences based on class, another important distinction among immigrant groups. For example, the Chinese and Japanese people who came in the nineteenth century and early twentieth century to work on plantations in Hawai'i, as loggers in Oregon, or building roads and railroads in several western states were poor and from rural areas of China and Japan. The 1965 immigration law made way for "the second wave" of Asian immigration (Takaki 1987). It set preferences for professionals, highly skilled workers, and members of the middle and upper-middle classes, making this group "the most highly skilled of any immigrant group our country has ever had" (quoted in Takaki 1987, p. 420). The first wave of Vietnamese refugees who immigrated between the mid-1970s and 1980 were from the middle and upper classes, and many were professionals; by contrast, the second wave of immigrants from Vietnam was composed of poor and rural people. The class backgrounds of immigrants affect not only their sense of themselves and their expectations but also how they can succeed as strangers in a foreign land. For example, a poor woman who arrives with no literacy skills in her own language will have a more difficult time learning to become literate in English than one who has formal schooling in her country of origin that may have included basic English.

Multiple Identities, Social Location, and Contradictions

The social features of one's identity incorporate individual, community, societal, and global factors [. . .]. Social location is a way of expressing the core of a person's existence in the social and political world. It places us in particular relationships to others, to the dominant culture of the United States, and to the rest of the world. It determines the kinds of power and privilege we have access to and can exercise, as well as situations in which we have less power and privilege.

Because social location is where all the aspects of one's identity meet, our experience of our own complex identities is sometimes contradictory, conflictual, and paradoxical. We live with multiple identities that can be both enriching and contradictory and that push us to confront questions of loyalty to individuals and groups. [. . .]

It is also through the complexity of social location that we are forced to differentiate our inclinations, behaviors, self-definition, and politics from how we are classified by larger societal institutions. An inclination toward bisexuality, for example, does not mean that one will necessarily act on that inclination. Defining oneself as working class does not necessarily lead to activity in progressive politics based on a class consciousness.

Social location is also where we meet others socially and politically. Who are we in relation to people who are both like us and different from us? How do we negotiate the inequalities in power and privilege? How do we both accept and appreciate who we and others are, and grow and change to meet the challenges of a multicultural world? [. . .]

Study Questions

1. What do Kirk and Okazawa-Rey claim are the most important factors that shape our identities?

2. Explain the macro, meso, and micro levels of social relations. Which of Kirk's and Okazawa-Rey's examples are most helpful to you in understanding these concepts? Which of these levels have had the most impact on the formation of your identity? Why?

3. Do you agree with Kirk and Okazawa-Rey that we all live with multiple identities? Using yourself as an example, explain your agreement/disagreement.

4. Explain "social location" in your own words. Is "social location" a useful concept for analysis in thinking about your own identity formation? Why or why not?

References

Blauner, R. *Racial Oppression in America*. New York: Harper & Row, 1972.

Fuchs, L. "The Reaction of Black Americans to Immigration," *Immigration Reconsidered*. Ed. V. Yans-McLaughlin. New York: Oxford University Press, 1990.

Roediger, D. R. *The Wages of Whiteness: Race and the Making of the American Working Class.* New York: Verso, 1991.

Stonequist, E. V. *The Marginal Man: A Study in Personality and Cultural Conflict*. New York: Scribner & Sons, 1961.

Takaki, R. *Strangers from a Different Shore: Perspectives on Race and Ethnicity*. New York: Oxford University Press, 1987.

Yans-McLaughlin, V. Ed. *Immigration Reconsidered*. New York: Oxford University Press, 1990.

Young, M. E., M. A. Nosek, C. A. Howland, G. Chanpong, and D. H. Rintala. "Prevalence of Abuse in Women with Disabilities." *Archives of Physical Medicine and Rehabilitation* 78: S34–S38 (1997).

Zinn, H. *People's History of the United States: 1492– Present*. Rev. and updated ed. New York: HarperPerennial, 1995.

Discussion Questions

Utilize Discussion Questions at end of article

What are the ethical implications of social location as described in the following quote on p. 13, "People are to know their place" and how does this relate to the idea that America is a meritocracy (American Dream)?

Define essentialism in your own words. Choose a community you do not know much about. What do you believe are qualities characterizing that community? Use your phone, laptop, or tablet to find a prominent figure from that community. Do they fit your previous description of someone from that community? Are there other characteristics that contribute to their identity you did not include?

Chapter 3

How do you see the world?

INSIDE THE MINDSETS

Carol S. Dweck

When I was a young woman, I wanted a prince-like mate. Very handsome, very successful. A big cheese. I wanted a glamorous career, but nothing too hard or risky. And I wanted it all to come to me as validation of who I was.

It would be many years before I was satisfied. I got a great guy, but he was a work in progress. I have a great career, but boy, is it a constant challenge. Nothing was easy. So why am I satisfied? I changed my mindset.

I changed it because of my work. One day my doctoral student, Mary Bandura, and I were trying to understand why some students were so caught up in proving their ability, while others could just let go and learn. Suddenly we realized that there were *two* meanings to ability, not one: a fixed ability that needs to be proven, and a changeable ability that can be developed through learning.

That's how the mindsets were born. I knew instantly which one I had. I realized why I'd always been so concerned about mistakes and failures. And I recognized for the first time that I had a choice.

More Resilient

More Engaged

When you enter a mindset, you enter a new world. In one world—the world of fixed traits—success is about proving you're smart or talented. Validating yourself. In the other—the world of changing qualities—it's about stretching yourself to learn something new. Developing yourself.

In one world, failure is about having a setback. Getting a bad grade. Losing a tournament. Getting fired. Getting rejected. It means you're not smart or talented. In the other world, failure is about not growing. Not reaching for the things you value. It means you're not fulfilling your potential.

Not Doing Well vs. Not Trying

In one world, effort is a bad thing. It, like failure, means you're not smart or talented. If you were, you wouldn't need effort. In the other world, effort is what *makes* you smart or talented.

You have a choice. Mindsets are just beliefs. They're powerful beliefs, but they're just something in your mind, and you can change your mind. As you read, think about where you'd like to go and which mindset will take you there.

Is Success About Learning—Or Proving You're Smart?

Benjamin Barber, an eminent sociologist, once said, "I don't divide the world into the weak and the strong, or the successes and the failures. . . . *I divide the world into the learners and nonlearners."*

What on earth would make someone a nonlearner? Everyone is born with an intense drive to learn. Infants stretch their skills daily. Not just ordinary skills, but the most difficult tasks of a lifetime, like learning to walk and talk. They never decide it's too hard or not worth the effort. Babies don't worry about making mistakes or humiliating themselves. They walk, they fall, they get up. They just barge forward.

What could put an end to this exuberant learning? The fixed mindset. As soon as children become able to evaluate themselves, some of them become afraid of challenges. They become afraid of not being smart. I have studied thousands of people from preschoolers on, and it's breathtaking how many reject an opportunity to learn.

We offered four-year-olds a choice: They could redo an easy jigsaw puzzle or they could try a harder one. Even at this tender age, children with the fixed mindset—the ones who believed in fixed traits—stuck with the safe one. Kids who are born smart "don't do mistakes," they told us.

Children with the growth mindset—the ones who believed you could get smarter—thought it was a strange choice. *Why are you asking me this, lady? Why would anyone want to keep doing the same puzzle over and over?* They chose one hard one after another. "I'm *dying* to figure them out!" exclaimed one little girl.

So children with the fixed mindset want to make sure they succeed. Smart people should always succeed. But for children with the growth mindset, success is about stretching themselves. It's about becoming smarter.

Proving Curent Level vs. Increasing Level.

One seventh-grade girl summed it up. "I think intelligence is something you have to work for . . . it isn't just given to you. . . . Most kids, if they're not sure of an answer, will not raise their hand to answer the question. But what I usually do is raise my hand, because if I'm wrong, then my mistake will be corrected. Or I will raise my hand and say, 'How would this be solved?' or 'I don't get this. Can you help me?' Just by doing that I'm increasing my intelligence."

Beyond Puzzles

It's one thing to pass up a puzzle. It's another to pass up an opportunity that's important to your future. To see if this would happen, we took advantage of an unusual situation. At the University of Hong Kong, everything is in English. Classes are in English, textbooks are in English, and exams are in English. But some students who enter the university are not fluent in English, so it would make sense for them to do something about it in a hurry.

As students arrived to register for their freshman year, we knew which ones were not skilled in English. And we asked them a key question: If the faculty offered a course for students who need to improve their English skills, would you take it?

We also measured their mindset. We did this by asking them how much they agreed with statements like this: "You have a certain amount of intelligence, and you can't really do much to change it." People who agree with this kind of statement have a fixed mindset.

Those who have a growth mindset agree that: "You can always substantially change how intelligent you are."

Later, we looked at who said yes to the English course. Students with the growth mindset said an emphatic yes. But those with the fixed mindset were not very interested.

Believing that success is about learning, students with the growth mindset seized the chance. But those with the fixed mindset didn't want to expose their deficiencies. Instead, to feel smart in the short run, they were willing to put their college careers at risk.

Life after college @ risk + general life satisfaction

This is how the fixed mindset makes people into nonlearners.

Brain Waves Tell the Story

You can even see the difference in people's brain waves. People with both mindsets came into our brain-wave lab at Columbia. As they answered hard questions and got feedback, we were curious about when their brain waves would show them to be interested and attentive.

People with a fixed mindset were only interested when the feedback reflected on their ability. Their brain waves showed them paying close attention when they were told whether their answers were right or wrong.

F = feedback on ability = brain activity

But when they were presented with information that could help them learn, there was no sign of interest. Even when they'd gotten an answer wrong, they were not interested in learning what the right answer was.

Only people with a growth mindset paid close attention to information that could stretch their knowledge. Only for them was learning a priority.

G = info to learn = brain activity

What's Your Priority?

If you had to choose, which would it be? Loads of success and validation or lots of challenge?

It's not just on intellectual tasks that people have to make these choices. People also have to decide what kinds of relationships they want: ones that bolster their egos or ones that challenge them to grow? Who is your ideal mate? We put this question to young adults, and here's what they told us.

People with the fixed mindset said the ideal mate would:

Put them on a pedestal.

$$F = \text{Confirm qualities}$$

Make them feel perfect.
Worship them.

In other words, the perfect mate would enshrine their fixed qualities. My husband says that he used to feel this way, that he wanted to be the god of a one-person (his partner's) religion. Fortunately, he chucked this idea before he met me.

People with the growth mindset hoped for a different kind of partner. They said their ideal mate was someone who would:

$$G = \text{encourage growth}$$

See their faults and help them to work on them.
Challenge them to become a better person.
Encourage them to learn new things.

Certainly, they didn't want people who would pick on them or undermine their self-esteem, but they did want people who would foster their development. They didn't assume they were fully evolved, flawless beings who had nothing more to learn.

Are you already thinking, *Uh-oh, what if two people with different mindsets get together?* A growth-mindset woman tells about her marriage to a fixed-mindset man:

> I had barely gotten all the rice out of my hair when I began to realize I made a big mistake. Every time I said something like "Why don't we try to go out a little more?" or "I'd like it if you consulted me before making decisions," he was devastated. Then instead of talking about the issue I raised, I'd have to spend literally an hour repairing the damage and making him feel good again. Plus he would then run to the phone to call his mother, who always showered him with the constant adoration he seemed to need. We were both young and new at marriage. I just wanted to communicate.

So the husband's idea of a successful relationship—total, uncritical acceptance—was not the wife's. And the wife's idea of a successful relationship—confronting problems—was not the husband's. One person's growth was the other person's nightmare.

CEO Disease

Speaking of reigning from atop a pedestal and wanting to be seen as perfect, you won't be surprised that this is often called "CEO disease." Lee Iacocca had a bad

case of it. After his initial success as head of Chrysler Motors, Iacocca looked remarkably like our four-year-olds with the fixed mindset. He kept bringing out the
same car models over and over with only superficial changes. Unfortunately, they
were models no one wanted anymore.

Meanwhile, Japanese companies were completely rethinking what cars should
look like and how they should run. We know how this turned out. The Japanese
cars rapidly swept the market.

CEOs face this choice all the time. Should they confront their shortcomings or
should they create a world where they have none? Lee Iacocca chose the latter. He
surrounded himself with worshipers, exiled the critics—and quickly lost touch with
where his field was going. Lee Iacocca had become a nonlearner.

But not everyone catches CEO disease. Many great leaders confront their
shortcomings on a regular basis. Darwin Smith, looking back on his extraordinary
performance at Kimberly-Clark, declared, "I never stopped trying to be qualified
for the job." These men, like the Hong Kong students with the growth mindset,
never stopped taking the remedial course.

CEOs face another dilemma. They can choose short-term strategies that boost
the company's stock and make themselves look like heroes. Or they can work for
long-term improvement—risking Wall Street's disapproval as they lay the foundation for the health and growth of the company over the longer haul.

Albert Dunlap, a self-professed fixed mindsetter, was brought in to turn around
Sunbeam. He chose the short-term strategy of looking like a hero to Wall Street.
The stock soared but the company fell apart.

Lou Gerstner, an avowed growth mindsetter, was called in to turn around IBM.
As he set about the enormous task of overhauling IBM culture and policies, stock
prices were stagnant and Wall Street sneered. They called him a failure. A few years
later, however, IBM was leading its field again.

Stretching

People in a growth mindset don't just *seek* challenge, they thrive on it. The bigger
the challenge, the more they stretch. And nowhere can it be seen more clearly than
in the world of sports. You can just watch people stretch and grow.

Mia Hamm, the greatest female soccer star of her time, says it straight out. "All
my life I've been playing up, meaning I've challenged myself with players older,
bigger, more skillful, more experienced—in short, better than me." First she played
with her older brother. Then at ten, she joined the eleven-year-old boys' team. Then
she threw herself into the number one college team in the United States. "Each
day I attempted to play up to their level . . . and I was improving faster than I ever
dreamed possible."

Patricia Miranda was a chubby, unathletic high school kid who wanted to wrestle.
After a bad beating on the mat, she was told, "You're a joke." First she cried, then
she felt: "That really set my resolve . . . I had to keep going and had to know if effort and focus and belief and training could somehow legitimize me as a wrestler."
Where did she get this resolve?

Miranda was raised in a life devoid of challenge. But when her mother died of
an aneurysm at age forty, ten-year-old Miranda came up with a principle. "When
you're lying on your deathbed, one of the cool things to say is, 'I really explored
myself.' This sense of urgency was instilled when my mom died. If you only go

through life doing stuff that's easy, shame on you." So when wrestling presented a challenge, she was ready to take it on.

Her effort paid off. At twenty-four, Miranda was having the last laugh. She won the spot for her weight group on the U.S. Olympic team and came home from Athens with a bronze medal. And what was next? Yale Law School. People urged her to stay where she was already on top, but Miranda felt it was more exciting to start at the bottom again and see what she could grow into this time.

Stretching Beyond the Possible

Sometimes people with the growth mindset stretch themselves so far that they do the impossible. In 1995, Christopher Reeve, the actor, was thrown from a horse. His neck was broken, his spinal cord was severed from his brain, and he was completely paralyzed below the neck. Medical science said, *So sorry. Come to terms with it.*

Reeve, however, started a demanding exercise program that involved moving all parts of his paralyzed body with the help of electrical stimulation. Why *couldn't* he learn to move again? Why couldn't his brain once again give commands that his body would obey? Doctors warned that he was in denial and was setting himself up for disappointment. They had seen this before and it was a bad sign for his adjustment. But, really, what else was Reeve doing with his time? Was there a better project?

Five years later, Reeve started to regain movement. First it happened in his hands, then his arms, then legs, and then torso. He was far from cured, but brain scans showed that his brain was once more sending signals to his body that the body was responding to. Not only did Reeve stretch his abilities, he changed the entire way science thinks about the nervous system and its potential for recovery. In doing so, he opened a whole new vista for research and a whole new avenue of hope for people with spinal cord injuries.

Thriving on the Sure Thing

Clearly, people with the growth mindset thrive when they're stretching themselves. When do people with the fixed mindset thrive? When things are safely within their grasp. If things get too challenging—when they're not feeling smart or talented—they lose interest.

I watched it happen as we followed pre-med students through their first semester of chemistry. For many students, this is what their lives have led up to: becoming a doctor. And this is the course that decides who gets to be one. It's one heck of a hard course, too. The average grade on each exam is C+, for students who've rarely seen anything less than an A.

F = doing well keeps students motivated engaged.

Most students started out pretty interested in chemistry. Yet over the semester, something happened. Students with the fixed mindset stayed interested *only when they did well right away.* Those who found it difficult showed a big drop in their interest and enjoyment. If it wasn't a testimony to their intelligence, they couldn't enjoy it.

"The harder it gets," reported one student, "the more I have to force myself to read the book and study for the tests. I was excited about chemistry before, but now every time I think about it, I get a bad feeling in my stomach."

In contrast, students with the growth mindset continued to show the same high level of interest even when they found the work very challenging. "It's a lot more difficult for me than I thought it would be, but it's what I want to do, so that only makes me more determined. When they tell me I can't, it really gets me going." Challenge and interest went hand in hand.

We saw the same thing in younger students. We gave fifth graders intriguing puzzles, which they all loved. But when we made them harder, children with the fixed mindset showed a big plunge in enjoyment. They also changed their minds about taking some home to practice. "It's okay, you can keep them. I already have them," fibbed one child. In fact, they couldn't run from them fast enough.

This was just as true for children who were the best puzzle solvers. Having "puzzle talent" did not prevent the decline.

Children with the growth mindset, on the other hand, couldn't tear themselves away from the hard problems. These were their favorites and these were the ones they wanted to take home. "Could you write down the name of these puzzles," one child asked, "so my mom can buy me some more when these ones run out?"

Not long ago I was interested to read about Marina Semyonova, a great Russian dancer and teacher, who devised a novel way of selecting her students. It was a clever test for mindset. As a former student tells it, "Her students first have to survive a trial period while she watches to see how you react to praise and to correction. Those more responsive to the correction are deemed worthy."

In other words, she separates the ones who get their thrill from what's easy—what they've already mastered—from those who get their thrill from what's hard.

I'll never forget the first time I heard myself say, "This is hard. This is fun." That's the moment I knew I was changing mindsets.

When Do You Feel Smart: When You're Flawless or When You're Learning?

The plot is about to thicken, for in the fixed mindset it's not enough just to succeed. It's not enough just to look smart and talented. You have to be pretty much flawless. And you have to be flawless right away.

We asked people, ranging from grade schoolers to young adults, "When do you feel smart?" The differences were striking. People with the fixed mindset said:

F = immediate perfection

"It's when I don't make any mistakes."
"When I finish something fast and it's perfect."
"When something is easy for me, but other people can't do it."
It's about being perfect right now. But people with the growth mindset said:
"When it's really hard, and I try really hard, and I can do something I couldn't do before."
Or "[When] I work on something a long time and I start to figure it out."
For them it's not about immediate perfection. It's about learning something over time: confronting a challenge and making progress.

G = Prolonged skill acquisition

If You Have Ability, Why Should You Need Learning?

Actually, people with the fixed mindset expect ability to show up on its own, before any learning takes place. After all, if you have it you have it, and if you don't you don't. I see this all the time.

Out of all the applicants from all over the world, my department at Columbia admitted six new graduate students a year. They all had amazing test scores, nearly perfect grades, and rave recommendations from eminent scholars. Moreover, they'd been courted by the top grad schools.

It took one day for some of them to feel like complete imposters. Yesterday they were hotshots; today they're failures. Here's what happens. They look at the faculty with our long list of publications. "Oh my God, I can't do that." They look at the advanced students who are submitting articles for publication and writing grant proposals. "Oh my God, I can't do that." They know how to take tests and get A's but they don't know how to do *this*—yet. They forget the *yet*.

Isn't that what school is for, to teach? They're there to learn how to do these things, not because they already know everything.

I wonder if this is what happened to Janet Cooke and Stephen Glass. They were both young reporters who skyrocketed to the top—on fabricated articles. Janet Cooke won a Pulitzer Prize for her *Washington Post* articles about an eight-year-old boy who was a drug addict. The boy did not exist, and she was later stripped of her prize. Stephen Glass was the whiz kid of *The New Republic,* who seemed to have stories and sources reporters only dream of. The sources did not exist and the stories were not true.

Did Janet Cooke and Stephen Glass need to be perfect right away? Did they feel that admitting ignorance would discredit them with their colleagues? Did they feel they should already be like the big-time reporters before they did the hard work of learning how? "We were stars—precocious stars," wrote Stephen Glass, "and that was what mattered." The public understands them as cheats, and cheat they did. But I understand them as talented young people—desperate young people—who succumbed to the pressures of the fixed mindset.

There was a saying in the 1960s that went: "Becoming is better than being." The fixed mindset does not allow people the luxury of becoming. They have to already be.

A Test Score Is Forever

Let's take a closer look at why, in the fixed mindset, it's so crucial to be perfect right now. It's because one test—or one evaluation—can measure you forever.

Twenty years ago, at the age of five, Loretta and her family came to the United States. A few days later, her mother took her to her new school, where they promptly gave her a test. The next thing she knew, she was in her kindergarten class—*but it was not the Eagles,* the elite kindergarten class.

As time passed, however, Loretta was transferred to the Eagles and she remained with that group of students until the end of high school, garnering a bundle of academic prizes along the way. Yet she never felt she belonged.

That first test, she was convinced, diagnosed her fixed ability and said that she was not a true Eagle. Never mind that she had been five years old and had just made a radical change to a new country. Or that maybe there hadn't been room in the Eagles for a while. Or that maybe the school decided she would have an easier transition in a more low-key class. There are so many ways to understand what happened and what it meant. Unfortunately, she chose the wrong one. For in the world of the fixed mindset, there is no way to *become* an Eagle. If you were a true Eagle, you would have aced the test and been hailed as an Eagle at once.

Is Loretta a rare case, or is this kind of thinking more common than we realize?

To find out, we showed fifth graders a closed cardboard box and told them it had a test inside. This test, we said, measured an important school ability. We told them nothing more. Then we asked them questions about the test. First, we wanted to make sure that they'd accepted our description, so we asked them: How much do you think this test measures an important school ability? All of them had taken our word for it.

Next we asked: Do you think this test measures *how smart you are?* And: Do you think this test measures *how smart you'll be when you grow up?*

Students with the growth mindset had taken our word that the test measured an important ability, but they didn't think it measured how *smart* they were. And they certainly didn't think it would tell them how smart they'd be when they grew up. In fact, one of them told us, "No way! Ain't no test can do that."

But the students with the fixed mindset didn't simply believe the test could measure an important ability. They also believed—just as strongly—that it could measure how smart they were. *And* how smart they'd be when they grew up.

They granted one test the power to measure their most basic intelligence now and forever. They gave this test the power to define them. That's why every success is so important.

Another Look at Potential

This leads us back to the idea of "potential" and to the question of whether tests or experts can tell us what our potential is, what we're capable of, what our future will be. The fixed mindset says yes. You can simply measure the fixed ability right now and project it into the future. Just give the test or ask the expert. No crystal ball needed.

So common is the belief that potential can be known right now that Joseph P. Kennedy felt confident in telling Morton Downey Jr. that he would be a failure. What had Downey—later a famous television personality and author—done? Why, he had worn red socks and brown shoes to the Stork Club.

"Morton," Kennedy told him, "I don't know anybody I've ever met in my life wearing red socks and brown shoes who ever succeeded. Young man, let me tell you now, you do stand out, but you don't stand out in a way that people will ever admire you."

Many of the most accomplished people of our era were considered by experts to have no future. Jackson Pollock, Marcel Proust, Elvis Presley, Ray Charles, Lucille Ball, and Charles Darwin were all thought to have little potential for their chosen fields. And in some of these cases, it may well have been true that they did not stand out from the crowd early on.

But isn't potential someone's capacity to *develop* their skills with effort over time? And that's just the point. How can we know where effort and time will take someone? Who knows—maybe the experts were right about Jackson, Marcel, Elvis,

Ray, Lucille, and Charles—in terms of their skills at the time. Maybe they were not yet the people they were to become.

I once went to an exhibit in London of Paul Cézanne's early paintings. On my way there, I wondered who Cézanne was and what his paintings were like before he was the painter we know today. I was intensely curious because Cézanne is one of my favorite artists and the man who set the stage for much of modern art. Here's what I found: Some of the paintings were pretty bad. They were overwrought scenes, some violent, with amateurishly painted people. Although there were some paintings that foreshadowed the later Cézanne, many did not. Was the early Cézanne not talented? Or did it just take time for Cézanne to become Cézanne?

People with the growth mindset know that it takes time for potential to flower. Recently, I got an angry letter from a teacher who had taken one of our surveys. The survey portrays a hypothetical student, Jennifer, who had gotten 65 percent on a math exam. It then asks teachers to tell us how they would treat her.

Teachers with the fixed mindset were more than happy to answer our questions. They felt that by knowing Jennifer's score, they had a good sense of who she was and what she was capable of. Their recommendations abounded. Mr. Riordan, by contrast, was fuming. Here's what he wrote.

To Whom It May Concern:

Having completed the educator's portion of your recent survey, I must request that my results be excluded from the study. I feel that the study itself is scientifically unsound. . . .

Unfortunately, the test uses a faulty premise, asking teachers to make assumptions about a given student based on nothing more than a number on a page. . . . Performance cannot be based on one assessment. You cannot determine the slope of a line given only one point, as there is no line to begin with. A single point in time does not show trends, improvement, lack of effort, or mathematical ability. . . .

Sincerely,
Michael D. Riordan

I was delighted with Mr. Riordan's critique and couldn't have agreed with it more. An assessment at one point in time has little value for understanding someone's ability, let alone their potential to succeed in the future.

It was disturbing how many teachers thought otherwise, and that was the point of our study.

The idea that one evaluation can measure you forever is what creates the urgency for those with the fixed mindset. That's why they must succeed perfectly and immediately. Who can afford the luxury of trying to grow when everything is on the line right now?

Is there another way to judge potential? NASA thought so. When they were soliciting applications for astronauts, they rejected people with pure histories of success and instead selected people who had had significant failures and bounced back from them. Jack Welch, the celebrated CEO of General Electric, chose executives on the basis of "runway," their capacity for growth. And remember Marina Semyonova, the famed ballet teacher, who chose the students who were energized by criticism. They were all rejecting the idea of fixed ability and selecting instead for mindset.

Proving You're Special

When people with the fixed mindset opt for success over growth, what are they *really* trying to prove? That they're special. Even superior.

When we asked them, "When do you feel smart?" so many of them talked about times they felt like a special person, someone who was different from and better than other people.

Until I discovered the mindsets and how they work, I, too, thought of myself as more talented than others, maybe even more worthy than others because of my endowments. The scariest thought, which I rarely entertained, was the possibility of being ordinary. This kind of thinking led me to need constant validation. Every comment, every look was meaningful—it registered on my intelligence scorecard, my attractiveness scorecard, my likability scorecard. If a day went well, I could bask in my high numbers.

One bitter cold winter night, I went to the opera. That night, the opera was everything you hope for, and everyone stayed until the very end—not just the end of the opera, but through all the curtain calls. Then we all poured into the street, and we all wanted taxis. I remember it clearly. It was after midnight, it was seven degrees, there was a strong wind, and, as time went on, I became more and more miserable. There I was, part of an undifferentiated crowd. What chance did I have? Suddenly, a taxi pulled up right next to me. The handle of the back door lined up perfectly with my hand, and as I entered, the driver announced, "You were different." I lived for these moments. Not only was I special. It could be detected from a distance.

The self-esteem movement encourages this kind of thinking and has even invented devices to help you confirm your superiority. I recently came across an ad for such a product. Two of my friends send me an illustrated list each year of the top ten things they *didn't* get me for Christmas. From January through November, they clip candidate items from catalogs or download them from the Internet. In December, they select the winners. One of my all-time favorites is the pocket toilet, which you fold up and return to your pocket after using. This year my favorite was the I LOVE ME mirror, a mirror with I LOVE ME in huge capital letters written across the bottom half. By looking into it, you can administer the message to yourself and not wait for the outside world to announce your specialness.

Of course, the mirror is harmless enough. The problem is when *special* begins to mean *better than others*. A more valuable human being. A superior person. An entitled person.

Special, Superior, Entitled

John McEnroe had a fixed mindset: He believed that talent was all. He did not love to learn. He did not thrive on challenges; when the going got rough, he often folded. As a result, by his own admission, he did not fulfill his potential.

But his talent was so great that he was the number one tennis player in the world for four years. Here he tells us what it was like to be number one.

McEnroe used sawdust to absorb the sweat on his hands during a match. This time the sawdust was not to his liking, so he went over to the can of sawdust and knocked it over with his racket. His agent, Gary, came dashing over to find out what was wrong.

> "You call that sawdust?" I said. I was actually screaming at him: The sawdust was ground too fine! "This looks like rat poison. Can't you get anything right?" So Gary

ran out and, twenty minutes later, came back with a fresh can of coarser sawdust . . . and twenty dollars less in his pocket: He'd had to pay a union employee to grind up a two-by-four. This is what it was like to be number one.

He goes on to tell us about how he once threw up all over a dignified Japanese lady who was hosting him. The next day she bowed, apologized to him, and presented him with a gift. "This," McEnroe proclaims, "is also what it was like to be number one."

"Everything was about *you* . . . 'Did you get everything you need? Is everything okay? We'll pay you this, we'll do that, we'll kiss your behind.' You only have to do what you want; your reaction to anything else is, 'Get the hell out of here.' For a long time I didn't mind it a bit. Would you?"

So let's see. If you're successful, you're better than other people. You get to abuse them and have them grovel. In the fixed mindset, this is what can pass for self-esteem.

As a contrast, let's look at Michael Jordan—growth-minded athlete par excellence—whose greatness is regularly proclaimed by the world: "Superman," "God in person," "Jesus in tennis shoes." If anyone has reason to think of himself as special, it's he. But here's what he said when his return to basketball caused a huge commotion: "I was shocked with the level of intensity my coming back to the game created. . . . People were praising me like I was a religious cult or something. That was very embarrassing. I'm a human being like everyone else."

Jordan knew how hard he had worked to develop his abilities. He was a person who had struggled and grown, not a person who was inherently better than others.

Tom Wolfe, in *The Right Stuff,* describes the elite military pilots who eagerly embrace the fixed mindset. Having passed one rigorous test after another, they think of themselves as special, as people who were born smarter and braver than other people. But Chuck Yeager, the hero of *The Right Stuff,* begged to differ. "There is no such thing as a natural-born pilot. Whatever my aptitude or talents, becoming a proficient pilot was hard work, really a lifetime's learning experience. . . . The best pilots fly more than the others; that's why they're the best." Like Michael Jordan, he was a human being. He just stretched himself farther than most.

In summary, people who believe in fixed traits feel an urgency to succeed, and when they do, they may feel more than pride. They may feel a sense of superiority, since success means that their fixed traits are better than other people's.

However, lurking behind that self-esteem of the fixed mindset is a simple question: If you're *somebody* when you're successful, what are you when you're unsuccessful?

Mindsets Change the Meaning of Failure

The Martins worshiped their three-year-old Robert and always bragged about his feats. There had never been a child as bright and creative as theirs. Then Robert did something unforgivable—he didn't get into the number one preschool in New York. After that, the Martins cooled toward him. They didn't talk about him the same way, and they didn't treat him with the same pride and affection. He was no longer their brilliant little Robert. He was someone who had discredited himself and shamed them. At the tender age of three, he was a failure.

As a *New York Times* article points out, failure has been transformed from an action (I failed) to an identity (I am a failure). This is especially true in the fixed mindset.

When I was a child, I, too, worried about meeting Robert's fate. In sixth grade, I was the best speller in my school. The principal wanted me to go to a citywide competition, but I refused. In ninth grade, I excelled in French, and my teacher wanted me to enter a citywide competition. Again, I refused. Why would I risk turning from a success into a failure? From a winner into a loser?

Ernie Els, the great golfer, worried about this too. Els finally won a major tournament after a five-year dry spell, in which match after match slipped away from him. What if he had lost this tournament, too? "I would have been a different person," he tells us. He would have been a loser.

Each April when the skinny envelopes—the rejection letters—arrive from colleges, countless failures are created coast to coast. Thousands of brilliant young scholars become "The Girl Who Didn't Get into Princeton" or the "The Boy Who Didn't Get into Stanford."

Defining Moments

Even in the growth mindset, failure can be a painful experience. But it doesn't define you. It's a problem to be faced, dealt with, and learned from.

Jim Marshall, former defensive player for the Minnesota Vikings, relates what could easily have made him into a failure. In a game against the San Francisco 49ers, Marshall spotted the football on the ground. He scooped it up and ran for a touchdown as the crowd cheered. But he ran the wrong way. He scored for the wrong team and on national television.

It was the most devastating moment of his life. The shame was overpowering. But during halftime, he thought, "If you make a mistake, you got to make it right. I realized I had a choice. I could sit in my misery or I could do something about it." Pulling himself together for the second half, he played some of his best football ever and contributed to his team's victory.

Nor did he stop there. He spoke to groups. He answered letters that poured in from people who finally had the courage to admit their own shameful experiences. He heightened his concentration during games. Instead of letting the experience define him, he took control of it. He *used* it to become a better player and, he believes, a better person.

In the fixed mindset, however, the loss of one's self to failure can be a permanent, haunting trauma. Bernard Loiseau was one of the top chefs in the world. Only a handful of restaurants in all of France receive the supreme rating of three stars from the *Guide Michelin*, the most respected restaurant guide in Europe. His was one of them. Around the publication of the 2003 *Guide Michelin*, however, Mr. Loiseau committed suicide. He had lost two points in another guide, going from a nineteen (out of twenty) to a seventeen in the *GaultMillau*. And there were rampant rumors that he would lose one of his three stars in the new *Guide*. Although he did not, the idea of failure had possessed him.

Loiseau had been a pioneer. He was one of the first to advance the "nouvelle cuisine," trading the traditional butter and cream sauces of French cooking for the brighter flavors of the foods themselves. A man of tremendous energy, he was also an entrepreneur. Besides his three-star restaurant in Burgundy, he had created three eateries in Paris, numerous cookbooks, and a line of frozen foods. "I'm like Yves Saint Laurent," he told people. "I do both haute couture and ready-to-wear."

A man of such talent and originality could easily have planned for a satisfying future, with or without the two points or the third star. In fact, the director of the *GaultMillau* said it was unimaginable that their rating could have taken his life. But in the fixed mindset, it *is* imaginable. Their lower rating gave him a new definition of himself: Failure. Hasbeen.

It's striking what counts as failure in the fixed mindset. So, on a lighter note . . .

My Success Is Your Failure

Last summer my husband and I went to a dude ranch, something very novel since neither of us had ever made contact with a horse. One day, we signed up for a lesson in fly fishing. It was taught by a wonderful eighty-year-old cowboy-type fisherman who showed us how to cast the fishing line, and then turned us loose.

We soon realized that he had not taught us how to recognize when the trout bit the lure (they don't tug on the line; you have to watch for a bubble in the water), what to do when the trout bit the lure (tug upward), or how to reel the trout in if by some miracle we got that far (pull the fish along the water; do not hoist it into the air). Well, time passed, the mosquitoes bit, but not so the trout. None of the dozen or so of us made the slightest progress. Suddenly, I hit the jackpot. Some careless trout bit hard on my lure and the fisherman, who happened to be right there, talked me through the rest. I had me a rainbow trout.

Reaction #1: My husband, David, came running over beaming with pride and saying, "Life with you is so exciting!"

Reaction #2: That evening when we came into the dining room for dinner, two men came up to my husband and said, "David, how're you coping?" David looked at them blankly; he had no idea what they were talking about. Of course he didn't. He was the one who thought my catching the fish was exciting. But I knew exactly what they meant. They had expected him to feel diminished, and they went on to make it clear that that's exactly what my success had done to them.

Shirk, Cheat, Blame: Not a Recipe for Success

Beyond how traumatic a setback can be in the fixed mindset, this mindset gives you no good recipe for overcoming it. If failure means you lack competence or potential—that you *are* a failure—where do you go from there?

In one study, seventh graders told us how they would respond to an academic failure—a poor test grade in a new course. Those with the growth mindset, no big surprise, said they would study harder for the next test. But those with the fixed mindset said they would study *less* for the next test. If you don't have the ability, why waste your time? And, they said, they would seriously consider cheating! If you don't have the ability, they thought, you just have to look for another way.

What's more, instead of trying to learn from and repair their failures, people with the fixed mindset may simply try to repair their self-esteem. For example, they may go looking for people who are even worse off than they are.

College students, after doing poorly on a test, were given a chance to look at tests of other students. Those in the growth mindset looked at the tests of people who had done far better than they had. As usual, they wanted to correct their deficiency.

But students in the fixed mindset chose to look at the tests of people who had done *really* poorly. That was their way of feeling better about themselves.

Jim Collins tells in *Good to Great* of a similar thing in the corporate world. As Procter & Gamble surged into the paper goods business, Scott Paper—which was then the leader—just gave up. Instead of mobilizing themselves and putting up a fight, they said, "Oh, well . . . at least there are people in the business worse off than we are."

Another way people with the fixed mindset try to repair their self-esteem after a failure is by assigning blame or making excuses. Let's return to John McEnroe.

It was never his fault. One time he lost a match because he had a fever. One time he had a backache. One time he fell victim to expectations, another time to the tabloids. One time he lost to a friend because the friend was in love and he wasn't. One time he ate too close to the match. One time he was too chunky, another time too thin. One time it was too cold, another time too hot. One time he was under-trained, another time overtrained.

His most agonizing loss, and the one that still keeps him up nights, was his loss in the 1984 French Open. Why did he lose after leading Ivan Lendl two sets to none? According to McEnroe, it wasn't his fault. An NBC cameraman had taken off his headset and a noise started coming from the side of the court.

Not his fault. So he didn't train to improve his ability to concentrate or his emotional control.

John Wooden, the legendary basketball coach, says you aren't a failure until you start to blame. What he means is that you can still be in the process of learning from your mistakes until you deny them.

When Enron, the energy giant, failed—toppled by a culture of arrogance—whose fault was it? Not mine, insisted Jeffrey Skilling, the CEO and resident genius. It was the world's fault. The world did not appreciate what Enron was trying to do. What about the Justice Department's investigation into massive corporate deception? A "witch hunt."

Jack Welch, the growth-minded CEO, had a completely different reaction to one of General Electric's fiascos. In 1986, General Electric bought Kidder, Peabody, a Wall Street investment banking firm. Soon after the deal closed, Kidder, Peabody was hit with a big insider trading scandal. A few years later, calamity struck again in the form of Joseph Jett, a trader who made a bunch of fictitious trades, to the tune of hundreds of millions, to pump up his bonus. Welch phoned fourteen of his top GE colleagues to tell them the bad news and to apologize personally. "I blamed myself for the disaster," Welch said.

Mindset and Depression

Maybe Bernard Loiseau, the French chef, was just depressed. Were you thinking that?

As a psychologist and an educator, I am vitally interested in depression. It runs wild on college campuses, especially in February and March. The winter is not over, the summer is not in sight, work has piled up, and relationships are often frayed. Yet it's been clear to me for a long time that different students handle depression in dramatically different ways. Some let everything slide. Others, though feeling wretched, hang on. They drag themselves to class, keep up with their work, and take care of themselves—so that when they feel better, their lives are intact.

Not long ago, we decided to see whether mindsets play a role in this difference. To find out, we measured students' mindsets and then had them keep an online "diary" for three weeks in February and March. Every day they answered questions about their mood, their activities, and how they were coping with problems. Here's what we discovered.

First, the students with the fixed mindset had higher levels of depression. Our analyses showed that this was because they ruminated over their problems and setbacks, essentially tormenting themselves with the idea that the setbacks meant they were incompetent or unworthy: "It just kept circulating in my head: You're a dope." "I just couldn't let go of the thought that this made me less of a man." Again, failures labeled them and left them no route to success.

And the more depressed they felt, the more they let things go; the less they took action to solve their problems. For example, they didn't study what they needed to, they didn't hand in their assignments on time, and they didn't keep up with their chores.

Although students with the fixed mindset showed more depression, there were still plenty of people with the growth mindset who felt pretty miserable, this being peak season for depression. And here we saw something really amazing. The *more* depressed people with the growth mindset felt, the *more* they took action to confront their problems, the *more* they made sure to keep up with their schoolwork, and the *more* they kept up with their lives. The worse they felt, the more determined they became!

In fact, from the way they acted, it might have been hard to know how despondent they were. Here is a story a young man told me.

> I was a freshman and it was the first time I had been away from home. Everyone was a stranger, the courses were hard, and as the year wore on I felt more and more depressed. Eventually, it reached a point where I could hardly get out of bed in the morning. But every day I forced myself to get up, shower, shave, and do whatever it was I needed to do. One day I really hit a low point and I decided to ask for help, so I went to the teaching assistant in my psychology course and asked for her advice.
>
> "Are you going to your classes?" she asked.
>
> "Yes," I replied.
>
> "Are you keeping up with your reading?"
>
> "Yes."
>
> "Are you doing okay on your exams?"
>
> "Yes."
>
> "Well," she informed me, "then you're not depressed."

Yes, he was depressed, but he was coping the way people in the growth mindset tend to cope—with determination.

Doesn't temperament have a lot to do with it? Aren't some people sensitive by nature, while others just let things roll off their backs? Temperament certainly plays a role, but mindset is the most important part of the story. When we *taught* people the growth mindset, it completely changed the way they reacted to their depressed mood. The worse they felt, the more motivated they became and the more they confronted the problems that faced them.

In short, when people believe in fixed traits, they are always in danger of being measured by a failure. It can define them in a permanent way. Smart or talented as they may be, this mindset seems to rob them of their coping resources.

When people believe their basic qualities can be developed, failures may still hurt, but failures don't define them. And if abilities can be expanded—if change and growth are possible—then there are still many paths to success.

Mindsets Change the Meaning of Effort

As children, we were given a choice between the talented but erratic hare and the plodding but steady tortoise. The lesson was supposed to be that slow and steady wins the race. But, really, did any of us ever want to be the tortoise?

No, we just wanted to be a less foolish hare. We wanted to be swift as the wind and a bit more strategic—say, not taking quite so many snoozes before the finish line. After all, everyone knows you have to show up in order to win.

The story of the tortoise and the hare, in trying to put forward the power of effort, gave effort a bad name. It reinforced the image that effort is for the plodders and suggested that in rare instances, when talented people dropped the ball, the plodder could sneak through.

The little engine that could, the saggy, baggy elephant, and the scruffy tugboat—they were cute, they were often overmatched, and we were happy for them when they succeeded. In fact, to this day I remember how fond I was of those little creatures (or machines), but no way did I identify with them. The message was: If you're unfortunate enough to be the runt of the litter—if you lack endowment—you don't have to be an utter failure. You can be a sweet, adorable little slogger, and maybe (if you really work at it and withstand all the scornful onlookers) even a success.

Thank you very much, I'll take the endowment.

The problem was that these stories made it into an either–or. Either you have ability *or* you expend effort. And this is part of the fixed mindset. Effort is for those who don't have the ability. People with the fixed mindset tell us, "If you have to work at something, you must not be good at it." They add, "Things come easily to people who are true geniuses."

I was a young assistant professor in the psychology department at the University of Illinois. Late one night, I was passing the psychology building and noticed that the lights were on in some faculty offices. Some of my colleagues were working late. *They must not be as smart as I am,* I thought to myself.

It never occurred to me that they might be just as smart and more hardworking! For me it was either–or. And it was clear I valued the either over the or.

Malcolm Gladwell, the author and *New Yorker* writer, has suggested that as a society we value natural, effortless accomplishment over achievement through effort. We endow our heroes with superhuman abilities that led them inevitably toward their greatness. It's as if Midori popped out of the womb fiddling, Michael Jordan dribbling, and Picasso doodling. This captures the fixed mindset perfectly. And it's everywhere.

A report from researchers at Duke University sounds an alarm about the anxiety and depression among female undergraduates who aspire to "effortless perfection." They believe they should display perfect beauty, perfect womanhood, and perfect scholarship all without trying (or at least without appearing to try).

Americans aren't the only people who disdain effort. French executive Pierre Chevalier says, "We are not a nation of effort. After all, if you have savoir-faire [a mixture of know-how and cool], you do things effortlessly."

People with the growth mindset, however, believe something very different. For them, even geniuses have to work hard for their achievements. And what's so heroic, they would say, about having a gift? They may appreciate endowment, but they admire effort, for no matter what your ability is, effort is what ignites that ability and turns it into accomplishment.

Seabiscuit

Here was a horse who was so broken, he was supposed to be put to sleep. In fact, here was a whole team of people—the jockey, the owner, the trainer—who were damaged in one way or another. Yet through their dogged determination and against all odds, they transformed themselves into winners. A down-and-out nation saw this horse and rider as a symbol of what could be accomplished through grit and spirit.

Equally moving is the parallel story about *Seabiscuit*'s author, Laura Hillenbrand. Felled in her college years by severe, recurrent chronic fatigue that never went away, she was often unable to function. Yet something in the story of the "horse who could" gripped and inspired her, so that she was able to write a heartfelt, magnificent story about the triumph of will. The book was a testament to Seabiscuit's triumph and her own, equally.

Seen through the lens of the growth mindset, these are stories about the transformative power of effort—the power of effort to change your ability and to change you as a person. But filtered through the fixed mindset, it's a great story about three men and a horse, all with deficiencies, who *had* to try very hard.

High Effort: The Big Risk

From the point of view of the fixed mindset, effort is only for people with deficiencies. And when people already know they're deficient, they have nothing to lose by trying. But if your claim to fame is not having any deficiencies—if you're considered a genius, a talent, or a natural—then you have a lot to lose. Effort can *reduce* you.

Nadja Salerno-Sonnenberg made her violin debut at the age of ten with the Philadelphia Orchestra. Yet when she arrived at Juilliard to study with Dorothy DeLay, the great violin teacher, she had a repertoire of awful habits. Her fingerings and bowings were awkward and she held her violin in the wrong position, but she refused to change. After several years, she saw the other students catching up and even surpassing her, and by her late teens she had a crisis of confidence. "I was used to success, to the prodigy label in newspapers, and now I felt like a failure."

This prodigy was afraid of trying. "Everything I was going through boiled down to fear. Fear of trying and failing. . . . If you go to an audition and don't really try, if you're not really prepared, if you didn't work as hard as you could have and you don't win, you have an excuse. . . . Nothing is harder than saying, 'I gave it my all and it wasn't good enough.'"

The idea of trying and still failing—of leaving yourself without excuses—is the worst fear within the fixed mindset, and it haunted and paralyzed her. She had even stopped bringing her violin to her lesson!

Then, one day, after years of patience and understanding, DeLay told her, "Listen, if you don't bring your violin next week, I'm throwing you out of my class." Salerno-Sonnenberg thought she was joking, but DeLay rose from the couch and calmly informed her, "I'm not kidding. If you are going to waste your talent, I don't want to be a part of it. This has gone on long enough."

Why is effort so terrifying?

There are two reasons. One is that in the fixed mindset, great geniuses are not supposed to need it. So just needing it casts a shadow on your ability. The second is that, as Nadja suggests, it robs you of all your excuses. Without effort, you can always say, "I could have been [fill in the blank]." But once you try, you can't say that anymore. Someone once said to me, "I could have been Yo-Yo Ma." If she had really tried for it, she wouldn't have been able to say that.

Salerno-Sonnenberg was terrified of losing DeLay. She finally decided that trying and failing—an honest failure—was better than the course she had been on, and so she began training with DeLay for an upcoming competition. For the first time she went all out, and, by the way, won. Now she says, "This is something I know for a fact: You have to work hardest for the things you love most. And when it's music you love, you're in for the fight of your life."

Fear of effort can happen in relationships, too, as it did with Amanda, a dynamic and attractive young woman.

> I had a lot of crazy boyfriends. A lot. They ranged from unreliable to inconsiderate. "How about a nice guy for once?" my best friend Carla always said. It was like, "You deserve better."
>
> So then Carla fixed me up with Rob, a guy from her office. He was great, and not just on day one. I loved it. It was like, "Oh, my God, a guy who actually shows up on time." Then it became serious and I freaked. I mean, this guy really liked me, but I couldn't stop thinking about how, if he really knew me, he might get turned off. I mean, what if I really, really tried and it didn't work? I guess I couldn't take that risk.

Low Effort: The Big Risk

In the growth mindset, it's almost inconceivable to want something badly, to think you have a chance to achieve it, and then do nothing about it. When it happens, the *I could have been* is heartbreaking, not comforting.

There were few American women in the 1930s through 1950s who were more successful than Clare Boothe Luce. She was a famous author and playwright, she was elected to Congress twice, and she was ambassador to Italy. "I don't really understand the word 'success,'" she has said. "I know people use it about me, but I don't understand it." Her public life and private tragedies kept her from getting back to her greatest love: writing for the theater. She'd had great success with plays like *The Women*, but it just wouldn't do for a political figure to keep penning tart, sexy comedies.

For her, politics did not provide the personal creative effort she valued most, and looking back she couldn't forgive herself for not pursuing her passion for theater. "I often thought," she said, "that if I were to write an autobiography, my title would be *The Autobiography of a Failure*."

Billie Jean King says it's all about what you want to look back and say. I agree with her. You can look back and say, "I could have been . . .," polishing your unused endowments like trophies. Or you can look back and say, "I gave my all for the things I valued." Think about what you want to look back and say. Then choose your mindset.

Turning Knowledge into Action

Sure, people with the fixed mindset have read the books that say: Success is about being your best self, not about being better than others; failure is an opportunity, not a condemnation; effort is the key to success. But they can't put this into practice because their basic mindset—their belief in fixed traits—is telling them something entirely different: that success *is* about being more gifted than others, that failure *does* measure you, and that effort is for those who can't make it on talent.

Discussion Questions

What is the difference between a fixed mindset and a growth mindset in your own words? Which do you think is most prevalent amongst your peers? Why?

What are some of the consequences of having a fixed mindset as described by Dweck (2006)? A growth mindset?

What changes could you make so you have more of a growth mindset?

HAPPINESS EXPLAINED

Tal Ben-Shahar

Happiness is the meaning and the purpose of life, the whole aim and end of human existence.

—Aristotle

We are all familiar with children's insatiable curiosity. Once they begin to question a certain phenomenon in the wonder-filled world around them, they do not relent. Why does it rain? Why does water rise to the sky? Why does water become gas? Why do the clouds not fall? Whether or not children get actual answers to their questions is of little relevance. Their relentless probing follows the pattern of the "infinitely regressive *why*"—regardless of the answer to a question, the child persists with another "Why?"

However, one question allows an adult to end the onslaught of "whys" without any feelings of guilt or inadequacy. This question is "Why do you want to be happy?" When questioning why we want certain things, other than happiness, we can always question their value with another "Why?" For example, why are you training so hard? Why do you want to win this prize? Why do you want to be rich and famous? Why do you want a fancy car, a promotion at work, a year off from work?

When the question is "Why do you want to be happy?" the answer is simple and definitive. We pursue happiness because it is in our nature to do so. When the answer to a question is "Because it will make me happy," nothing can challenge the validity and finality of the answer. Happiness is the highest on the hierarchy of goals, the end toward which all other ends lead.

The British philosopher David Hume argues that "the great end of all human industry is the attainment of happiness. For this were arts invented, sciences cultivated, laws ordained, and societies modeled." Wealth, fame, admiration, and all other goals are subordinate and secondary to happiness; whether our desires are material or social, they are *means* toward one end: happiness.

> Do the "infinitely regressive *why*" exercise for a couple of things that you want—whether a bigger house, a promotion, or anything else. Notice how many "whys" it takes you to reach happiness.

For those not convinced by the argument that happiness should be pursued because it is the highest end, there is much research that suggests that happiness is also a means toward higher levels of overall success. In a review of the research on well-being, psychologists Sonja Lyubomirsky, Laura King, and Ed Diener note, "Numerous studies show that happy individuals are successful across multiple life domains, including marriage, friendship, income, work performance, and health." The research illustrates that the relationship between happiness and success is reciprocal: not only can success—be it at work or in love—contribute to happiness, but happiness also leads to more success.

All else being equal, happy people have better relationships, are more likely to thrive at work, and also live better and longer. Happiness is a worthwhile pursuit, whether as an end in itself or as a means toward other ends.

Happiness Is . . .

Just when we believe that we have satisfied a child's curiosity, she will come up with another ploy. From the "infinitely regressive *why*," she will change course to the "infinitely regressive *what*" and the "infinitely regressive *how*." The questions "What is happiness?" and "How can we attain happiness?" require a more elaborate answer.

I define happiness as "the overall experience of pleasure and meaning."[1] A happy person enjoys positive emotions while perceiving her life as purposeful. The definition does not pertain to a single moment but to a generalized aggregate of one's experiences: a person can endure emotional pain at times and still be happy overall.

We may think about this definition in terms of the happiness archetype. Pleasure is about the experience of positive emotions in the here and now, about present benefit; meaning comes from having a sense of purpose, from the future benefit of our actions.

Pleasure

Emotion, of course, plays a pivotal role in all our pursuits—including our pursuit of happiness. It is nearly impossible for us to imagine a life devoid of emotion. Think of an emotionless robot that, other than the capacity for emotions, has exactly the same physical and cognitive attributes as humans. The robot thinks and behaves in the same way that humans do. It can discuss deep philosophical issues and follow complex logic; it can dig ditches and build skyscrapers.

As sophisticated as the robot is, however, it lacks all motivation to act. This is because even the most basic drives are dependent on emotions—the one thing this robot lacks. The robot could not feel the satisfaction of eating or the need to eat; it could not experience the pain associated with hunger or the satisfaction of satiation. The robot would not pursue food and, given that it has the same physical needs of humans, would soon die.

But let us assume that the robot has been programmed to eat and drink regularly. Even then, despite continuing to live on the physical level, the robot would have neither motivation nor incentive to act. Attaining social standing, acquiring wealth, or falling in love would make no difference to it.

Emotions cause *motion*; they provide a *motive* that drives our action. The very language we use suggests an essential truth—that emotion, motion, and motivation are intimately linked. In Latin, *movere* (motion) means "to move," and the prefix *e-* means "away." The word *motive*, source of *motivation*, comes from *motivum*, which means "a moving cause." Emotions *move us away* from a desireless state, providing us motivation to act.

The neurologist Antonio Damasio provides an illuminating real-life example of the link between emotion and motivation. Following surgery for a brain tumor, one of Damasio's patients, Eliot, retained all of his cognitive abilities—his memory, mathematical ability, perceptual ability, and language skills. However, the part of Eliot's frontal lobe connected to the ability to experience emotions was damaged in the operation. Eliot's condition was similar to that of the emotionless robot: he had all the physical and cognitive characteristics of a normal human being, but the system "involved in feeling and emotion" was damaged.

Eliot's life changed dramatically. Prior to the surgery, he was a happily married, successful lawyer, but after the operation, despite the fact that his "rational brain" was not damaged, Eliot's behavior became so unbearable for those around him that his wife left him, he lost his job, and he was unable to hold another job for very long. The most striking thing about his predicament was his apathetic reaction: he no longer cared about his relationship or his career.

If we were devoid of emotion and hence of motivation to act, we would aspire to nothing. We would remain indifferent to our actions and thoughts, as well as their ramifications. Because emotion is the foundation of motivation, it naturally plays a central role in our motivation to pursue happiness.

However, merely being capable of emotion—any emotion—is not enough. To be happy, we need the experience of positive emotion; pleasure is a prerequisite for a fulfilling life. According to the psychologist Nathaniel Branden, "Pleasure for man is not a luxury, but a profound psychological need." The total absence of pleasure and the experience of constant emotional pain preclude the possibility of a happy life.

When I speak of pleasure, I am not referring to the experience of a constant "high" or ecstasy. We all experience emotional highs and lows. We can experience sadness at times—when we suffer loss or failure—and still lead a happy life. In fact, the unrealistic expectation of a constant high will inevitably lead to disappointment and feelings of inadequacy and hence to negative emotions. Happiness does not require a constant experience of ecstasy, nor does it require an unbroken chain of positive emotions.[2]

While the happy person experiences highs and lows, his overall state of being is positive. Most of the time he is propelled by positive emotions such as joy and affection rather than negative ones such as anger and guilt. Pleasure is the rule; pain, the exception. To be happy, we have to feel that, on the whole, whatever sorrows, trials, and tribulations we may encounter, we still experience the joy of being alive.

> Make a mental list of things—from little things to big ones—that provide you with pleasure.

But is living an emotionally gratifying life really enough? Is experiencing positive emotions a sufficient condition for happiness? What of a psychotic who experiences euphoric delusions? What of those who consume ecstasy-inducing drugs or spend their days leisurely sprawled on the beach? Are these people happy? The answer is no. Experiencing positive emotions is necessary but not *sufficient* for happiness.

Meaning

The philosopher Robert Nozick, in *Anarchy, State, and Utopia,* describes a thought experiment that can help us differentiate between the experience of a person on ecstasy-inducing drugs and an experience of true happiness. Nozick asks us to imagine a machine that could provide us with "the experience of writing a great poem or bringing about world peace or loving someone and being loved in return" or any other experience we might desire. The machine could afford us the emotional experience of being in love, which would feel the same as actually being in love. We would be unaware that we were plugged into the machine (that is, we would believe that we were actually spending time with our beloved). Nozick asks whether, given the opportunity, we would *choose* to plug into the machine for the rest of our lives. Another way of asking this question is, would we be *happy* if we were plugged into the machine for the rest of our lives?

The answer for most of us would clearly be no. We would not want to be hooked up to a machine permanently because we care about "things in addition to how our lives *feel* to us from the inside." Few of us would think that "only a person's experiences matter." We want not only to take pleasure in experiences, we "want them to be so." There is, then, more to happiness than positive emotions.

Circumventing the cause of these emotions, through a machine or drugs, would be tantamount to living a lie. Given the choice between a machine-generated feeling that we had brought about world peace and a less powerful feeling derived from actually helping one person, we would most likely choose the latter. It is as if we have an internal mechanism that demands more than the present sensation that we feel—we need the *cause* of our emotions to be meaningful. We want to know that our actions have an *actual* effect in the world, not just that we *feel* that they do.

As far as emotions are concerned, human beings are not far removed from animals, and some of the higher animals, like chimpanzees, have an emotional brain similar to ours. This is not surprising because without emotions (or sensations, in the case of some animals), there would be no drive to do anything, and a living organism would not sustain itself. Without emotions or sensations, animals, like the emotionless robot, would not move.

However, while our capacity for emotions is similar to that of other animals, we are fundamentally different. The fact that we can reflect on the cause of our emotions is one of the characteristics that distinguish us. We have the capacity to reflect on our feelings, thoughts, and actions; we have the capacity to be conscious of our consciousness and our experiences.

We also have the capacity for spirituality. The *Oxford English Dictionary* defines spirituality as "the real sense of significance of something." Animals cannot live a spiritual life; they cannot endow their actions with meaning beyond the pleasure or pain that those actions yield.

When speaking of a meaningful life, we often talk of having a sense of purpose, but what we sometimes fail to recognize is that finding this sense of purpose entails more than simply setting goals. Having goals or even reaching them does not guarantee that we are leading a purposeful existence. To experience a sense of purpose, the goals we set for ourselves need to be intrinsically meaningful.

We could set ourselves the goal of scoring top grades in college or owning a large house, yet still feel empty. To live a meaningful life, we must have a self-generated purpose that possesses personal significance rather than one that is dictated by society's standards and expectations. When we do experience this sense of purpose, we often feel as though we have found our calling. As George Bernard Shaw said, "This is the true joy in life, the being used for a *purpose* recognized by yourself as a mighty one."

Different people find meaning in different things. We may find our calling in starting up a business, working in a homeless shelter, raising children, practicing medicine, or making furniture. The important thing is that *we* choose our purpose in accordance with our own values and passions rather than conforming to others' expectations. An investment banker who finds meaning and pleasure in her work—who is in it for the right reasons—leads a more spiritual and fulfilling life than a monk who is in his field for the wrong reasons.

Idealism and Realism

I once asked a friend what his calling in life was. He told me that he does not think about his life in terms of calling or some higher purpose. "I am not an idealist," he said, "but a realist."

The realist is considered the pragmatist, the person who has both feet firmly planted on the ground. The idealist is seen as the dreamer, the person who has her eyes toward the horizon and devotes her time to thinking about calling and purpose.

Yet when we set realism and idealism in opposition to one another—when we live as though having ideals and dreams were unrealistic and detached— we are allowing a false dichotomy to hold us back. Being an idealist *is* being a realist in the deepest sense—it is being true to our *real* nature. We are so constituted that we actually need our lives to have meaning. Without a higher purpose, a calling, an ideal, we cannot attain our full potential for happiness. While I am not advocating dreaming over doing (both are important), there is a significant truth that many realists—rat racers mostly—ignore: *to be idealistic is to be realistic.*

Being an idealist is about having a sense of purpose that encompasses our life as a whole; but for us to be happy, it is not enough to experience our life as meaningful on the general level of the big picture. We need to find meaning on the specific level of our daily existence as well. For example, in addition to having the general purpose of creating a happy family or dedicating our life to liberating the oppressed, we also need a specific purpose related to those goals, such as having lunch with our child or taking part in protest marches. It is often difficult to sustain ourselves with the thought of a general sense of purpose that lies far off on the horizon: we need a more specific and tangible sense that we are doing something meaningful next week, tomorrow, later today.

> Think of the things that provide you with meaning. What can, or already does, provide a sense of purpose to your life as a whole? What daily or weekly activities provide you with meaning?

According to French Renaissance philosopher Michel de Montaigne, "The great and glorious masterpiece of man is to live with purpose." Having a purpose, a goal that provides a sense of direction, imbues our individual actions with meaning—and from experiencing life as a collection of disjointed pieces, we begin to experience it as a masterpiece. An overarching purpose can unify individual activities, just like the overarching theme of a symphony unifies the individual notes. In and of itself, a note does not amount to much, but it becomes significant—and beautiful—when part of a common theme, a common purpose.

Potential and Happiness

When thinking about the most meaningful life for ourselves, we must also consider our potential and how to make full use of our capacities. While a cow might seem content with a life spent grazing in the pasture, we cannot be happy living simply to gratify our physical desires. Our inborn potential as humans dictates that we do more, that we utilize our full capacities. "The happiness that is genuinely satisfying," writes the philosopher Bertrand Russell, "is accompanied by the fullest exercise of our faculties and the fullest realization of the world in which we live."

This does not mean that a woman who has the potential to be the most influential person in her country cannot be happy unless she becomes president or prime minister, or that a person with the potential to be successful in business cannot be happy unless she makes millions. Becoming the president or a millionaire are *external* manifestations of potential. What I am referring to are *internal* measures of potential. The person with the capacity to be the president could be happy as a scholar of ancient Sanskrit; the person with the capacity to be a millionaire could lead a fulfilling life as a journalist. They can find satisfaction if they feel, *from within,* that they are doing things that challenge them, things that use them fully and well.[3]

What pursuits would challenge you and fulfill your potential?

Success and Happiness

Some people might be concerned that pursuing meaning and pleasure over accolades and wealth could come at the price of success. If, for example, grades and getting into the best institutions no longer constitute a strong motivation, might not a student lose his commitment to his schoolwork? If promotions and raises are no longer the ultimate driving force in the workplace, will employees dedicate fewer hours to their jobs?

I had similar concerns about my own success as I was contemplating the shift toward the happiness archetype. The "no pain, no gain" formula had served me well, in terms of quantifiable success, and I feared that my resolve would weaken—that the next milestone would lose its appeal and no longer sustain me as it did when I was a rat racer. What happened, however, was the exact opposite.

The shift from being a rat racer to pursuing happiness is not about working less or with less fervor but about working as hard or harder at the right activities—those that are a source of both present and future benefit. Similarly, the shift from hedonism to the pursuit of happiness does not entail having less fun; the difference is that the fun the happy person experiences is sustainable, whereas the fun of the hedonist is ephemeral. The happy person defies the "no pain, no gain" formula: she enjoys the journey and, dedicating herself to a purpose in which she believes, attains a better outcome.

The Need for Meaning and Pleasure

Just as pleasure is not sufficient for the attainment of happiness, neither is a sense of purpose. First, it is exceedingly difficult to sustain long-term action, regardless of the meaning we assign to it, without enjoying emotional gratification in the present. The prospect of a brighter future can usually keep us motivated for only a limited time. Second, even if we did sustain our denial of immediate gratification, as rat racers often do, we most certainly would not be happy.

In his book *Man's Search for Meaning,* Viktor Frankl talks about how victims of the Holocaust were able to find meaning in their lives. Despite the physical and emotional torture that these people endured in the concentration camps, some of them found meaning, a sense of purpose, in their meager existence. Their purpose could have been to reunite with loved ones or to someday write about what they had lived through. However, even to suggest that these people were happy while in the camp is absurd. In order to be happy, having meaning in life is not enough. We need the experience of meaning *and* the experience of positive emotions; we need present *and* future benefit.

My theory of happiness draws on the works of Freud as well as Frankl. Freud's pleasure principle says that we are fundamentally driven by the instinctual need for pleasure. Frankl argues that we are motivated by a will to meaning rather than by a will to pleasure—he says that "striving to find meaning in one's life is the primary motivational force in man." In the context of finding happiness, there is some truth in both Freud's and Frankl's theories. We need to gratify both the will for pleasure and the will for meaning if we are to lead a fulfilling, happy life.[4]

We, especially in the United States, are often criticized for being a society obsessed with happiness: self-help books offering quick-fix solutions and a struggle-free life are selling at an unprecedented rate, and there are psychiatrists who prescribe medication at the first sign of emotional discomfort. While the criticism is, to some extent, justified, it identifies the wrong obsession: the obsession is with pleasure, not with happiness.

The brave new world of quick fixes does not take into consideration long-term benefits and ignores our need for meaning. True happiness involves some emotional discomfort and difficult experiences, which some self-help books and psychiatric medication attempt to circumvent. Happiness presupposes our having to overcome obstacles. In the words of Frankl, "What man actually needs is not a tensionless state but rather the striving and struggling for some goal worthy of him. What he needs is not the discharge of tension at any cost, but the call of a potential meaning waiting to be fulfilled by him." As the science of psychiatry advances, it is likely that more and more people are going to be put on medication. While there are certainly many cases in which the use of psychiatric drugs is warranted and necessary, I am taking issue with the ease with which such medication is dispensed. There is a real danger that with the struggle, meaning too will be medicated away.

We should also remember that going through difficult times augments our capacity for pleasure: it keeps us from taking pleasure for granted, reminds us to be grateful for all the large and small pleasures in our lives. Being grateful in this way can *itself* be a source of real meaning and pleasure.

There is a synergistic relationship between pleasure and meaning, between present and future benefit. When we derive a sense of purpose from what we do, our experience of pleasure is intensified; and taking pleasure in an activity can make our experience of it all the more meaningful.[5]

Think back to a difficult or painful experience you had. What did you learn from it? In what ways did you grow?

Quantity and Quality

We all enjoy and derive meaning from different activities, and to varying degrees. For example, writing provides me with both present and future benefit, but writing for more than three hours a day bores me. Watching two movies a week contributes to my happiness, whereas spending four hours a day in front of a screen, over time, will most likely frustrate me. Just because an activity provides us with meaning and pleasure does not mean that we can be happy doing it all the time.

To extend the food motif beyond the hamburger, I will introduce what I've come to call the *lasagna principle*—the notion that our capacity to enjoy different activities is limited and unique. Lasagna is my favorite food, and every time I visit my parents, my mother prepares a tray of it, which I promptly devour. This does not, however, mean that I want to eat lasagna all day and every day. The same principle applies to my favorite activities, such as writing and watching movies, as well as to my favorite people. Just because my family is the most meaningful thing in my life does not mean that spending eight hours a day with them is what would make me happiest; and not wanting to spend all my waking hours with them does not imply that I love them any less. I derive a great deal of pleasure and meaning from being with other people, but I also need my daily quota of solitude. Identifying the right activity, and then the right quantity for each activity, leads to the highest quality of life.

The best method of maximizing our levels of happiness is trial and error, paying attention to the quality of our inner experiences. Yet most of us do not take the time to ask ourselves the question of questions—because we are too busy. As Thoreau says, however, "Life is too short to be in a hurry." If we are always on the go, we are *reacting* to the exigencies of day-to-day life rather than allowing ourselves the space to *create* a happy life.

Abraham Maslow maintains that a person "cannot choose wisely for a life unless he dares to listen to himself, his own self, at each moment in life." It is important to put time aside to take Maslow's dare, to ask ourselves the type of questions that can help us choose wisely: Are the things that I am doing meaningful to me? Are they pleasurable? Is my mind telling me that I should be doing different things with my time? Is my heart telling me that I must change my life? We have to listen, really listen, to our hearts *and* minds—our emotions *and* our reason.

EXERCISES

Mapping Your Life

Though it is difficult to quantify internal states of mind and heart, it is still possible to evaluate our lives in terms of happiness and gain insight into how we can become happier. We could begin by recording our daily activities and evaluating them according to how pleasurable and meaningful they are.

Devoting a few minutes at the end of each day to write down and reflect upon how we spent our time can help us recognize important patterns. For example, we might realize that we spend a significant proportion of our time in activities that provide future benefit but that we do not enjoy, or doing things that provide us with neither meaning nor pleasure. We can then evaluate our lives through the lens of happiness and decide to add more meaningful and pleasurable experiences.

While there are basic principles that can guide us toward the good life—finding meaning and pleasure, for instance—there is no universal prescription for it. It is self-evident that human beings are complex, multifaceted, and different; each person is unique, a world unto himself. By zooming in on my day-to-day activities, I can see beyond the general principles that govern *a* life and identify the unique needs and wants of *my* life.

For a period of a week or two, record your daily activities. At the end of each day, write down how you spent your time, from half an hour e-mailing to two hours watching TV. This does not need to be a precise by-the-minute account of your day, but it should provide you with an overall sense of what your days look like.

At the end of the week, create a table listing each of your activities, the amount of time you devoted to each one, and how much meaning and pleasure each one provides (you can use a scale of 1 through 5, with 1 indicating no meaning or pleasure, and 5 signifying very high meaning or pleasure). Next to the amount of time, indicate whether you would like to spend more or less of your time on the activity. If you'd like to spend more time, write "+" next to it; if you'd like to spend a lot more time doing it, put down "++." If you'd like to spend less time on the activity, put "−" next to it; for a lot less time, write "− −." If you are satisfied with the amount of time you are spending on a particular activity, or if it is not possible to change the amount of time you devote to it at the moment, write "=" next to it.

Here is an example of part of such a weekly map:

Activity	Meaning	Pleasure	Time/week
Spending time with family	5	4	2.2 hours ++
Meetings at work	4	2	11 hours =
Watching TV	2	3	8.5 hours −

Integrity Mirror

Make a list of the things that are most meaningful and pleasurable to you, that make you happiest. For example, a list could include family, exercising, promoting human rights around the world, listening to music, and so on.

Next to each of the items on your list, write down how much time per week or month you devote to it. With or without the help of the map you made in the preceding exercise, ask yourself whether you are living your highest values. Are you spending quality time with your partner and children? Are you exercising three times a week? Are you active in a human rights organization? Do you put time aside to listen to music at home and attend concerts?

This exercise raises a mirror to your life and helps you determine whether or not there is congruence—integrity—between your highest values and the way you live. With increased integrity comes increased happiness.[6] Given that we're often blind to the discrepancy between what we say is important to us and what we actually do, it may be useful to do this exercise with someone who knows you well and cares about you enough to be willing to help you evaluate your life honestly.[7]

How much time we choose to spend on our highest values depends on personal preferences and availability. Just because family is my highest value does not imply that to increase my integrity and therefore happiness I need to reallocate all the time I currently spend on my hobby to my family (remember the lasagna principle). A person who must work two jobs to get enough food on the table for his family is living in accordance with his highest values even though he gets to spend little time playing with his children.

Often, however, we are pulled away from the life that would make us happier by internal and external forces that we have some control over—such as our habits, our fears, or other people's expectations. Given that time is a finite and limited resource, we may need to give up some activities that are lower on our list of importance—say "no" to certain opportunities so that we can say "yes" to ones that are more valuable to us.

Repeat this exercise regularly. Change, especially of deeply ingrained habits and patterns, does not happen overnight. Most important, once again, is to ritualize your activities. In addition to creating a habit of activities that you want to engage in, introduce negative rituals—times during which you refrain from doing certain things. For example, if feasible, create an Internet-free time zone, each day between certain hours. We spend an increasing amount of time on the Web; checking our e-mail every few minutes takes away from our productivity and creativity and ultimately makes us less happy.[8] You can also introduce phone-free or meetings-free time zones, when you can fully focus on other activities, whether getting work done or spending time with your friends.

Discussion Questions

Think of an example of a time when a personal success led to an increase in happiness. Was that experience reciprocal – i.e., did your success and happiness lead to more success or less?

How effective are your current behaviors at achieving the two elements of happiness: pleasure and meaning?

What changes could you make to increase your happiness level?

How does emotion drive motion in people with a fixed mindset? A growth mindset?

What influence do others have on your pursuit of purpose?

What can be done to ensure one lives a life in which they create instead of react?

BODY RITUAL AMONG THE NACIREMA

Horace Miner

THE anthropologist has become so familiar with the diversity of ways in which different peoples behave in similar situations that he is not apt to be surprised by even the most exotic customs. In fact, if all of the logically possible combinations of behavior have not been found somewhere in the world, he is apt to suspect that they must be present in some yet undescribed tribe. This point has, in fact, been expressed with respect to clan organization by Murdock (1949:71). In this light, the magical beliefs and practices of the Nacirema present such unusual aspects that it seems desirable to describe them as an example of the extremes to which human behavior can go.

Professor Linton first brought the ritual of the Nacirema to the attention of anthropologists twenty years ago (1936:326), but the culture of this people is still very poorly understood. They-are a North American group living in the territory between the Canadian Cree, the Yaqui and Tarahumare of Mexico, and the Carib and Arawak of the Antilles. Little is known of their origin, although tradition states that they came from the east. According to Nacirema mythology, their nation was originated by a culture hero, Notgnihsaw, who is otherwise known for two great feats of strength—the throwing of a piece of wampum across the river Pa-To-Mac and the chopping down of a cherry tree in which the Spirit of Truth resided.

Nacirema culture is characterized by a highly developed market economy which has evolved in a rich natural habitat. While much of the people's time is devoted to economic pursuits, a large part of the fruits of these labors and a considerable portion of the day are spent in ritual activity. The focus of this activity is the human body, the appearance and health of which loom as a dominant concern in the ethos of the people. While such a concern is certainly not unusual, its ceremonial aspects and associated philosophy are unique.

The fundamental belief underlying the whole system appears to be that the human body is ugly and that its natural tendency is to debility and disease. Incarcerated in such a body, man's only hope is to avert these characteristics through the use of the powerful influences of ritual and ceremony. Every household has one or more shrines devoted to this purpose. The more powerful individuals in the society have several shrines in their houses and, in fact, the opulence of a house is often referred to in terms of the number of such ritual centers it possesses. Most houses are of wattle and daub construction, but the shrine rooms of the more wealthy are walled with stone. Poorer families imitate the rich by applying pottery plaques to their shrine walls.

While each family has at least one such shrine, the rituals associated with it are not family ceremonies but are private and secret. The rites are normally only

---

Source: Miner, H. (1956). "Body ritual among the Nacirema." *The American Anthropologist*, 58, 503–507.

discussed with children, and then only during the period when they are being initiated into these mysteries. I was able, however, to establish sufficient rapport with the natives to examine these shrines and to have the rituals described to me.

The focal point of the shrine is a box or chest which is built into the wall. In this chest are kept the many charms and magical potions without which no native believes he could live. These preparations are secured from a variety of specialized practitioners. The most powerful of these are the medicine men, whose assistance must be rewarded with substantial gifts. However, the medicine men do not provide the curative potions for their clients, but decide what the ingredients should be and then write them down in an ancient and secret language. This writing is understood only by the medicine men and by the herbalists who, for another gift, provide the required charm.

The charm is not disposed of after it has served its purpose, but is placed in the charm-box of the household shrine. As these magical materials are specific for certain ills, and the real or imagined maladies of the people are many, the charm-box is usually full to overflowing. The magical packets are so numerous that people forget what their purposes were and fear to use them again. While the natives are very vague on this point, we can only assume that the idea in retaining all the old magical materials is that their presence in the charm-box, before which the body rituals are conducted, will in some way protect the worshipper.

Beneath the charm-box is a small font. Each day every member of the family, in succession, enters the shrine room, bows his head before the charmbox, mingles different sorts of holy water in the font, and proceeds with a brief rite of ablution. The holy waters are secured from the Water Temple of the community, where the priests conduct elaborate ceremonies to make the liquid ritually pure.

In the hierarchy of magical practitioners, and below the medicine men in prestige, are specialists whose designation is best translated "holy-mouth-men." The Nacirema have an almost pathological horror of and fascination with the mouth, the condition of which is believed to have a supernatural influence on all social relationships. Were it not for the rituals of the mouth, they believe that their teeth would fall out, their gums bleed, their jaws shrink, their friends desert them, and their lovers reject them. They also believe that a strong relationship exists between oral and moral characteristics. For example, there is a ritual ablution of the mouth for children which is supposed to improve their moral fiber.

The daily body ritual performed by everyone includes a mouth-rite. Despite the fact that these people are so punctilious about care of the mouth, this rite involves a practice which strikes the uninitiated stranger as revolting. It was reported to me that the ritual consists of inserting a small bundle of hog hairs into the mouth, along with certain magical powders, and then moving the bundle in a highly formalized series of gestures.

In addition to the private mouth-rite, the people seek out a holy-mouth-man once or twice a year. These practitioners have an impressive set of paraphernalia, consisting of a variety of augers, awls, probes, and prods. The use of these objects in the exorcism of the evils of the mouth involves almost unbelievable ritual torture of the client. The holy-mouth-man opens the client's mouth and, using the above mentioned tools, enlarges any holes which decay may have created in the teeth. Magical materials are put into these holes. If there are no naturally occurring holes in the teeth, large sections of one or more teeth are gouged out so that the supernatural substance can be applied. In the client's view, the purpose of these ministrations is to arrest decay and to draw friends. The extremely sacred and traditional character of the rite is evident in the fact that the natives return to the holy-mouth-men year after year, despite the fact that their teeth continue to decay.

It is to be hoped that, when a thorough study of the Nacirema is made, there will be careful inquiry into the personality structure of these people. One has but to watch the gleam in the eye of a holy-mouth-man, as he jabs an awl into an exposed nerve, to suspect that a certain amount of sadism is involved. If this can be established, a very interesting pattern emerges, for most of the population shows definite masochistic tendencies. It was to these that Professor Linton referred in discussing a distinctive part of the daily body ritual which is performed only by men. This part of the rite involves scraping and lacerating the surface of the face with a sharp instrument. Special women's rites are performed only four times during each lunar month, but what they lack in frequency is made up in barbarity. As part of this ceremony, women bake their heads in small ovens for about an hour. The theoretically interesting point is that what seems to be a preponderantly masochistic people have developed sadistic specialists.

The medicine men have an imposing temple, or *lati pso,* in every community of any size. The more elaborate ceremonies required to treat very sick patients can only be performed at this temple. These ceremonies involve not only the thaumaturge but a permanent group of vestal maidens who move sedately about the temple chambers in distinctive costume and headdress.

The *latipso* ceremonies are so harsh that it is phenomenal that a fair proportion of the really sick natives who enter the temple ever recover. Small children whose indoctrination is still incomplete have been known to resist attempts to take them to the temple because "that is where you go to die." Despite this fact, sick adults are not only willing but eager to undergo the protracted ritual purification, if they can afford to do so. No matter how ill the supplicant or how grave the emergency, the guardians of many temples will not admit a client if he cannot give a rich gift to the custodian. Even after one has gained admission and survived the ceremonies, the guardians will not permit the neophyte to leave until he makes still another gift.

The supplicant entering the temple is first stripped of all his or her clothes. In every-day life the Nacirema avoids exposure of his body and its natural functions. Bathing and excretory acts are performed only in the secrecy of the household shrine, where they are ritualized as part of the body-rites. Psychological shock results from the fact that body secrecy is suddenly lost upon entry into the *latipso.* A man, whose own wife has never seen him in an excretory act, suddenly finds himself naked and assisted by a vestal maiden while he performs his natural functions into a sacred vessel. This sort of ceremonial treatment is necessitated by the fact that the excreta are used by a diviner to ascertain the course and nature of the client's sickness. Female clients, on the other hand, find their naked bodies are subjected to the scrutiny, manipulation and prodding of the medicine men.

Few supplicants in the temple are well enough to do anything but lie on their hard beds. The daily ceremonies, like the rites of the holy-mouth-men, involve discomfort and torture. With ritual precision, the vestals awaken their miserable charges each dawn and roll them about on their beds of pain while performing ablutions, in the formal movements of which the maidens are highly trained. At other times they insert magic wands in the supplicant's mouth or force him to eat substances which are supposed to be healing. From time to time the medicine men come to their clients and jab magically treated needles into their flesh. The fact that these temple ceremonies may not cure, and may even kill the neophyte, in no way decreases the people's faith in the medicine men.

There remains one other kind of practitioner, known as a "listener." This witch-doctor has the power to exorcise the devils that lodge in the heads of people who have been bewitched. The Nacirema believe that parents bewitch their own children. Mothers are particularly suspected of putting a curse on children while teaching them the secret body rituals. The counter-magic of the witch-doctor is unusual in its lack of ritual. The patient simply tells the "listener" all his troubles and fears, beginning with the earliest difficulties he can remember. The memory displayed by the Nacirema in these exorcism sessions is truly remarkable. It is not uncommon for the patient to bemoan the rejection he felt upon being weaned as a babe, and a few individuals even see their troubles going back to the traumatic effects of their own birth.

In conclusion, mention must be made of certain practices which have their base in native esthetics but which depend upon the pervasive aversion to the natural body and its functions. There are ritual fasts to make fat people thin and ceremonial feasts to make thin people fat. Still other rites are used to make women's breasts larger if they are small, and smaller if they are large. General dissatisfaction with breast shape is symbolized in the fact that the ideal form is virtually outside the range of human variation. A few women afflicted with almost inhuman hypermammary development are so idolized that they make a handsome living by simply going from village to village and permitting the natives to stare at them for a fee.

Reference has already been made to the fact that excretory functions are ritualized, routinized, and relegated to secrecy. Natural reproductive functions are similarly distorted. Intercourse is taboo as a topic and scheduled as an act. Efforts are made to avoid pregnancy by the use of magical materials or by limiting intercourse to certain phases of the moon. Conception is actually very infrequent. When pregnant, women dress so as to hide their condition. Parturition takes place in secret, without friends or relatives to assist, and the majority of women do not nurse their infants.

Our review of the ritual life of the Nacirema has certainly shown them to be a magic-ridden people. It is hard to understand how they have managed to exist so long under the burdens which they have imposed upon themselves. But even such exotic customs as these take on real meaning when they are viewed with the insight provided by Malinowski when he wrote (1948:70):

Looking from far and above, from our high places of safety in the developed civilization, it is easy to see all the crudity and irrelevance of magic. But without its power and guidance early man could not have mastered his practical difficulties as he has done, nor could man have advanced to the higher stages of civilization.

References

LINTON, RALPH
    1936 The Study of Man. New York, D. Appleton-Century Co.
MALINOWSKI, BRONISLAW
    1948 Magic, Science, and Religion. Glencoe, The Free Press.
MURDOCK, GEORGE P.
    1949 Social Structure. New York, The Macmillan Co.

Discussion Questions

What assumptions can you make about the Nacirema based on the rituals described in the article?

How does your cultural worldview impact your perception of the Nacirema (and other cultures)?

What does it mean to be ethnocentric and how does that relate to your perceptions of the Nacirema?

GRIT

THE POWER *OF* PASSION *AND* PERSEVERANCE

Angela Duckworth

Preface

Growing up, I heard the word *genius* a lot.

It was always my dad who brought it up. He liked to say, apropos of nothing at all, "You know, you're no genius!" This pronouncement might come in the middle of dinner, during a commercial break for *The Love Boat,* or after he flopped down on the couch with the *Wall Street Journal.*

I don't remember how I responded. Maybe I pretended not to hear.

My dad's thoughts turned frequently to genius, talent, and who had more than whom. He was deeply concerned with how smart he was. He was deeply concerned with how smart his family was.

I wasn't the only problem. My dad didn't think my brother and sister were geniuses, either. By his yardstick, none of us measured up to Einstein. Apparently, this was a great disappointment. Dad worried that this intellectual handicap would limit what we'd eventually achieve in life.

Two years ago, I was fortunate enough to be awarded a MacArthur Fellowship, sometimes called the "genius grant." You don't apply for the MacArthur. You don't ask your friends or colleagues to nominate you. Instead, a secret committee that includes the top people in your field decides you're doing important and creative work.

When I received the unexpected call telling me the news, my first reaction was one of gratitude and amazement. Then my thoughts turned to my dad and his offhand diagnoses of my intellectual potential. He wasn't wrong; I didn't win the MacArthur because I'm leagues smarter than my fellow psychologists. Instead, he had the right answer ("No, she's not") to the wrong question ("Is she a genius?").

There was about a month between the MacArthur call and its official announcement. Apart from my husband, I wasn't permitted to tell anyone. That gave me time to ponder the irony of the situation. A girl who is told repeatedly that she's no genius ends up winning an award for being one. The award goes to her because she has discovered that what we eventually accomplish may depend more on our passion and perseverance than on our innate talent. She has by then amassed degrees from some pretty tough schools, but in the third grade, she didn't test high enough for the gifted and talented program. Her parents are Chinese immigrants, but she didn't get lectured on the salvation of hard work. Against stereotype, she can't play a note of piano or violin.

The morning the MacArthur was announced, I walked over to my parents' apartment. My mom and dad had already heard the news, and so had several "aunties," who were calling in rapid succession to offer congratulations. Finally, when the phone stopped ringing, my dad turned to me and said, "I'm proud of you."

I had so much to say in response, but instead I just said, "Thanks, Dad."

There was no sense rehashing the past. I knew that, in fact, he *was* proud of me.

Still, part of me wanted to travel back in time to when I was a young girl. I'd tell him what I know now.

I would say, "Dad, you say claim I'm no genius. I won't argue with that. You know plenty of people who are smarter than I am." I can imagine his head nodding in sober agreement.

"But let me tell you something. I'm going to grow up to love my work as much as you love yours. I won't just have a job; I'll have a calling. I'll challenge myself every day. When I get knocked down, I'll get back up. I may not be the smartest person in the room, but I'll strive to be the grittiest."

And if he was still listening: "In the long run, Dad, grit may matter more than talent."

All these years later, I have the scientific evidence to prove my point. What's more, I know that grit is mutable, not fixed, and I have insights from research about how to grow it.

This book summarizes everything I've learned about grit.

When I finished writing it, I went to visit my dad. Chapter by chapter, over the course of days, I read him every line. He's been battling Parkinson's disease for the last decade or so, and I'm not entirely sure how much he understood. Still, he seemed to be listening intently, and when I was done, he looked at me. After what felt like an eternity, he nodded once. And then he smiled.

Part I What Grit is and Why It Matters

Chapter 1 SHOWING UP

By the time you set foot on the campus of the United States Military Academy at West Point, you've earned it.

The admissions process for West Point is at least as rigorous as for the most selective universities. Top scores on the SAT or ACT and outstanding high school grades are a must. But when you apply to Harvard, you don't need to start your application in the eleventh grade, and you don't need to secure a nomination from a member of Congress, a senator, or the vice president of the United States. You don't, for that matter, have to get superlative marks in a fitness assessment that includes running, push-ups, sit-ups, and pull-ups.

Each year, in their junior year of high school, more than 14,000 applicants begin the admissions process. This pool is winnowed to just 4,000 who succeed in getting the required nomination. Slightly more than half of those applicants—about

2,500—meet West Point's rigorous academic and physical standards, and from that select group just 1,200 are admitted and enrolled. Nearly all the men and women who come to West Point were varsity athletes; most were team captains.

And yet, one in five cadets will drop out before graduation. What's more remarkable is that, historically, a substantial fraction of dropouts leave in their very first summer, during an intensive seven-week training program named, even in official literature, Beast Barracks. Or, for short, just Beast.

Who spends two years trying to get into a place and then drops out in the first two months?

Then again, these are no ordinary months. Beast is described in the West Point handbook for new cadets as "the most physically and emotionally demanding part of your four years at West Point . . . designed to help you make the transition from new cadet to Soldier."

A Typical Day at Beast Barracks

5:00 a.m.	Wake-up
5:30 a.m.	Reveille Formation
5:30 to 6:55 a.m.	Physical Training
6:55 to 7:25 a.m.	Personal Maintenance
7:30 to 8:15 a.m.	Breakfast
8:30 to 12:45 p.m.	Training/Classes
1:00 to 1:45 p.m.	Lunch
2:00 to 3:45 p.m.	Training/Classes
4:00 to 5:30 p.m.	Organized Athletics
5:30 to 5:55 p.m.	Personal Maintenance
6:00 to 6:45 p.m.	Dinner
7:00 to 9:00 p.m.	Training/Classes
9:00 to 10:00 p.m.	Commander's Time
10:00 p.m.	Taps

The day begins at 5:00 a.m. By 5:30, cadets are in formation, standing at attention, honoring the raising of the United States flag. Then follows a hard workout—running or calisthenics—followed by a nonstop rotation of marching in formation, classroom instruction, weapons training, and athletics. Lights out, to the bugled notes of taps, occurs at ten p.m. And on the next day the routine starts over again. Oh, and there are no weekends, no breaks other than meals, and virtually no contact with family and friends outside of West Point.

One cadet's description of Beast: "You are challenged in a variety of ways in every developmental area—mentally, physically, militarily, and socially. The system will find your weaknesses, but that's the point—West Point toughens you."

––––––––

So, who makes it through Beast?

It was 2004 and my second year of graduate school in psychology when I set about answering that question, but for decades, the U.S. Army has been asking the same thing. In fact, it was in 1955—almost fifty years before I began working on this puzzle—that a young psychologist named Jerry Kagan was drafted into the army, ordered to report to West Point, and assigned to test new cadets for the purpose of identifying who would stay and who would leave. As fate would have it, Jerry was not only the first psychologist to study dropping out at West Point, he was also the first psychologist I met in college. I ended up working part-time in his lab for two years.

Jerry described early efforts to separate the wheat from the chaff at West Point as dramatically unsuccessful. He recalled in particular spending hundreds of hours showing cadets cards printed with pictures and asking the young men to make up stories to fit them. This test was meant to unearth deep-seated, unconscious motives, and the general idea was that cadets who visualized noble deeds and courageous accomplishments should be the ones who would graduate instead of dropping out. Like a lot of ideas that sound good in principle, this one didn't work so well in practice. The stories the cadets told were colorful and fun to listen to, but they had absolutely nothing to do with decisions the cadets made in their actual lives.

Since then, several more generations of psychologists devoted themselves to the attrition issue, but not one researcher could say with much certainty why some of the most promising cadets routinely quit when their training had just begun.

Soon after learning about Beast, I found my way to the office of Dr. Mike Matthews, a military psychologist who had been a West Point faculty member for years. Mike explained that the West Point admissions process successfully identified men and women who had the potential to thrive there. In particular, admissions staff calculate for each applicant something called the Whole Candidate Score, a weighted average of SAT or ACT exam scores, high school rank adjusted for the number of students in the applicant's graduating class, expert appraisals of leadership potential, and performance on objective measures of physical fitness.

You can think of the Whole Candidate Score as West Point's best guess at how much talent applicants have for the diverse rigors of its four-year program. In other words, it's an estimate of how easily cadets will master the many skills required of a military leader.

The Whole Candidate Score is the single most important factor in West Point admissions, and yet it *didn't* reliably predict who would make it through Beast. In fact, cadets with the highest Whole Candidate Scores were just as likely to drop out as those with the lowest. And this was why Mike's door was open to me.

From his own experience joining the air force as a young man, Mike had a clue to the riddle. While the rigors of his induction weren't quite as harrowing as those of West Point, there were notable similarities. The most important were challenges that exceeded current skills. For the first time in their lives, Mike and the other recruits were being asked, on an hourly basis, to do things they couldn't yet do. "Within two weeks," Mike recalls, "I was tired, lonely, frustrated, and ready to quit—as were all of my classmates."

Some did quit, but Mike did not.

What struck Mike was that rising to the occasion had almost nothing to do with talent. Those who dropped out of training rarely did so from lack of ability. Rather, what mattered, Mike said, was a "never give up" attitude.

———

Around that time, it wasn't just Mike Matthews who was talking to me about this kind of hang-in-there posture toward challenge. As a graduate student just beginning to probe the psychology of success, I was interviewing leaders in business, art, athletics, journalism, academia, medicine, and law: *Who are the people at the very top of your field? What are they like? What do you think makes them special?*

Some of the characteristics that emerged in these interviews were very field-specific. For instance, more than one businessperson mentioned an appetite for taking financial risks: "You've got to be able to make calculated decisions about millions of dollars and still go to sleep at night." But this seemed entirely beside the point for artists, who instead mentioned a drive to create: "I like making stuff. I don't know why, but I do." In contrast, athletes mentioned a different kind of motivation, one driven by the thrill of victory: "Winners love to go head-to-head with other people. Winners hate losing."

In addition to these particulars, there emerged certain commonalities, and they were what interested me most. No matter the field, the most successful people were lucky and talented. I'd heard that before, and I didn't doubt it.

But the story of success didn't end there. Many of the people I talked to could also recount tales of rising stars who, to everyone's surprise, dropped out or lost interest before they could realize their potential.

Apparently, it was critically important—and not at all easy—to keep going after failure: "Some people are great when things are going well, but they fall apart when things aren't." High achievers described in these interviews really stuck it out: "This one guy, he wasn't actually the best writer at the beginning. I mean, we used to read his stories and have a laugh because the writing was so, you know, clumsy and melodramatic. But he got better and better, and last year he won a Guggenheim." And they were constantly driven to improve: "She's never satisfied. You'd think she would be, by now, but she's her own harshest critic." The highly accomplished were paragons of perseverance.

Why were the highly accomplished so dogged in their pursuits? For most, there was no realistic expectation of ever catching up to their ambitions. In their own eyes, they were never good enough. They were the opposite of complacent. And yet, in a very real sense, they were satisfied being unsatisfied. Each was chasing something of unparalleled interest and importance, and it was the chase—as much as the capture—that was gratifying. Even if some of the things they had to do were boring, or frustrating, or even painful, they wouldn't dream of giving up. Their passion was enduring.

In sum, no matter the domain, the highly successful had a kind of ferocious determination that played out in two ways. First, these exemplars were unusually resilient and hardworking. Second, they knew in a very, very deep way what it was they wanted. They not only had determination, they had *direction.*

It was this combination of passion and perseverance that made high achievers special. In a word, they had grit.

———

For me, the question became: How do you measure something so intangible? Something that decades of military psychologists hadn't been able to quantify? Something those very successful people I'd interviewed said they could recognize on sight, but couldn't think of how to directly test for?

I sat down and looked over my interview notes. And I started writing questions that captured, sometimes verbatim, descriptions of what it means to have grit.

Half of the questions were about perseverance. They asked how much you agree with statements like "I have overcome setbacks to conquer an important challenge" and "I finish whatever I begin."

The other half of the questions were about passion. They asked whether your "interests change from year to year" and the extent to which you "have been obsessed with a certain idea or project for a short time but later lost interest."

What emerged was the Grit Scale—a test that, when taken honestly, measures the extent to which you approach life with grit.

————————

In July 2004, on the second day of Beast, 1,218 West Point cadets sat down to take the Grit Scale.

The day before, cadets had said good-bye to their moms and dads (a farewell for which West Point allocates exactly ninety seconds), gotten their heads shaved (just the men), changed out of civilian clothing and into the famous gray and white West Point uniform, received their footlockers, helmets and other gear, and, though they may have mistakenly thought they already knew how, were instructed by a fourth-year cadet in the proper way to stand in line ("Step up to my line! Not on my line, not over my line, not behind my line. Step up *to* my line!").

Initially, I looked to see how grit scores lined up with aptitude. Guess what? Grit scores bore absolutely no relationship to the Whole Candidate Scores that had been so painstakingly calculated during the admissions process. In other words, how talented a cadet was said nothing about their grit, and vice versa.

The separation of grit from talent was consistent with Mike Matthews's observations of air force training, but when I first stumbled onto this finding it came as a real surprise. After all, why *shouldn't* the talented endure? Logically, the talented should stick around and try hard, because when they do, they do phenomenally well. At West Point, for example, among cadets who ultimately make it through Beast, the Whole Candidate Score is a marvelous predictor of every metric West Point tracks. It not only predicts academic grades, but military and physical fitness marks as well.

So it's surprising, really, that talent is no guarantee of grit. In this book, we'll explore the reasons why.

————————

By the last day of Beast, seventy-one cadets had dropped out.

Grit turned out to be an astoundingly reliable predictor of who made it through and who did not.

The next year, I returned to West Point to run the same study. This time, sixty-two cadets dropped out of Beast, and again grit predicted who would stay.

In contrast, stayers and leavers had indistinguishable Whole Candidate Scores. I looked a little closer at the individual components that make up the score. Again, no differences.

So, what matters for making it through Beast?

Not your SAT scores, not your high school rank, not your leadership experience, not your athletic ability.

Not your Whole Candidate Score.

What matters is grit.

————————

Does grit matter beyond West Point? To find out, I looked for other situations so challenging that a lot of people drop out. I wanted to know whether it was just the rigors of Beast that demanded grit, or whether, in general, grit helped people stick to their commitments.

The next arena where I tested grit's power was sales, a profession in which daily, if not hourly, rejection is par for the course. I asked hundreds of men and women employed at the same vacation time-share company to answer a battery of personality questionnaires, including the Grit Scale. Six months later, I revisited the company, by which time 55 percent of the salespeople had dropped out. Grit predicted who stayed and who left. Moreover, no other commonly measured personality trait—including extroversion, emotional stability, and conscientiousness—was as effective as grit in predicting job retention.

Around the same time, I received a call from the Chicago Public Schools. Like the psychologists at West Point, researchers there were eager to learn more about the students who would successfully earn their high school diplomas. That spring, thousands of high school juniors completed an abbreviated Grit Scale, along with a battery of other questionnaires. More than a year later, 12 percent of those students failed to graduate. Students who did graduate were grittier, and grit was a more powerful predictor than how much students cared about school, how conscientious they were about their studies, and even how safe they felt at school.

Likewise, in two large American samples, I found that grittier adults were more likely to get further in their formal schooling. Adults who'd earned an MBA, PhD, MD, JD, or another graduate degree were grittier than those who'd only graduated from four-year colleges, who were in turn grittier than those who'd accumulated some college credits but no degree. Interestingly, adults who'd successfully earned degrees from two-year colleges scored slightly higher than graduates of four-year colleges. This puzzled me at first, but I soon learned that the dropout rates at community colleges can be as high as 80 percent. Those who defy the odds are especially gritty.

In parallel, I started a partnership with the Army Special Operations Forces, better known as the Green Berets. These are among the army's best-trained soldiers, assigned some of the toughest and most dangerous missions. Training for the Green Berets is a grueling, multistage affair. The stage I studied comes *after* nine weeks of boot camp, four weeks of infantry training, three weeks of airborne school, and four weeks of a preparation course focused on land navigation. All these preliminary training experiences are very, very hard, and at every stage there are men who don't make it through. But the Special Forces Selection Course is even harder. In the words of its commanding general, James Parker, this is "where we decide who will and who will not" enter the final stages of Green Beret training.

The Selection Course makes Beast Barracks look like summer vacation. Starting before dawn, trainees go full-throttle until nine in the evening. In addition to daytime and nighttime navigation exercises, there are four- and six-mile runs and marches, sometimes under a sixtyfive-pound load, and attempts at an obstacle course informally known as "Nasty Nick," which includes crawling through water under barbed wire, walking on elevated logs, negotiating cargo nets, and swinging from horizontal ladders.

Just getting to the Selection Course is an accomplishment, but even so, 42 percent of the candidates I studied voluntarily withdrew before it was over. So what distinguished the men who made it through? Grit.

What else, other than grit, predicts success in the military, education, and business? In sales, I found that prior experience helps—novices are less likely to keep their jobs than those with experience. In the Chicago public school system, a supportive teacher made it more likely that students would graduate. And for aspiring Green Berets, baseline physical fitness at the start of training is essential.

But in each of these domains, when you compare people matched on these characteristics, grit still predicts success. Regardless of specific attributes and advantages that help someone succeed in each of these diverse domains of challenge, grit matters in all of them.

————

The year I started graduate school, the documentary *Spellbound* was released. The film follows three boys and five girls as they prepare for and compete in the finals of the Scripps National Spelling Bee.

To get to the finals—an adrenaline-filled three-day affair staged annually in Washington, DC, and broadcast live on ESPN, which normally focuses its programming on high-stakes sports matchups—these kids must first "outspell" thousands of other students from hundreds of schools across the country. This means spelling increasingly obscure words without a single error, in round after round, first besting all the other students in the contestant's classroom, then in their grade, school, district, and region.

Spellbound got me wondering: To what extent is flawlessly spelling words like *schottische* and *cymotrichous* a matter of preternatural verbal talent, and to what extent is grit at play?

I called the bee's executive director, a dynamic woman (and former champion speller herself) named Paige Kimble. Kimble was as curious as I was to learn more about the psychological makeup of winners. She agreed to send out questionnaires to all 273 spellers just as soon as they qualified for the finals, which would take place several months later. In return for the princely reward of a $25 gift card, about two-thirds of the spellers returned the questionnaires to my lab. The oldest respondent was fifteen years old, the absolute age limit according to competition rules, and the youngest was just seven.

In addition to completing the Grit Scale, spellers reported how much time they devoted to spelling practice. On average, they practiced more than an hour a day on weekdays and more than two hours a day on weekends. But there was a lot of variation around these averages: some spellers were hardly studying at all, and some were studying as much as nine hours on a given Saturday!

Separately, I contacted a subsample of spellers and administered a verbal intelligence test. As a group, the spellers demonstrated unusual verbal ability. But there was a fairly wide range of scores, with some kids scoring at the verbal prodigy level and others just "average" for their age.

When ESPN aired the final rounds of the competition, I watched all the way through to the concluding suspenseful moments when, at last, thirteen-year-old Anurag Kashyap correctly spelled A-P-P-O-G-G-I-A-T-U-R-A (a musical term for a kind of grace note) to win the championship.

Then, with the final rankings in hand, I analyzed my data.

Here's what I found: measurements of grit taken months before the final competition predicted how well spellers would eventually perform. Put simply, grittier kids went further in competition. How did they do it? By studying many more hours and, also, by competing in more spelling bees.

What about talent? Verbal intelligence also predicted getting further in competition. But there was no relationship at all between verbal IQ and grit. What's more, verbally talented spellers did not study any more than less able spellers, nor did they have a longer track record of competition.

The separation of grit and talent emerged again in a separate study I ran on Ivy League undergraduates. There, SAT scores and grit were, in fact, inversely correlated. Students in that select sample who had higher SAT scores were, on average, just slightly less gritty than their peers. Putting together this finding with the other data I'd collected to that point, I came to a fundamental insight that would guide my future work: *Our potential is one thing. What we do with it is quite another.*

Discussion Questions

What messages did you receive about intelligence growing up, from whom, and how do you think it influences your current behavior?

In Grit, a West Point cadet describes the Beast program by stating, "You are challenged in a variety of ways in every developmental area – mentally, physically, militarily, and socially. The system will find your weaknesses, but that's the point" (p. 5). Compare this quote to your idea of and experience at college.

Do you think grit is more important than other characteristics in determining the success and happiness of an individual? Why or why not?

APPRECIATIVE INQUIRY

A POSITIVE APPROACH TO CHANGE

Edwin C. Thomas

Introduction

Maybe it is because we have just emerged from the midst of election season. Or perhaps it is the constant barrage of negative news about virtually every aspect of our existence, whether it is about issues of significance (terrorism, hunger, and genocide) or about matters so trivial one wonders how spoiled we have become. We are awash in a sea of negativity. It seems that no matter what we do, who does it, or how it is done, there is a never-ending supply of critics and complainers just waiting to tell us what is wrong. As John Gardner puts it, we are increasingly engaged in a self-destructive "war of the parts against the whole."[1]

There is evidence to support the notion that this is just the natural tendency of the human animal. Negativity certainly seems to be the normal state of the culture in all too many of our organizations and communities. And few things bring out negative reactions in people, organizations and communities more than efforts to change what is perceived to be wrong.

The traditional approach to change is problem solving in nature. It starts off from a negative perspective—something is broken, something could be done better, something needs to be fixed. Thus we engage in problem identification, root cause analysis, brainstorming possible solutions, action planning, implementation of changes, and hopefully, evaluation of the results. Indeed this is precisely what managers are trained to do—identify problems and fix them. However well intended, problem solving approaches to change are notoriously difficult and often unsuccessful. (See John Kotter's book *Leading Change* for an excellent treatment of change and the traditional change process.)[2]

Resistance to change is a well-established fact of organizational life, and for good reason. Change always involves uncertainty. Invariably it involves more work. And we have learned by experience that change is not always for the better.

Change causes many in the organization to feel incompetent, needy and powerless. It creates confusion and unpredictability throughout the organization. It generates conflict, and ultimately creates loss (of certainty, control, ownership, or even jobs).[3]

While the literature on change helps us to diagnose and understand resistance to change efforts and provides us with various strategies for designing processes to overcome resistance, success is still illusive.

Maybe we should try a completely different approach to change.

Thomas, Edwin C. 2008. "Appreciative Inquiry: A Positive Approach to Change." Columbia, S.C.: USC Institute for Public Service and Policy Research. Reprinted by permission.

Appreciative Inquiry

In the 1980s, David Cooperrider, professor at the Weatherhead School of Management at Case Western Reserve University, developed a new model for organizational development and change which he termed "appreciative inquiry."

Appreciation has to do with both recognition and enhancing value. It is about affirming past and present strengths, assets, and potentials. Inquiry refers to both exploration and discovery. It is about asking questions, study, and learning.[4]

Appreciative inquiry (AI) is a positive way to embrace organizational change based on a simple assumption:

> Every organization has something that works right—things that give life when it most alive, effective, successful, and connected in healthy ways to its stakeholders and communities. AI begins by identifying what is positive and connecting to it in ways that heighten energy and vision for change.[5]

AI assumes that human systems, e.g., organizations and groups, are not like machines that can be taken apart and fixed, but rather are social systems. As such, they are more like organisms—living, breathing entities that stay healthiest when they are focused on their positive life-giving characteristics, rather than their problematic aspects.

Thus, AI starts from the positive perspective. Rather than looking at what is wrong, it looks at what it right in the organization. It is the discovery of the best in people, their organizations, and the world around them. It is the art and practice of asking the unconditional positive questions that strengthen a system's capacity to apprehend, anticipate, and heighten positive potential.

AI is an approach to organizational analysis and learning that is intended for discovering, understanding, and fostering innovations in social organizational arrangements and processes. In this context, AI refers to two things:

- A search for knowledge; and,
- A theory of collective action designed to evolve the vision and will of a group, an organization, or society as a whole.

Instead of negation, criticism and spiraling diagnosis, there is discover, dream, design and destiny. It works from accounts of the "positive change core." AI links the energy of the positive core directly to any change agenda and changes never before thought possible are suddenly and democratically mobilized.

The Positive Core

As noted, and it is worth reemphasizing, all organizations have something about their past to value. This element must be appreciated in order that change becomes a positive experience, without encountering unnecessary resistance from the sense of disruption, failure, and powerlessness. The AI process helps one to honor the past (continuity) and search for newness (novelty) in order to embrace movement toward the new future (transition).

The organization's positive core can be found by looking at its . . .

- Achievements
- Strategic opportunities
- Product strengths
- Technical assets
- Innovations
- Best business practices
- Positive emotions
- Financial assets
- Cooperative moments
- Organizational wisdom
- Core competencies
- Visions of possibilities
- Vital traditions and values
- Social capital
- Embedded knowledge
- Business ecosystems, e.g., suppliers, partners, competitors, customers.[6]

It is here that we can find those things that give us satisfaction, provide meaning from our efforts, give us pride in our work, our organizations and our communities. Here we find those things of which we would like more.

The Four Stages of Appreciative Inquiry

The AI process involves four stages which have been labeled discovery, dream, design, and destiny known as the 4-D Cycle.

1. Discovery

The Discovery phase is a diligent and extensive search to understand the "best of what is" and "what has been." It begins with a collaborative act of crafting appreciative interview questions and constructing and an appreciative interview guide.

Appreciative interview questions are written as affirmative probes into an organization's positive core, in the topic areas selected. They are written to generate stories, to enrich the images and inner dialogue within the organization, and to bring the positive core more fully into focus.

2. Dream

The Dream phase is an energizing exploration of "what might be": a time for people to explore their hopes and dreams for their work, their working relationships, their organization, and the world at large. It is a time for groups of people to engage in thinking big, and thinking out of the boundaries of what has been in the past. The intent of the Dream phase is to identify and spread generative, affirmative and hopeful images of the future.

3. Design

The Design phase involves making choices about "what should be" within the organization or system. It is a conscious re-creation or transformation, through which such things as systems, structures, strategies, processes and images will become more fully aligned with the organization's positive past (Discovery) and highest potential (Dream).

4. Destiny

The Destiny phase initiates a series of inspired actions that support ongoing learning and innovation—or "what will be." Since the entire 4-D cycle provides an open forum for employees to contribute and step forward in the service of the organization, change occurs in all phases of an appreciative inquiry process.

The Destiny phase, however, focuses specifically on personal and organizational commitments and paths forward which result in changes in organizational systems, structure, processes or procedures.

The Affirmative Topic Choice

The 4-D Cycle begins with the affirmative question, which grows out of the choice of affirmative topic. Thus the choice of both topic and question are critical to the direction of the change process. AI is premised, in part, on the belief that human systems grow in the direction of what they study, talk about, and focus on. People, organizations, and communities construct and exist in worlds of their own making, which in turn act back on them.[7]

An interesting example of the use of the AI comes from British Airways (BA). At one point the airline had a great deal of concern about its handling of baggage and their customers' "arrival experience." To put it succinctly, customers and their baggage did not always arrive on the same flight. This, of course, cost BA considerable money, time, and goodwill.

Using the AI model, BA employees focused, not on what was wrong (lost baggage), but rather on what they wanted. In this case, they wanted more "exceptional arrival experiences." So an appreciative question was to "describe times when customers had an exceptional arrival experience." In an interview process using this question, employees identified the components of an "exceptional arrival experience." This inquiry led to the discovery of a number of best practices that could be implemented at BA as a part of their quest for world class service. What's more, it did it in an inclusive, energizing manner that inspired the group rather than criticizing it for past failures.[8]

Does AI Work?

There are numerous anecdotal examples and case studies of success using the AI model. Research as to why it works indicates that, among other things, it gives people the experience of personal and collective power, and the exercise of that power for the good of the whole. It enhances self-esteem and self-expression. It gives people the freedom to be heard and to make a positive contribution. Indeed it addresses many of the causes of resistance to change as experienced in the traditional approaches to change.

Beyond that, there is convincing evidence about the power of positive thinking that also makes this model appealing.

And finally, how refreshing it would be to approach the many issues we have in our organizations and our society from the positive perspective, seeking what we would like to have more of, rather than always bemoaning what is wrong with everything. Rather than being constantly at war with one another about virtually everything, how productive would it be to try and appreciate the good that we have accomplished, and to explore ways to have more of that success?

Of course some might be skeptical! But as Tom White, then head of GTE Telephone Operations stated:

> Don't get me wrong. I'm not advocating mindless happy talk. Appreciative inquiry is a complex science designed to make things better. We can't ignore problems—we just need to approach them from the other side.[9]

For More Information:

For the reader who might be intrigued by this approach, there are a number of excellent resources available. Here are three that I would recommend as a starting place:

The Power of Appreciative Inquiry: A Practical Guide to Positive Change by Diana Whitney and Amanda Trosten-Bloom.

Appreciative Inquiry Handbook by David L. Cooperrider, Diana Whitney and Jacqueline M. Stavros.

"The Appreciative Inquiry Commons," a website devoted to the sharing of academic resources and practical tools on AI has an excellent collection of articles on the rapidly growing discipline of positive change. See http://appreciativeinquiry.case.edu/.

About the Author

Edwin C. Thomas, B.S., M.E., and M.P.A., is the Director of the Governmental Research and Service Unit at the University of South Carolina's Institute for Public Service and Policy Research. Mr. Thomas has been engaged in public service and public administration for more than three decades. He received his degrees from the University of South Carolina.

Discussion Questions

According to this article, a traditional approach to change starts and ends with a negative perspective. Do you agree or disagree, and why?

What affect do you believe perspective has on your ability to deal with change?

Create positive questions you might use to assess this class/your first semester progress. How might utilizing these questions help us improve our UNI experience/you improve your experience?

Endnotes

1. Gardner, J. (1990). *On leadership*. New York, NY: The Free Press, p. 95.
2. Kotter, J. (1996). *Leading change*. Boston, MA: Harvard Business School Press.
3. Bolman and Deal. (1991). *Reframing organizations: artistry, choice, and leadership*. San Francisco, CA: Jossey-Bass, p. 377.
4. Whitney, D. & Trosten-Bloom, A. (2003). *The power of appreciative inquiry: a practical guide to positive change*. San Francisco, CA: Berrett-Koehler, pp. 2-3.
5. Cooperrider, D., Whitney, D., and Stavros, J. (2005). *Appreciative inquiry handbook*. San Francisco, CA: Berrett-Koehler, p. xvii.
6. Ibid., p. 31.
7. Op. Cit. Whitney, D. & Trosten-Bloom, A. (2003), p. 132.
8. Ibid., pp. 133-134.
9. Op. Cit. Cooperrider, D., Whitney, D., and Stavros, J. (2005), p. xx.

Chapter 5

Why are you here?

"ONLY CONNECT"

THE CONTINUING VALUE AND RELEVANCE OF THE LIBERAL ARTS

Michael Wentworth

"Having recognized the need for education within a democracy, we need to determine the appropriate content of that education. In addition to an understanding and appreciation of the democratic system itself, what knowledge, skills, and values are necessary to enable individuals to live intelligently and responsibly as free persons in a free society?"

— Stephen Cahn (2003)

"It is time that we had uncommon schools, that we did not leave off our education when we begin to be men and women. It is time that villages were universities, and their elder inhabitants the fellows of universities, with leisure . . . to pursue liberal studies the rest of their lives."

— Henry David Thoreau (1910)

A number of years ago, a colleague in political science called and left a message in my mailbox in the English Department that went something like this: "Mike, wouldn't you like to speak on the value of the liberal arts at the upcoming dinner honoring the newly inducted members of the Phi Eta Sigma Honor Society? Nothing fancy or elaborate. Fifteen to twenty minutes should cover it."

I read the message to its conclusion with an accelerating sense of panic, and suddenly I saw myself in high school speech class standing in front of my fellow orators, including the love of my life at the time, who was in love with some four-letter ace who drove a flaming crimson, gorp-heavy Bonneville convertible and had

Wentworth, M. (2016). "Only connect: The continuing value and relevance of the liberal arts." In D. Ashe & C. Clements (Eds.). *Best Practices in University Teaching, 2nd Ed.* (pp. 217–231). Wilmington, NC: UNCW Center for Teaching Excellence. Reprinted by permission of UNCW Center for Teaching Excellence and Mike Wentworth.

everything going for him, unlike me, who stood dumbfounded and goofy like the scarecrow in *The Wizard of Oz,* frantically restuffing his innards after the attack of the flying monkeys. I don't remember the topic of the speech, but like every other speech that fateful year, I – elocutionally challenged – stammered through to the end.

Returning to the present, I sadly acknowledged the fact that there was no way out of this one; for no apparent reason, my colleague in political science obviously had it in for me. He was clearly evening some score I wasn't even aware of. Compared to the current proliferation of construction projects and the escalating student enrollment, it was a much smaller campus at the time and, like the song goes, there was "nowhere to run, nowhere to hide." And besides, I could hardly refuse. The word would get out that "Wentworth over in English doesn't even know the value of the liberal arts." Yes, I was definitely stuck all right.

Morosely, I went home, overcome with a shuddering fit of the shakes. I somehow managed to eat dinner and afterwards turned on the TV, flipped a few channels, and there it was: *Jeopardy.* The first-round categories had already been revealed: history, philosophy, the planets, bodies of water, presidential elections, and the Wild West. "No sweat," I thought, as I proceeded to answer question after question with a mounting sense of self-satisfaction and realized that, at least on this particular evening, I would have outscored the contestants and walked away with the big money. Then, with a sudden flash of inspiration, I sensed a possible connection with my topic — the value of the liberal arts — and the diversified information base of the successful *Jeopardy* contestant. Just for the fun of it, I jotted down a number of answers:

- According to the World Almanac, he's the last U.S. president to run with no opposition (That's right, "no opposition"!).
- The axiom "Cogito ergo sum" ("I think, therefore I am") is his most famous formulation.
- This Wild West horse thief with a glamorous name was dubbed "the female Robin Hood" by the popular press.
- She was known as Rebecca Rolfe when she died in England of a sudden illness in 1617.

Well, by the time the show had ended, I began to have second thoughts, triggered perhaps by the fact that I had missed the Final Jeopardy question and, consequently, lost all my imaginary earnings (naturally, I had risked everything). No doubt chastened, I began to realize that the value of the liberal arts very possibly involved more than a flashy display of erudition, and erudition that relied more on the reflexive regurgitation of stored facts (the modus operandi of one Thomas Gradgrind, sir, and his trusty and trusting protégé Mr. McChoakmchild, so wonderfully pilloried by Charles Dickens in *Hard Times*) than any measure of judgment and genuine problem-solving. The whole *"Jeopardy* trip," not to mention any number of evenings when I'd "run the table" in "Trivial Pursuit," suddenly struck me as pretty mercenary and self-serving.

"Come on," I told myself. "You know the value of the liberal arts." Well, sure I did, didn't I? Evidently not, as I spent several uninspired hours at the drawing board. Reassured by the fact that if worst came to worst, I could always fall back on the official UNCW catalogue (Surely, there would be something in there!) or Cardinal Newman's *The Idea of a University* – which admittedly I'd never read, and still haven't – though I could handle the relevant *Jeopardy* question, I finally went to bed. I fidgeted about for maybe six or seven hours, but eventually dozed off and had this weird sort of dream – or it seemed weird at the time. I don't remember all the details, but it went something like this: There's a shipload of people (the ship looked like something out of some pirate movie with Bob Hope and Virginia Mayo I'd seen as a kid), and the people looked like they had maybe shopped off the back rack at some Army-Navy surplus store before there even were Army-Navy surplus stores. Well, they arrive and disembark at their destination, some uncivilized wilderness they'd only heard or dreamt about in their worst nightmare.

There were no houses, schools, or hospitals, no malls, no video rental stores, no buy-one-and-get-one free pizza franchises, and, perhaps most distressing, no Krispy Kreme donut shops. The climate, together with much of the vegetation and wildlife, was equally strange and unfamiliar. Shortly after landing, our ragged crew came into contact with what appeared to be native residents, though they, too, seemed strange and, evidently unfamiliar with the Queen's English, spoke a language totally incomprehensible to our landing party. It wasn't long before one faction among the party had seen enough and was determined to head back home even though things weren't much better there. But the leader of the group, with rhetorical pluck that would have made Dale Carnegie proud, somehow convinced everyone that "we can make this work." Then, somewhere off-stage, a disembodied, but authoritative, voice (amazing that disembodied voices often assume an authoritative register) pronounced, "And so they did."

Before "The End" flashed up on the screen, the alarm sounded, and I awoke in a feverish sweat and a high state of agitation before discovering that, unlike the alien wilderness of my dream, I was lying in my bed, right here in Wilmington, North Carolina, the very nexus of comfort and civilization. I didn't think much of this dream until I arrived at the university to teach my first class of the day: American Literature to 1870. Then, as I opened my dog-eared anthology to the assigned text, there it was: Anne Bradstreet's poem "To My Dear and Loving Husband." Bradstreet and her husband were members of a party led by John Winthrop, who left England for the New World of "America" in 1630 to escape religious persecution. Though beset throughout her life by a series of misfortunes, ranging from rheumatic fever and smallpox to lameness, fever, and frequent fainting spells, Anne, much to the disapproval of local townswomen, managed to write poetry in her spare time and produced, as it turns out, the first published volume of poetry in colonial America. Not only Anne, but her fellow colonists, were afflicted by every conceivable form of discomfort and personal tragedy upon landing in a wilderness where, according to Anne's father, "many died weekly, yea, almost daily."

Yet, whatever the personal adversity and hardship, they made it work. And beyond their courage, stamina, and vision, the eventual success of their enterprise was enabled by an assiduous application of — and, yes, you're probably five steps ahead of me — nearly every one of the liberal arts included in your typical college catalog. Try building a house, a church, a community center without some knowledge of mathematics, physics, engineering, and architectural design; try designing an equitable form of government without some knowledge of political and social philosophy; try establishing an agriculturally based economy without some knowledge of natural science on the one hand, and marketing and economics on the other; try operating harmoniously and purposefully as a society without some awareness of the dynamic sociological principles that define any functional social community; try preserving the triumphs and failures of any social experiment without an understanding of history as the recorded measure of human achievement; try surviving the accumulated rigors of life in a strange land without the recreational, but nonetheless essential, diversion of music, storytelling, and the visual arts and crafts; try negotiating amicable relations with indigenous cultures (which, regrettably, with the notable exception of Roger Williams, we more often than not failed, and are still failing, to do) without the anthropologist's respect for cultural relativism or the linguist's concern for language as the fundamental basis for human communication and understanding.

The point, of course, as I myself realized at the time, is that nothing less than American civilization and the cultivated understanding of its diverse peoples and folkways, its landscape and physical resources, its continuing evolution as a social experiment should convince the most smugly snickering of skeptics about the value of the liberal arts. Amazingly, such an achievement, in terms of early American history, was more a matter of natural aptitude and acquired skill than formal education. True enough, such early colonial leaders as John Winthrop, Samuel Sewall, and Cotton Mather had graduated from university, though educational historians would be quick to point out that such graduates would have been totally unfamiliar with the modern liberal arts curriculum.

Consider, for example, the rigidly classical curriculum at Harvard College in 1636 when first-year students — all men, by the way — would have been expected to take logic, Greek, Hebrew, rhetoric, and theology in addition to more familiar courses in history and plant biology. As recently as 1916, North Carolina novelist Thomas Wolfe's first semester of study as a freshman at the University of North Carolina at Chapel Hill included Greek, Latin, philosophy, and English literature. Still, however unselfconsciously, the early colonists must have intuitively understood the value of what we now recognize as the liberal arts in domesticating what was often described as a "savage and desert wilderness." In fact, it's not entirely fanciful to think of the earliest colonial settlements as open classrooms or informal campus communities, though daily assignments involved a constant array of unanticipated problem-solving situations, and a passing grade was more often than not survival itself.

But what about the value of the liberal arts for the contemporary college student? Several years ago, I conducted a survey among my undergraduate classes to see what they thought and was disappointed, if not entirely surprised, to discover that many didn't know or viewed general education requirements as a waste of time or something to get out of the way (like cleaning the attic or mowing the lawn). Other responses were more encouraging and ranged from such profound insights as "The liberal arts enable you to interpret life in terms that reflect 'the poetry of being'" to a more typical response: "I believe that a liberal arts education allows you to broaden your horizons and get a different view of life. You become a well-rounded person who is able to carry on a conversation about anything." Now, I'm all in favor of conversational facility though I'm wary of a further proliferation of talk-show hosts in an already glutted media market, and far be it from me to quibble with the notion of well-roundedness, though here again I'm uncomfortably reminded of my expanding waistline or some department-store Santa Claus.

So, let me suggest a number of additional advantages. Students will expectedly and rightfully continue to question the value of the liberal arts until educators and administrators make a convincing and compelling case for the liberal arts as a coherent, interrelated, intrinsically <u>and</u> extrinsically meaningful system of knowledge, the individual components of which should complement and reinforce one another. Even the most comprehensive curriculum, even the most inspired classroom instruction will inevitably fail unless students are encouraged to discover the connections between and among disciplines and the relevance of other disciplines to their own chosen field of major concentration.

As novelist and cultural historian David Madden (2000) observes,

> The premise behind interdisciplinary studies is that just as no person is an island, no subject exists in isolation from all others; that a complex examination of a subject is rewarding; that several disciplines provide the milieu for that relationship; and that each discipline is enriched and made more powerful by interaction with other disciplines. (p. 2)

It's impossible, for example, to fully appreciate the poet William Wordsworth's autobiographical narrative *The Prelude* without some understanding of the role of the French Revolution in the formative development of Wordsworth and his contemporaries, and it's likewise impossible to fully appreciate the romantic spirit of the age without an awareness of such philosophers as Locke and Rousseau, such composers as Berlioz, Beethoven, and Chopin, such painters as Constable, Turner, Gericault, and Delacroix. It's impossible to understand our good friend Anne Bradstreet's poetry in isolation from matters of history, economics, and religious beliefs that provided the practical and ideological frame of reference for her personal history, and, of course, it's no less shortsighted to ignore the social, political, philosophical, and cultural variables that frame our own personal histories.

In short, it's all a matter of "making connections," in regard to which the titular heroine in Willy Russell's (1986) popular drama *Educating Rita* (the basis for an equally popular film featuring Julie Waters and Michael Caine) provides a revealing and telling case in point. Russell's drama, inspired by his own working-class background outside of Liverpool and, as such, his own unlikely educational aspirations, involves the working class hairdresser Rita (at one time, Russell himself was a hairdresser), who undertakes an "open university" course in literature at "a Victorian-built university in the north of England," with a cynical burnt-out alcoholic English professor, Frank.

Following their introductory tutorial, Frank lends Rita, whose taste in literature runs toward Rita Mae Brown and Harold Robbins, a copy of E. M. Forster's *Howard's End*. During their next tutorial, Rita dismisses *Howard's End* as "crap," an estimate based on what she perceives as the elitist orientation of the novel and later raises the question, "Does Forster's repeated use of the phrase 'only connect' suggest that he was really a frustrated electrician?" (p.189). Frank, who has been invigorated by Rita's wit, humor, spontaneity, and unrehearsed charm, for the moment lets Rita's question ride. Rita doesn't catch up with the actual import of Forster's phrase until later when she provides a probing analysis of the lack of meaning in her working-class milieu:

> There's somethin' wrong. An' like the worst thing is that y' know the people who are supposed to like represent the people on our estate, y' know the *Daily Mirror* an' the

Sun, an' ITV an' the Unions, what are they tellin' the people to do. They just tell them to go out an' get more money, don't they? But they don't want more money; it's like me, isn't it? Y' know, buyin' new dresses all the time, isn't it? The Unions tell them to go out an' get more money an' ITV an' the papers tell them what to spend it on so the disease is always covered up" (p. 195).

Rita then observes that her husband, Denny, who resents her ambition "to sing a better song,"

tried to stop me comin' tonight. He tried to get me to go out to the pub with him an' his mates. He hates me comin' here. It's like drug addicts, isn't it? They hate it when one of them tries to break away. It makes me stronger comin' here. That's what Denny's frightened of (p. 195).

Frank then remarks, "Only connect," to which Rita responds, "Oh, not friggin' Forster again." Frank then identifies various connections she's unselfconsciously expressed: "Your dresses/ITV and the *Daily Mirror.* Addicts/you and your husband." In a clarifying moment of illumination, Rita reflects, "An'—an' in that book, no one does connect." She then asks Frank, "Why didn't y' just tell me from the start?" in response to which Frank explains, "I could have told you, but you'll have a much better understanding of something if you discover it in your own terms" (p. 195).

Frank's response to Rita's question reveals an enlightened pedagogy that creatively, by way of a calculated reticence and faith in Rita's innate intelligence, facilitates learning on students' "own terms," though the risk, of course, is that students may fail to successfully meet such a "deferred pedagogical agenda," but that's the challenge confronting any teacher at any level. No less tellingly, the exchange between Rita and Frank models the self-educating process of making connections between the social and cultural variables that define students' backgrounds and their own personal aspirations, as well as making connections between "book learning" (Forster's novel, in Rita's case) and the "real world" that should underscore and characterize the learning experience of students in the college classroom. This, in no small measure, constitutes a primary outcome of a liberal arts education.

But beyond promoting such a facility – no inconsequential achievement in itself – any authentic, meaningful liberal arts curriculum should promote an informed, active citizenship in assessing and responsibly responding to various local, regional, national, and global concerns. Ralph Waldo Emerson (1960), in "The American Scholar," often regarded as America's "intellectual declaration of independence," identifies and discusses the "main influences" on the mind of the scholar, or "Man Thinking." First and foremost is the "book of nature," followed by "the mind of the Past," as recorded and preserved in books. Yet Emerson ultimately holds that knowledge, whether acquired through the direct and studious observation of nature or through the assiduous study of the "inscribed" genius of the past, must culminate in "action," which, for the "true scholar," as opposed to the cloistered "recluse," is "essential," for "without it he is not yet man." Emerson (1960) then elaborates:

I do not see how any man can afford, for the sake of his nerves and his nap, to spare any action in which he can partake. . . . The true scholar grudges every opportunity of action past by, as a loss of power. It is the raw material out of which the intellect moulds her splendid products (p. 70).

The "true scholar's" necessary commitment to action is aptly illustrated by Henry David Thoreau, Emerson's friend and neighbor. Like Emerson, he was a Harvard graduate, who, in his refusal to support the Mexican War – a war he viewed as an immoral pretext to extend institutional slavery to the American West – withheld a proportionate portion of his assigned tax as a result of which he was arrested by local authorities and spent a night in jail. The philosophical, ethical, and political considerations that informed Thoreau's defiance are eloquently articulated in his well-known and influential essay "Resistance to Civil Government."

Thoreau's principled resistance is as relevant and timely today as it was more than a century and a half ago in illustrating the ethical dilemma of those singular individuals who choose to turn their backs to a government whose policies they find oppressive. Thoreau's example would later prove instructive to Gandhi in India and Martin Luther King, Jr., in the American South, both of whom applied the lesson of Thoreau's passive resistance and civil disobedience to pressing social inequities of their own day. Yet Thoreau's passive resistance was hardly an original concept or stance since he had been anticipated nearly two thousand years before by Jesus Christ and even earlier than that by the titular heroine of Sophocles' *Antigone*. What was true for Antigone, Jesus, Thoreau, Gandhi, and Martin Luther King, Jr., is no less true for those students with whom we come into contact on a regular basis.

To summarize, then, any set of general education requirements should validate the value of the liberal arts by stimulating the sort of critical thinking that facilitates the discovery of connections among disciplines, encourages meaningful links to the real world, both on and off campus, and promotes an informed and principled notion of active citizenship. For philosopher of education Stephen Cahn (2003), an integral component of liberal arts education is developing an "understanding of public issues," culminating in such a notion of "active citizenship":

> In a democracy public issues cover an enormous range of topics, for every action of a government is an appropriate subject for open discussion, and such actions typically involve social, political, economic, scientific, and historical factors. Consider some of the critical issues confronting the world today: poverty, overpopulation, pollution, ideological conflict, the dangers of nuclear warfare, and the possible benefits of space research. How can these matters be intelligently discussed or even understood by those ignorant of the physical structure of the world, the forces that shape society, or the ideas and events that form the background of present crises? Thus, substantial knowledge of natural science, social science, world history, and national history is required for all those called upon to think about public issues, and in a democracy such participation is required of everyone (p. 202).

In this spirit, the University of North Carolina Wilmington has recently revised its longstanding basic studies requirements and adopted a more current, relevant, integrative set of "University Studies" requirements, which, beyond an overarching agenda "to cultivate [the student's] skills and capacities [within and across disciplines] to respond to and anticipate the complexities of modern citizenship in an inclusive and creative manner," incorporates a number of additional innovative features. Students, for example, are required to take a three-course sequence within a self-selected "transdisciplinary cluster," the purpose of which is to engage students "in the type of cross-disciplinary study that will help them to seek creative solutions to difficulties they will encounter when dealing with the complex problems that shape our modern world." Representative clusters not only include such traditional topical themes as ancient thought and culture and Judaism and the Jewish people, but such timely topical themes as immigration, climate change and society, gender and social justice, global diversity, and evolution, which address current social, ethnic, gender, legal, environmental, and scientific issues that require a well-informed, well-reasoned measure of critical judgment and discrimination.

In a similar vein, UNCW has also developed a wide range of area studies minors that illustrates the sort of integrated curricular enterprise I've previously described. Such area studies minors include African-American Studies, Asian Studies, European Studies, Latin American Studies, Middle East/Islamic Studies, Native American Studies, Postcolonial Studies, and Women's Studies, thereby reinforcing UNCW's commitment to globalism, cultural diversity, and cross-disciplinary studies, though other more professionally oriented area studies minors include Digital Arts, Forensic Science, Information Technology, and Journalism.

I myself have adopted an interdisciplinary approach to various special topics courses I have taught in the past. In "America and the Great Depression," for example, students are invited to examine the Great Depression from a variety of disciplinary perspectives, ranging from literature, photography, popular music, and popular film to sociology, transportation geography, climatology, agronomy, politics, economics, public health, and education. Thus, in addition to John Steinbeck's *The Grapes of Wrath,* the reading-viewing-listening syllabus for the course includes Karen Hesse's *Out of the Dust* (a prize-winning young adult novel), Studs Terkel's *Hard Times: An Oral History of the Great Depression,* Jerry Stanley's *Children of the Dust Bowl: The True Story of the School at Weedpatch Camp, Dear Mrs. Roosevelt: Letters from Children of the Great Depression,* Timothy Egan's *The Worst Hard Time: The Untold Story of Those Who Survived the Great American Dust Bowl,* Errol Lincoln Uys' *Riding the Rails: Teenagers on the Move during the Great Depression,* Michael Wallis' *Route 66: The Mother Road,* Mildred Armstrong Kalish's *Little Heathens: Hard Times and High Spirits on an Iowa Farm during the Great Depression,* Woody Guthrie's "Dust Bowl Ballads," and *Children of the Great Depression,* a remarkable, often-haunting anthology of photographs by such legendary Farm Security Administration photographers as Dorothea Lange, Walker Evans, Russell Lee, and Arthur Rothstein.

But whatever the focus of the course, I typically incorporate a directive in the course syllabus encouraging students to establish possible complementary relations, as relevant, between assigned readings and 1) the current arena of local, regional, national, and international affairs, 2) other works of literature they have read, either independently or in other courses, and 3) other academic courses they have taken or are currently taking — e.g., American history, psychology, sociology, anthropology, economics, geography, philosophy and religion. The supposition is that a <u>real</u> liberal arts education should be consciously and purposefully interdisciplinary and, thereby, should encourage a sensitivity to the interconnectedness of both major and non-major courses.

However daunting and prohibitive the current tendency toward the "specialized major," students themselves should be encouraged to familiarize themselves with various course offerings outside their major and across disciplines and to assume a resourceful and creative initiative in mapping a meaningful and integrated scheme of courses that corresponds to their own special interests and aptitudes (though, admittedly, upon entering college or university, many students have yet to discover their "own special interests and aptitudes"). Such an initiative, especially for those students in the liberal arts who often enjoy a greater degree of flexibility in regard to elective hours than the more specialized professional major, might lead students to consider a double major, an academic minor, an area studies minor, or certificate program option outside their major.

Aside from a judicious and imaginative selection of distribution and elective courses, students should also be encouraged to broaden their cultural frame of reference by continuing their study of a foreign language beyond the minimal proficiency requirement or by taking a second language. Stephen Cahn notes (2003), in this regard,

> the significant value . . . derived from reading some foreign literature in its original language. Not only does great literature lose some of its richness in translation, but learning another language increases linguistic sensitivity and makes one more conscious of the unique potentialities and limitations of any particular tongue. Such study is also a most effective means of widening cultural horizons, for understanding another language is a key to understanding another culture (p. 203).

Likewise, French professor Michael Randall (2003) advocates the study of foreign language texts in their original language and, more specifically, older texts:

> These texts . . . demand that students drop their understanding of the world based on the present and become part of a reality not their own. . . . If I can draw students into the literary world of 400 to 500 years ago — even briefly — their present can become richer and more complex. . . . A student who has come to grips with a text from a foreign culture from many centuries ago no longer perceives the present in quite the same way. The awareness of the complexity of a difficult text from a foreign culture leads to an awareness of the complexity that marks our present culture. That makes for a less efficient consumer of facile marketing and political spin; but that inefficiency makes for a richer individual and more responsible citizen (p. 189-190).

Beyond self-enrichment and developing a greater understanding and sensitivity to cultural diversity and a recognition of parallels with the student's own native culture, advanced study in a foreign language carries pragmatic, potential career-oriented benefits, as well. Professional educators, as well as future health professionals, social workers, professional counselors, and public administration officials, among others, might be well-advised to develop an oral proficiency in Spanish, especially in view of the projection that in the not-too-distant future, Spanish rather than English will be the primary spoken language in the U.S. Then, too, given China's increasing economic prominence globally, business majors might consider developing a proficiency in Chinese. Currently, Chinese universities, who are far more progressive – though no doubt driven by pragmatic considerations – than their American counterparts, are anxious to hire English-as-a-second-language teachers — an inviting opportunity for liberal arts students considering the often demoralizing, debt-ridden prospect of "life after graduation."

Students should be further encouraged to involve themselves in the international campus community — which at UNCW currently includes exchange students from more than fifty different countries — and related social and cultural events and to explore travel and study abroad opportunities. The Office of International

Programs at UNCW sponsors study abroad programs with "adopted" universities in such countries as Chile, Costa Rica, the United Kingdom, Finland, Sweden, France, Germany, Spain, Italy, the Netherlands, South Africa, China, Japan, New Zealand, and Australia, many – though not all – of which are discipline-specific. Numerous academic departments at UNCW have well-established study abroad programs, most notably, the department of foreign languages, though the Cameron School of Business offers study abroad programs in international business in Bremen, Germany; Marseilles, France; and Valencia, Spain. Just recently, the Department of English has established a dual-exchange program with Nanjing University of Science and Technology in Nanjing, China.

Students should be further aware of applied learning and community-related internship initiatives. Such initiatives are, in fact, a curricular component in many academic departments at UNCW and are particularly meaningful not only in acquiring practical, hands-on experience beyond a formal classroom setting in a student's major and future profession, but in promoting active citizenship, developing social and oral communication skills, and dispelling the "Ivory Tower insularity" and elitism of the academy often held by the "real world outside."

In addition, students should be encouraged to extend the learning curriculum outside the classroom by attending music recitals, poetry and fiction readings, dramatic productions, foreign films, and art exhibits, as well as campus-sponsored lectures and performances, the latter of which can further heighten the student's awareness of pressing social, environmental, and political issues on a global, national, and regional scale, as well as enhancing what Stephen Cahn (2003) describes as the student's "sensitivity to aesthetic experience," for

> an appreciation and understanding of the literature, art, and music of various cultures enriches the imagination, refines the sensibilities, deepens feelings, and provides increased awareness of the world in which we live. In a society of aesthetic illiterates not only the quality of art suffers but also the quality of life (p. 203).

At UNCW, the University Presents series annually provides a wide range of lecture and performance events. Featured events over the upcoming 2013-2014 academic year include professional productions of *The Fantasticks* (the world's longest-running theatrical production of any kind) and *The Graduate* (previously, and memorably, adapted to film, from Charles Webb's novel, by Mike Nichols and starring Dustin Hoffman as an angst-ridden college graduate); Grammy Award-winning saxophonist Branford Marsalis; Mary Wilson, an original member of the Supremes; "Celtic Nights—Journey of Hope: Irish Voice, Music, and Dance"; and lectures by Donna Brazile (veteran political strategist, the first African American to manage a presidential campaign, and one of the *Washingtonian's* "top 100 most powerful women"), Jose Antonio Vargas (Pulitzer Prize-winning author and immigrant activist), and Dr. Daniel Pauly (the world's most well-known fisheries scientist). Various academic departments at UNCW have self-sponsored lecture series of their own, which typically feature scholars with a national and international reputation. By way of cross-disciplinary collaboration, various departments sponsor public symposia and forums on special topics ranging from Islamic culture, terrorism, the endangered coastal environment, elder care, and the local economy.

Finally then, and most importantly, students should be encouraged to avoid overspecialization at the expense of the stimulating range of learning experiences that a liberal arts education is intended to provide and to take advantage of extracurricular learning initiatives. Thus, like Olympic decathletes, students should be discouraged from over-investing in a single event at the expense of the total performance.

If I were to recommend a model – though Thomas Jefferson and Ben Franklin immediately come to mind – I can think of no better example than Sir Thomas More, the author of *Utopia* and the first lay lord chancellor of England, who served under the most notorious womanizer in English history, Henry VIII. More's interests, ranging from Greek and Latin studies, philosophy, theology, and law to medicine, zoology, music, astronomy, art, and political and economic theory, were so prodigious that the contemporary poet Henry Whittington once described More as "a man for all seasons." Such versatility in a world that increasingly demands nothing less is the ultimate challenge and continuing legacy of the liberal arts. Though their diplomas wouldn't necessarily say as much, upon graduation students should be positioned to take special pride and satisfaction in the fact that they not only leave campus as prospective accountants, teachers, nurses, or chemical engineers but as "men and women for all academic and worldly seasons."

References

Cahn, Stephen. (2003). The democratic framework. In R. K. Durst (Ed.), *You are here: Readings on higher education for college writers* (198-205). Upper Saddle, NJ: Prentice Hall.

Durst, R. K. (2003). *You are here: Readings on higher education for college writers.* Upper Saddle, NJ: Prentice Hall.

Emerson, R. W. (1960). The American scholar. In S. E. Whicher (Ed.), *Selections from Ralph Waldo Emerson: An organic anthology* (63-80). Boston: Houghton Mifflin.

Madden, D. (2000). The Civil War as a model for the scope of popular culture, or the United States Civil War Center and the Popular Culture Association: Myriad-minded interdisciplinarians. *Journal of American and Comparative Cultures,* 23, 1-9. doi:10.1111/j.1537-4726.2000.2301_1.x

Randall, M. (2003). A guide to good teaching: Be slow and inefficient. In R. K. Durst (Ed.), *You are here: Readings on higher education for college writers* (188-191). Upper Saddle, NJ: Prentice Hall.

Russell, W. (1986). *Two plays and a musical: Educating Rita/ stags and hens/ blood brothers.* London: Methuen.

Thoreau, H. D. (1910). *Walden.* New York: Thomas Y. Crowell & Company.

Walser, R. G. (1977). *Thomas Wolfe undergraduate.* Durham, NC: Duke University Press.

Discussion Questions

What do you believe is the most beneficial piece of advice Wentworth provides regarding taking advantage of a liberal arts education? Why?

What other ways will you take advantage of attending a liberal arts college outside of the classroom and how will this help you in the future?

Looking at our University Studies requirements, choose classes that will help you grow and prepare for your future outside of UNCW. Explain how each of these classes will assist you on your path.

CLAIMING AN EDUCATION

Adrienne Rich

IN THIS IMPORTANT ESSAY, Adrienne Rich (b. 1929) argues that education en-
tails being responsible for oneself—not just for women, but for all students.
Her emphasis is on clear thinking, active discussion, and the intellectual
and imaginative capacity to be persuaded that new ideas might be true.

Rich, a well-known feminist, has written numerous essays and many
volumes of poetry, including The Necessities of Life (1966), Leaflets (1969),
The Will to Change (1971), and An Atlas of the Difficult World (1991).
"Claiming an Education," a talk given at the Douglass College convocation
in 1977, was first printed in the magazine The Common Woman in 1977.

For this convocation, I planned to separate my remarks into two parts: some thoughts about you, the woman students here, and some thoughts about us who teach in a women's college. But ultimately, those two parts are indivisible. If university education means anything beyond the processing of human beings into expected roles, through credit hours, tests, and grades (and I believe that in a women's college especially it *might* mean much more), it implies an ethical and intellectual contract between teacher and student. This contract must remain intuitive, dynamic, unwritten; but we must turn to it again and again if learning is to be reclaimed from the depersonalizing and cheapening pressures of the present-day academic scene.

The first thing I want to say to you who are students, is that you cannot afford to think of being here to *receive* an education; you will do much better to think of yourselves as being here to *claim* one. One of the dictionary definitions of the verb "to claim" is: *to take as the rightful owner; to assert in the face of possible contradiction.* "To receive" is *to come into possession of; to act as receptacle or container for; to accept as authoritative or true.* The difference is that between acting and being acted-upon, and for women it can literally mean the difference between life and death.

One of the devastating weaknesses of university learning, of the store of knowledge and opinion that has been handed down through academic training, has been its almost total erasure of women's experience and thought from the curriculum, and its exclusion of women as members of the academic community. Today, with increasing numbers of women students in nearly every branch of higher learning, we still see very few women in the upper levels of faculty and administration in most institutions. Douglass College itself is a women's college in a university administered overwhelmingly by men, who in turn are answerable to the state legislature, again composed predominantly of men. But the most significant fact for you is that what you learn here, the very texts you read, the lectures you hear, the way your studies are divided into categories and fragmented one from the other—all this reflects, to a very large degree, neither objective reality, nor an accurate picture of the past, nor a group of rigorously tested observations about human behavior. What you can learn here (and I mean not only at Douglass but any college in any university) is how *men* have perceived and organized their experience, their history, their ideas of social relationships, good and evil, sickness and health, etc. When you read or hear about "great issues," "major texts," "the mainstream of Western thought," you are hearing about what men, above all white men, in their male subjectivity, have decided is important.

Black and other minority peoples have for some time recognized that their racial and ethnic experience was not accounted for in the studies broadly labeled human; and that even the sciences can be racist. For many reasons, it has been more difficult for women to comprehend our exclusion, and to realize that even the sciences can be sexist. For one thing, it is only within the last hundred years that higher education has grudgingly been opened up to women at all, even to white, middle-class women. And many of us have found ourselves poring eagerly over books with titles like: *The Descent of Man; Man and His Symbols; Irrational Man; The Phenomenon of Man; The Future of Man; Man and the Machine; From Man to Man; May Man Prevail?; Man, Science, and Society;* or *One-Dimensional Man*—books pretending to describe a "human" reality that does not include over one-half the human species.

Less than a decade ago, with the rebirth of a feminist movement in this country, women students and teachers in a number of universities began to demand and set up women's studies courses—to *claim* a woman-directed education. And, despite the inevitable accusations of "unscholarly," "group therapy," "faddism," etc., despite backlash and budget cuts, women's studies are still growing, offering to more and more women a new intellectual grasp on their lives, new understanding of our history, a fresh vision of the human experience, and also a critical basis for evaluating what they hear and read in other courses, and in the society at large.

But my talk is not really about women's studies, much as I believe in their scholarly, scientific, and human necessity. While I think that any Douglass student has everything to gain by investigating and enrolling in women's studies courses, I want to suggest that there is a more essential experience that you owe yourselves, one which courses in women's studies can greatly enrich, but which finally depends on you, in all your interactions with yourself and your world. This is the experience of *taking responsibility toward yourselves.* Our upbringing as women has so often told us that this should come second to our relationships and responsibilities to other people. We have been offered ethical models of the self-denying wife and mother; intellectual models of the brilliant but slapdash dilettante who never commits herself to anything the whole way, or the intelligent woman who denies her intelligence in order to seem more "feminine," or who sits in passive silence even when she disagrees inwardly with everything that is being said around her.

Responsibility to yourself means refusing to let others do your thinking, talking, and naming for you; it means learning to respect and use your own brains and instincts; hence, grappling with hard work. It means that you do not treat your body as a commodity with which to purchase superficial intimacy or economic security; for our bodies and minds are inseparable in this life, and when we allow our bodies to be treated as objects, our minds are in mortal danger. It means insisting that those to whom you give your friendship and love are able to respect your mind. It means being able to say, with Charlotte Brontë's Jane Eyre: "I have an inward treasure born with me, which can keep me alive if all the extraneous delights should be withheld or offered only at a price I cannot afford to give."

Responsibility to yourself means that you don't fall for shallow and easy solutions—predigested books and ideas, weekend encounters guaranteed to change your life, taking "gut" courses instead of ones you know will challenge you, bluffing at school and life instead of doing solid work, marrying early as an escape from real decisions, getting pregnant as an evasion of already existing problems. It means that you refuse to sell your talents and aspirations short, simply to avoid conflict and confrontation. And this, in turn, means resisting the forces in society which say that women should be nice, play safe, have low professional expectations, drown in love and forget about work, live through others, and stay in the places assigned to us. It means that we insist on a life of meaningful work, insist that work be as meaningful as love and friendship in our lives. It means, therefore, the courage to be "different"; not to be continuously available to others when we need time for ourselves and our work; to be able to demand of others—parents, friends, roommates, teachers, lovers, husbands, children—that they respect our sense of purpose and our integrity as persons. Women everywhere are finding the courage to do this, more and more, and we are finding that courage both in our study of women in the past who possessed it, and in each other as we look to other women for comradeship, community, and challenge. The difference between a life lived actively, and a life of passive drifting and dispersal of energies, is an immense difference. Once we begin to feel committed to our lives, responsible to ourselves, we can never again be satisfied with the old, passive way.

Now comes the second part of the contract. I believe that in a women's college you have the right to expect your faculty to take you seriously. The education of women has been a matter of debate for centuries, and old, negative attitudes about women's role, women's ability to think and take leadership, are still rife both in and outside the university. Many male professors (and I don't mean only at Douglass) still feel that teaching in a women's college is a secondrate career. Many tend to eroticize their women students—to treat them as sexual objects—instead of demanding the best of their minds. (At Yale a legal suit [*Alexander v. Yale*] has been brought against the university by a group of women students demanding a stated policy against sexual advances toward female students by male professors.) Many teachers, both men and women, trained in the male-centered tradition, are still handing the ideas and texts of that tradition on to students without teaching them to criticize its antiwoman attitudes, its omission of women as part of the species. Too often, all of us fail to teach the most important thing, which is that clear thinking, active discussion, and excellent writing are all necessary for intellectual freedom, and that these require *hard work*. Sometimes, perhaps in discouragement with a culture which is both anti-intellectual and antiwoman, we may resign ourselves to low expectations for our students before we have given them half a chance to become more thoughtful, expressive human beings. We need to take to heart the words of Elizabeth Barrett Browning, a poet, a thinking woman, and a feminist, who wrote in 1845 of her impatience with studies which cultivate a "passive recipiency" in the mind, and asserted that "women want to be made to *think actively*: their apprehension is quicker than that of men, but their defect lies for the most part in the logical faculty and in the higher mental activities." Note that she implies a defect which can be remedied by intellectual training, *not* an inborn lack of ability.

I have said that the contract on the student's part involves that you demand to be taken seriously so that you can also go on taking yourself seriously. This means seeking out criticism, recognizing that the most affirming thing anyone can do for you is demand that you push yourself further, show you the range of what you *can* do. It means rejecting attitudes of "take-it-easy," "why-be-so-serious," "why-worry-you'll-probably-get-married-anyway." It means assuming your share of responsibility for what happens in the classroom, because that affects the quality of your daily life here. It means that the student sees herself engaged *with* her teachers in an active, ongoing struggle for a real education. But for her to do this, her teachers must be committed to the belief that women's minds and experience are intrinsically valuable and indispensable to any civilization worthy the name; that there is no more exhilarating and intellectually fertile place in the academic world today than a women's college—*if* both students and teachers in large enough numbers are trying to fulfill this contract. The contract is really a pledge of mutual seriousness about women, about language, ideas, methods, and values. It is our shared commitment toward a world in which the inborn potentialities of so many women's minds will no longer be wasted, raveled-away, paralyzed, or denied.

Discussion Questions

The word feminism has garnered a strong connotative meaning in our current culture. Explain what you believe feminism is and how it related to this reading.

What is the message you received about your role in society and education and how has this affected your academic attitude and performance? Your social attitude and behaviors?

Are your current behaviors and attitudes toward education indicative of someone who is receiving an education or claiming one? How can you do to strengthen your path toward claiming an education?

BUILDING A COMPASS

Bill Burnett and Dave Evans

We have just three questions for you:

What is your name?

What is your quest?

What is the airspeed velocity of an unladen swallow?

If you're like most people, it was probably easy to answer two of those three questions. We all know our names, and a simple Google search can give us the other answer—twenty-four miles per hour. (For all of you hard-core Monty Python fans, that velocity is for a *European* swallow.)

So let's talk about the question that's a little bit harder—what is your quest? It's not hard to imagine that if we added up all the hours spent trying to *figure out* life, for some of us they would outweigh the hours spent actually *living* life. Really. Living. Life.

We all know how to worry about our lives. Analyze our lives. Even speculate about our lives. Worry, analysis, and speculation are not our best discovery tools, and most of us have, at one time or another, gotten incredibly lost and confused using them. They tend to keep us spinning in circles and spending weeks, months, or years sitting on that couch (or at a desk, or in a relationship) trying to figure out what to do next. It's as if life were this great big DIY project, but only a select few actually got the instruction manual.

This is not designing your life.

This is obsessing about your life.

We're here to change that.

And the questions we're ultimately asking are the same ones the Greeks started asking in the fifth century b.c. and we've all been asking ever since: What is the good life? How do you define it? How do you live it? Throughout the ages, people have been asking the same questions:

Why am I here?

What am I doing?

Why does it matter?

What is my purpose?

What's the point of it all?

Life design is a way for you to figure out your own answers to these perennial questions, and to figure out your own good life. Dave's answers to "Why am I here?" and "What am I doing?" and "Why does it matter?" are going to be different from Bill's answers, and our answers are going to be different from yours. But we are all asking the same questions. And we can all find answers for our own lives.

In the last chapter, you answered one of our favorite questions—"How's it going?"—a question we often ask in our office hours. If you filled in your life design dashboard, you now know where your gauges are full, and where they're running on empty, and knowing what's on your life design dashboard is the first step in designing your life.

The next step is building your compass.

Building Your Compass

You need two things to build your compass—a Workview and a Lifeview. To start out, we need to discover what work means to you. What is work for? Why do you do it? What makes good work good? If you discover and are able to articulate your philosophy of work (what it's for and why you do it), you will be less likely to let others design your life for you. Developing your own Workview is one component of the compass you are building; a Lifeview is second.

Now, Lifeview may sound a bit lofty, but it's really not—everyone has a Lifeview. You may not have articulated it before, but if you are alive, you have a Lifeview. A Lifeview is simply your ideas about the world and how it works. What gives life meaning? What makes your life worthwhile or valuable? How does your life relate to others in your family, your community, and the world? What do money, fame, and personal accomplishment have to do with a satisfying life? How important are experience, growth, and fulfillment in your life?

Once you've written your Workview and your Lifeview, and completed the simple exercise that follows, you'll have your compass and be on the path toward a well-designed life. Don't worry—we know that your Workview and Lifeview will change. It's obvious that the Workview and Lifeview you have as a teenager, as a young college grad, and as an empty nester will all be substantially different. The point is, you don't have to have it all figured out for the rest of your life; you just have to create the compass for what life is about for you right now.

Parker Palmer, a renowned educational reformer and author of *Let Your Life Speak,* says that at one point he suddenly realized he was doing a noble job of living someone else's life. Parker was emulating his great heroes—Martin Luther King, Jr., Gandhi—both great social justice leaders of the 1950s and '60s. Because he valued their sentiments and goals, he set his path in the world by their compass, not his own, and worked hard to change the educational system from within. He earned a Ph.D. at UC Berkeley and was on track to reach his goal of becoming a respected university president. That was all well and good, but Parker hated it. He came to the realization that he could be inspired by people like Martin Luther King and Gandhi, but that didn't mean he had to walk their same path. He ended up redesigning his life as a thought leader and writer—still working for the same goals, but in a way that was less about imitation and more about authenticity.

The point is, there are lots of powerful voices in the world, and lots of powerful voices in our heads, all telling us what to do or who to be. And because there are many models for how life is supposed to be lived, we all run the risk, like Parker, of accidentally using someone else's compass and living someone else's life. The best way to avoid this is to articulate clearly our own Workview and Lifeview, so we can build our own unique compass.

Our goal for your life is rather simple: *coherency*. A coherent life is one lived in such a way that you can clearly connect the dots between three things:

- **Who you are**
- **What you believe**
- **What you are doing**

For example, if in your Lifeview you believe in leaving the planet a better place for the next generation, and you work for a giant corporation that is polluting the planet (but for a really great salary), there is going to be a lack of coherency between what you believe and what you do—and as a result a lot of disappointment and discontent. Most of us have to make some trade-offs and compromises along the way, including some we may not like. If your Lifeview is that art is the only thing worth pursuing, and your Workview tells you that it's critical to make enough money so your kids have everything they need, you are going to make a compromise in your Lifeview while your children are dependent and at home. But that will be okay, because it's a conscious decision, which allows you to stay "on course" and coherent. Living coherently doesn't mean everything is in perfect order all the time. It simply means you are living in alignment with your values and have not sacrificed your integrity along the way. When you have a good compass guiding you, you have the power to cut these kinds of deals with yourself. If you can see the connections between who you are, what you believe, and what you are doing, you will know when you are on course, when there is tension, when there might need to be some careful compromises, and when you are in need of a major course correction. Our experience with our students has shown that the ability to connect these three dots increases your sense of self, and that helps you create more meaning in your life and have greater satisfaction.

So now it's time to build your compass and set out on your quest. Right now your quest is simple (and it's not to find the Holy Grail). Your quest is to design your life. We may all want the same things in life—a healthy and long life, work we enjoy and that matters, loving and meaningful relationships, and a hell of a lot of fun along the way—but how we think we'll get them is very different.

Workview Reflection

Write a short reflection about your Workview. We're not looking for a term paper here (and we're still not grading you), but we do want you really to write this down. Don't do it in your head. This should take about thirty minutes. Try to shoot for 250 words—less than a page of typed writing.

A Workview should address the critical issues related to what work is and what it means to you. It is not just a list of what you want from or out of work, but a general statement of your view of work. It's your definition for what good work deserves to be. A Workview may address such questions as:

- **Why work?**
- **What's work for?**
- **What does work mean?**
- **How does it relate to the individual, others, society?**
- **What defines good or worthwhile work?**

- **What does money have to do with it?**
- **What do experience, growth, and fulfillment have to do with it?**

In the years during which we've been helping people with this exercise, we've noticed that a Workview is a pretty new idea for most people. And we've noticed that when people get stuck on this exercise it is because they are just writing down what they're looking for in a job or an employment situation, which is a "job description." For this exercise, we're not interested in *what* work you want to do, but *why* you work.

What we're after is your philosophy of work—what it's for, what it means. This will essentially be your work manifesto. When using the term "work," we mean the broadest definition—not just what you do to make money or for "a job." Work is often the largest single component of most people's waking lives, and over a lifetime it occupies more of our attention and energy than anything else we do. Accordingly, we're suggesting you take the time to reflect and articulate what work and vocation mean to you (and perhaps what you hope work means for others as well).

Workviews can and do range widely in what they address and how they incorporate different issues, such as service to others and the world, money and standard of living, and growth, learning, skills, and talents. All of these can be part of the equation. We want you to address what you think is important. You do not have to address the question of service to others or any explicit connection to social issues. However, the positive psychologist Martin Seligman[1] found that the people who can make an explicit connection between their work and something socially meaningful to them are more likely to find satisfaction, and are better able to adapt to the inevitable stresses and compromises that come with working in the world. Since most people tell us they long for satisfying and meaningful work, we encourage you to explore the questions above and write down your Workview. Your compass won't be complete without it.

Lifeview Reflection

Just as you did with the Workview, please write a reflection on your Lifeview. This should also take no more than thirty minutes and be 250 words or so. Below are some questions often addressed in a Lifeview, just to get you started. The key thing is to write down whatever critical defining values and perspectives provide the basis for your understanding of life. Your Lifeview is what provides your definition of what have been called "matters of ultimate concern." It's what matters most to you.

- **Why are we here?**
- **What is the meaning or purpose of life?**
- **What is the relationship between the individual and others?**
- **Where do family, country, and the rest of the world fit in?**
- **What is good, and what is evil?**
- **Is there a higher power, God, or something transcendent, and if so, what impact does this have on your life?**
- **What is the role of joy, sorrow, justice, injustice, love, peace, and strife in life?**

We realize that these are somewhat philosophical questions, and we did just mention the "G" word. Some readers will see God as unimportant; others may have wanted us to address this up front as the most important issue. You've probably figured out by now that design is values-neutral, and we don't take sides. The questions, including the ones about God or spirituality, are given to provoke your thinking, and it's up to you to see which ones you want to try to answer. They are not talking points for religious or political debates, and there are no wrong answers—no wrong Lifeviews. The only way to do this incorrectly is not to do it at all. Besides that, be curious and think like a designer. Ask the questions that work for you, make up your own, and see what you discover.

Write down your answers.

Ready. Begin.

Coherency and Workview-Lifeview Integration

Read over your Workview and Lifeview, and write down a few thoughts on the following questions (please try to answer each of the questions):

- **Where do your views on work and life complement one another?**
- **Where do they clash?**
- **Does one drive the other? How?**

Please take some time to write up your thoughts on the integration of your two views. Our students tell us that this is where they often get the biggest "aha" moments, so please take this part of the exercise seriously and give the integration some thought. In most cases, this reflection will result in some editing of one or both of your views. By having your Workview and your Lifeview in harmony with each other, you increase your own clarity and ability to live a consciously coherent, meaningful life—one in which who you are, what you believe, and what you do are aligned. When you've got an accurate compass, you'll never stray off course for long.

True North

So now you have an articulated and integrated Lifeview and Workview. Ultimately, what these two views do is give you your "True North." They create your compass. They will help you know if you're on course or off course. At any moment you can assess where you are in relation to your True North. It's rare that people sail beautifully straight through their beautiful lives, always looking beautiful. In fact, as all sailors know, you can't chart a course of one straight line—you tack according to what the winds and the conditions allow. Heading True North, you may sail one way, then another direction, and then back the other way. Sometimes you sail close to the shoreline to avoid rough seas, adapting as needed. And sometimes storms hit and you get completely lost, or the entire sailboat tips over.

These are the times when it's best to have your Workview and your Lifeview handy to reorient yourself. Anytime you start to feel your life is not working, or you're going through a major transition, it's good to do a compass calibration. We do them at least once a year.

Rotate your tires.

Change the battery in your smoke detector.

Double-check your Workview and Lifeview and make sure they align.

Anytime you're changing your situation, or pursuing a new thing, or wondering what you're doing at a particular job—stop. Before you start, it's a good idea to check your compass and orient yourself. Now that you have your compass, it's time to "find your way."

This is a quest, after all.

Dysfunctional Belief: *I should know where I'm going!*

Reframe: *I won't always know where I'm going—but I can always know whether I'm going in the right direction.*

TRY STUFF
Workview and Lifeview

1. Write a short reflection about your Workview. This should take about thirty minutes. Shoot for about 250 words—less than a page of typed writing.

2. Write a short reflection about your Lifeview. This should also take no more than thirty minutes and be 250 words or so.

3. Read over your Lifeview and Workview, and answer each of these questions:

   a. Where do your views on work and life complement one another?

   b. Where do they clash?

   c. Does one drive the other? How?

Discussion Questions

What does it mean to you, to live a good life? Why is it important to define your idea of a good life?

How is your current state indicative of a coherent or incoherent life?

What are the implications of living your life according to someone else's compass?

Chapter 6

What do you want to do?

IT TAKES MORE THAN A MAJOR

EMPLOYER PRIORITIES FOR COLLEGE LEARNING AND STUDENT SUCCESS

Hart Research Associates

From January 9 to 13, 2013, Hart Research Associates conducted an online survey among 318 employers whose organizations have at least 25 employees and report that 25 percent or more of their new hires hold either an associate's degree from a two-year college or a bachelor's degree from a four-year college. Respondents are executives at private sector and nonprofit organizations, including owners, CEOs, presidents, c-suite level executives, and vice presidents.

This report provides a detailed analysis of employers' priorities for the kinds of learning today's college students need to succeed in today's economy. It also reports on changes in educational and assessment practices that employers recommend.

Overview

Innovation is a priority for employers today. Nearly all employers surveyed (95 percent) say they give hiring preference to college graduates with skills that will enable them to contribute to innovation in the workplace. More than nine in ten agree that "innovation is essential" to their organization's continued success.

Employers recognize capacities that cut across majors as critical to a candidate's potential for career success, and they view these skills as more important than a student's choice of undergraduate major. Nearly all those surveyed (93 percent) agree that "a candidate's demonstrated capacity to think critically, communicate clearly, and solve complex problems is *more important* than their undergraduate major." More than nine in ten of those surveyed say it is important that those they hire demonstrate ethical judgment and integrity, intercultural skills, and the capacity for continued new learning. More than three in four employers say they want colleges to place *more emphasis* on helping students develop five key learning outcomes, including critical thinking, complex problem solving, written and oral communication, and applied knowledge in real-world settings. Employers endorse several educational practices as potentially helpful in preparing college students for workplace success. These include practices that require students to conduct research and use evidence-based analysis; gain in-depth knowledge in the major and analytic, problem-solving, and communication skills; and apply their learning in real-world settings.

Employers recognize the importance of liberal education and the liberal arts. The majority of employers agree that having both field-specific knowledge and skills and a broad range of skills and knowledge is most important for recent college graduates to achieve long-term career success. Few think that having field-specific knowledge and skills alone is what is most needed for individuals' career success. Eighty percent of employers agree that, regardless of their major, every college student should acquire broad knowledge in the liberal arts and sciences. When read a description of a twenty-first-century liberal education, a large majority of employers recognize its importance; 74 percent would recommend this kind of education to a young person they know as the best way to prepare for success in today's global economy.

Employers endorse a blended model of liberal and applied learning. Across many areas tested, employers strongly endorse educational practices that involve students in active, effortful work—practices including collaborative problem solving, internships, research, senior projects, and community engagements. Employers consistently rank outcomes and practices that involve application of skills over acquisition of discrete bodies of knowledge. They also strongly endorse practices that require students to demonstrate both acquisition of knowledge and its application.

Employers think that more college graduates have the skills and preparation needed for entry-level positions than for advancement. A majority of employers (56 percent) express satisfaction with the job colleges and universities are doing to prepare graduates for success in the workplace, but more than two in five indicate room for improvement. Two in three employers (67 percent) believe most college graduates have the skills and knowledge they need to succeed in entry-level positions, but only 44 percent think they have what is required for advancement and promotion to higher levels.

Employers express interest in e-portfolios and partnerships with colleges to ensure college graduates' successful transition to the workplace. In addition to a resume or college transcript, more than four in five employers say an electronic portfolio would be useful to them in ensuring that job applicants have the knowledge and skills they need to succeed in their company or organization. Notable proportions of business and nonprofit leaders say they are already partnering with two-year and four-year colleges to advance the success of college students after graduation, and those who are not express interest in doing so to provide more hands-on learning opportunities and to help college students successfully make the transition from college into the workplace.

Eleven Key findings

1. *Employers are highly focused on innovation as critical to the success of their companies, and they report that the challenges their employees face today are more complex and require a broader skill set than in the past. Notably,*

employers indicate that they prioritize critical thinking, communication, and complex problem-solving skills over a job candidate's major field of study when making hiring decisions.

Employers point out that both the expectations and challenges their employees face are greater today than in the past. Majorities say their company or organization is asking employees to take on greater responsibilities and to use a broader set of skills (93 percent total agree; 52 percent strongly agree) while facing challenges today that are more complex than in the past (91 percent total agree; 50 percent strongly agree).

Employers today are highly focused on innovation and are giving priority to hiring employees who can help in this advancement. Fully 92 percent agree that innovation is essential to their company's continued success, including 51 percent who strongly agree. Additionally, 95 percent of employers agree (57 percent strongly) that their company "puts a priority on hiring people with the intellectual and interpersonal skills that will help them contribute to innovation in the workplace."

To achieve success at their companies in today's more complex environment, employers are in broad agreement that a candidate's demonstrated capacity to think critically, communicate clearly, and solve complex programs is *more* important than his or her undergraduate field of study (93 percent total agree; 59 percent strongly agree).

2. *While they may prioritize key skills over a job candidate's field of study, the majority of employers agree that having both field-specific knowledge and skills and a broad range of skills and knowledge is most important for recent college graduates to achieve long-term career success.* When asked whether having field-specific knowledge, a broad range of skills, or both is most important to achieving long-term career success, over half (55 percent) of employers say it is most important to have both. Among employers who chose just one category, more say having a broad range of skills and knowledge is important for career advancement (29 percent) than say having knowledge and skills that apply to a specific field or position is most important for college graduates' long-term success (16 percent).

3. *Employers' evaluation of two-year and four-year colleges and universities for the job they are doing preparing graduates to succeed and contribute to today's economy suggests that many see room for improvement. They register a greater sense of confidence in college graduates having the skills and knowledge to succeed in entry-level positions than to advance or be promoted within their companies or organizations.*

A 56 percent majority of employers think that higher education is doing an excellent (9 percent) or good job (47 percent) in preparing students for success in today's economy, compared with 44 percent who say the system is doing a fair (40 percent) or poor job (4 percent). It is notable that few employers give postsecondary institutions marks of either excellent or poor; most fall somewhere in the middle.

When asked to think about college graduates from both two-year and four-year colleges and universities, two-thirds of employers say that all (14 percent) or most (53 percent) graduates who apply to positions within their company or organization have the skills to succeed in entry-level positions, compared with one in three (33 percent) who say about half or fewer are qualified for entry-level positions.

Thinking specifically about the skills and knowledge needed to advance or be promoted within their company or organization, 44 percent of employers say that all (7 percent) or most (37 percent) graduates have what it takes to move beyond the entry level. Fifty-six percent of employers say that about half or fewer applicants who apply to positions within their company or organization have the skills and knowledge for advancement.

4. *Employers point to a variety of types of knowledge and skills as important considerations when hiring, placing the greatest priority on ethics, intercultural skills, and capacity for professional development.* While majorities of employers say that all skill and knowledge areas tested are important, they differentiate between those that are very important to the hiring decisions of their company or organization.

Employers place the greatest degree of importance on the following areas:
○ *Ethics:* "Demonstrate ethical judgment and integrity" (96 percent important, including 76 percent very important)
○ *Intercultural Skills:* "Comfortable working with colleagues, customers, and/or clients from diverse cultural backgrounds" (96 percent important, including 63 percent very important)
○ *Professional Development:* "Demonstrate the capacity for professional development and continued new learning" (94 percent important, including 61 percent very important)

While deemed important by majorities of employers, they place a lesser degree of emphasis on the following areas when it comes to hiring:
○ *Community Involvement:* "Show an interest in giving back to the communities in which our company or organization is located or those that it serves" (71 percent important, including 26 percent *very* important; 29 percent just somewhat/not important)
○ *Global Knowledge:* "Know about global cultures, histories, values, religions, and social systems" (55 percent important, including 16 percent very important; 45 percent just somewhat/not important)

5. *Majorities of employers believe two-year and four-year colleges and universities should place more emphasis on a variety of key learning outcomes in order to increase graduates' success in today's global economy. Few say less emphasis should be placed on any of the learning outcomes tested, but employers overall are most likely to believe there is a need to increase the focus on active skills such as critical thinking, complex problem solving, communication, and applying knowledge to real-world settings.*

Employers were asked whether colleges and universities should place more, less, or the same emphasis on seventeen different learning outcomes in order to help students succeed in today's global economy. Large majorities believe colleges and universities should place at least the same or greater emphasis on all these learning outcomes. Of the seventeen learning outcomes tested, majorities believe that colleges should place more emphasis on eleven of them, including seven for which more than seven in ten employers say colleges should increase their focus.

Employers say the most emphasis should be placed on the following areas:
○ critical thinking and analytical reasoning (82 percent more emphasis, 7 percent less)
○ complex problem solving and analysis (81 percent more emphasis, 6 percent less)

> o written and oral communication (80 percent more emphasis, 8 percent less)
> o the application of knowledge and skills in real-world settings (78 percent more emphasis, 6 percent less)
> o the location, organization, and evaluation of information from multiple sources (72 percent more emphasis, 9 percent less)
> o innovation and creativity (71 percent more emphasis, 9 percent less)

Employers see less need for colleges to heighten their focus on ensuring graduates demonstrate (1) proficiency in a foreign language, (2) knowledge about global issues/developments, (3) knowledge about cultural diversity/the role of the United States in the world, (4) civic knowledge/participation, and (5) an understanding of democratic institutions and values. Rather, majorities of employers would like higher education institutions to maintain their current level of emphasis in these areas.

6. *There is broad agreement among employers that all students, regardless of their chosen field of study, should have educational experiences that teach them about building civic capacity, broad knowledge about the liberal arts and sciences, and cultures outside the United States.*

Large majorities of employers agree with each of six tested goals for college (see fig. 1). Top among them, 91 percent of employers agree that all students should have experiences in college that teach them how to solve problems with people whose views are different from their own, including 57 percent who strongly agree with this statement. Other aims of college learning that earn high levels of agreement include teaching students about ethical issues and public debates important to their field (87 percent total agree; 43 percent strongly) and ensuring college students gain experience working with others to solve important problems in their community (86 percent total agree; 41 percent strongly).

While employers may not be clamoring for colleges to *increase* their emphasis on civic learning or on teaching about global issues, they widely agree that all students should receive civic education and learn about cultures outside the United States. Fully 82 percent agree (27 percent strongly) that every student should take classes that build civic capacity, and learning about societies and cultures outside the United States (78 percent total agree; 26 percent strongly) is widely valued for all students. Additionally, four in five agree (32 percent strongly) that all students should acquire broad knowledge in the liberal arts and sciences, regardless of a student's chosen field of study.

The variation in the proportion of employers who say they *strongly agree* with these goals for college do reveal some distinctions, however, suggesting the deepest commitment to the top goal of all students learning how to solve problems with people with different views.

7. *Among the ten existing and emerging educational practices tested, employers believe several have the potential to improve the education of today's college students and prepare graduates to succeed in the workplace.*

Employers express the greatest confidence in the following practices to help students succeed beyond graduation. Large majorities believe that colleges that set expectations for students to achieve these learning outcomes will do the most to prepare them for success:

> o work through ethical issues and debates to form their own judgments about the issues at stake (66 percent say "will help a lot/fair amount")
> o acquire hands-on or direct experience with the methods of science (69 percent say "will help a lot/fair amount")

○ develop the skills to conduct research collaboratively (74 percent say "will help a lot/fair amount")

○ complete an internship or community-based field project (78 percent say "will help a lot/fair amount")

○ complete a project prior to graduation that demonstrates their acquired knowledge and skills (79 percent say "will help a lot/fair amount")

○ develop research questions in their field and evidence-based analyses (83 percent say "will help a lot/fair amount")

A flipped classroom approach to learning also has broad appeal among employers. Three in five (59 percent) say an approach that deemphasizes lectures and devotes classroom time to dialogue, debate, and problem solving in groups or alone with the guidance of the instructor will help prepare students a lot or a fair amount for success beyond graduation.

Employers anticipate that other emerging educational practices would have a more muted impact in preparing students for success: expecting students to learn about points of view of people in societies outside of North America and Western Europe (47 percent a lot or fair amount), expecting them to learn about cultural and ethnic diversity in the context of the United States (44 percent a lot or fair amount), and expecting them to explore various challenges facing society (42 percent a lot or fair amount).

8. *In addition to a resume and college transcript, a large majority of employers say an electronic portfolio demonstrating a student's work and key skill and knowledge areas would be useful in evaluating potential candidates for hire.* Four in five (83 percent) employers say an electronic portfolio of student accomplishments would be very (43 percent) or fairly (40 percent) useful to them in ensuring applicants have the skills and knowledge to succeed in their company or organization. Just 17 percent say the portfolio would be only somewhat useful or less.

9. *A notable proportion of employers say their company or organization currently partners with a nearby college or university to offer internships to college students. Smaller proportions of employers report partnering with higher education institutions in other ways, but express interest in partnering to offer internships in the future.*

When it comes to partnering with two-year and four-year colleges to advance the success of college students after graduation, employers are most likely to say their company or organization offers internships and/or apprenticeships to students at nearby institutions (47 percent currently do this). An additional 42 percent of employers say they have a high (21 percent) or medium (21 percent) level of interest in developing this type of program in the future. Only 11 percent say they would have a low level of interest.

Other collaborative efforts between colleges and companies or organizations are less common among employers today; nevertheless, majorities of employers express interest in these initiatives:

○ working closely with the career services office of a nearby college to help students successfully make the transition from college into the workplace (26 percent currently do this; 51 percent do not currently do this, but would have a high/medium level of interest in doing so in the future)

○ partnering with colleges in the area to better align the curriculum and learning outcomes they teach to the skills and knowledge our company looks for in new hires (22 percent currently do this; 54 percent do not currently do this, but would have a high/medium level of interest in doing so in the future)

  ○ sponsoring a program at a nearby college to get students involved in more "real-world" or hands-on learning while they are still in college (18 percent currently do this; 53 percent do not currently do this, but would have a high/medium level of interest in doing so in the future)

10. *Across several areas tested, employers strongly endorse educational practices that involve students in active, effortful work—practices that involve such things as collaborative problem solving, research, senior projects, community engagement, and internships.*

Questions that ask employers about specific areas of "knowledge" with no reference to active learning or skill development receive lower scores than questions that address cross-cutting skills, or questions that address a combination of knowledge and skills. Even where employers considered particular kinds of knowledge very important or somewhat important (e.g., global knowledge, science and technology), they still place a higher priority on forms of learning that emphasize students' active development and application of intellectual and practical skills.

More than nine in ten of those surveyed say it is important that those they hire demonstrate ethical judgment and integrity, intercultural skills, and the capacity for continued new learning. More than 75 percent of employers say they want colleges to place more emphasis on helping students develop five key learning outcomes, including critical thinking, complex problem solving, written and oral communication, and applied knowledge in real-world settings.

In contrast, no more than 40 percent of employers indicate a desire for colleges to place more emphasis on helping students gain knowledge in areas including global issues, the role of the United States in the world, cultural diversity in America, civics, or democratic institutions and values. (Majorities would rather that colleges maintain their current level of emphasis on these knowledge areas.) The only knowledge area in which more than half of employers would like to see colleges place more emphasis is on knowledge about science and technology (56 percent would like to see more emphasis), but it is still a lower priority than active, effortful learning and skills development.

Employers endorse several educational practices as potentially helpful in preparing college students for workplace success. These include practices that require students to conduct research and use evidence-based analysis; gain in-depth knowledge in the major and analytic, problem-solving, and communication skills; and apply their learning in real-world settings.

11. *Employers recognize the importance of today's colleges and universities providing a liberal education—one that focuses on both broad knowledge in a variety of areas and knowledge in a specific field of interest, as well as intellectual and practical skills that span all areas of study and a sense of social responsibility. When given a description of the component elements of a liberal education, nearly all consider this kind of learning very or fairly important for colleges to provide, and a large majority would recommend this approach to young people they know.*

When presented with a description of liberal education, fully 94 percent of employers say it is important for today's colleges to provide this type of education, including half (51 percent) who say it is very important to do so (see fig. 2).

Moreover, nearly three in four employers (74 percent) say they would recommend that their own child or a young person they know pursue this type of education in order to achieve professional and career success in today's global economy (see fig. 2). Just 7 percent would not recommend this approach, and 19 percent say it depends. When forced to choose one way or the other (and without the "depends" option), fully 89 percent would recommend the described approach to a young person seeking advice on the type of college education they should pursue, and only 11 percent would not.

Hart Research Associates is a public opinion research firm. The results presented here are from a survey conducted on behalf of the Association of American Colleges and Universities.

Discussion Questions

How do you think a student can acquire innovation skills?

How does UNCW and your UNI course provide opportunities to gain necessary skills for employment?

Employers feel it is important that students can apply the knowledge gained in college in a practical manner. Thinking of the last week, how often did you acquire knowledge and how often were you asked to apply the knowledge acquired?

A BUTTERFLY FLAPS ITS WINGS AND YOU FIND A JOB

CHAOS AND YOUR CAREER PLANS

Katharine Brooks

You need chaos in your soul to give birth to a dancing star.

—FRIEDRICH NIETZSCHE, THUS SPAKE ZARATHUSTRA

Has it happened yet? Have you been asked **THE QUESTION?**

You know the one: it's the question that cuts to the core of your existence, the question that haunts you pretty much from the time you decide to be a college student to months, even years, after you graduate. Tt starts so innocently. Someone asks you what your major is, so you tell them.

There's a slight pause. Then comes **THE QUESTION:**

"What are You Going to do With That?"

OK, think fast.

"I'm going to law school," you say, even though you aren't really sure you want to, but it sure sounds good. Or "I'm thinking about med school," even though you have no interest in science classes.

The questioner's face relaxes; maybe he even smiles. He pats you on the shoulder. "Wow, that's great!"

And that's how the lie begins...

Do you feel sometimes there's a cosmic joke at work? That you chose this really interesting major but now you're wondering, was it worth it? Or perhaps you're just starting college and **THE QUESTION** is already making you nervous.

The Pressure of The Linear Path

The problem behind **THE QUESTION** is that it assumes a linear path between your major and your career. And the lure of the linear path is powerful. It's embedded in our thinking. From the time you played with fire trucks and people asked you if you wanted to be a firefighter, linear paths to careers have been assumed to be the natural state of things. So it seems only logical that you would pursue a major that would become your ultimate career. Business majors go into business. Engineering majors become engineers, philosophy majors become...? Hmm...

Your parents would probably be thrilled if you had a glitch-free linear path from school to work all worked out. You know, "I'm studying accounting so I can be an accountant," or "I'm going to be an English major so I can teach English." *You* might be secretly relieved as well.

But that's early twentieth-century thinking–1909 to be exact, when the trait-and-factor approach was designed to determine the best career choices for people. As America shifted from an agricultural to an industrial society, vocational researchers sought ways to determine the best fit between individuals and their jobs. Career tests were designed to match people's interests and skills with potential vocations. Society placed additional restraints on employment, with women and minorities relegated to narrow fields. Most people pursued education to learn a specific trade, and a college education was reserved for the elite few who would likely go on to teaching, medicine, law, or the ministry.

In the twenty-first century, a college education is wide open to many more individuals regardless of gender, race, or career goal. Many students now choose a college education because of the interesting subjects they can study, not necessarily because of a specific career plan.

Whatever your reason for pursing your major, you, like many others, are probably struggling with **THE QUESTION:** What do I *do* with this degree? Where is *my* linear path?

To help you envision such a path, here's a list of the actual careers of some recent graduates, drawn from alumni surveys from three institutions. Note the relatively direct relationship between their majors and their careers.

MAJOR	JOB
Art	Cartoonist
Asian American Studies	Teaching English as a second language in Korea
Chemistry	Veterinarian
Classics/Archaeology	Latin teacher
Dramatic Arts	MTV program developer
Economics	Bond trader on Wall Street
English	Editor, major publishing house
French and Spanish	Foreign service officer
Geography	High school geography teacher
Government	Special prosecutor, district attorney's office
Government	Republican National Committee PR staff
Psychology	Psychotherapist
Religion	Minister, single adults program

Can you see the linear relationship that exists between a major and a career? The symmetry between the job duties and the use of the graduates' skills? The English major is using her writing skills. The psychology major is helping people.

The economics major is working on Wall Street. It's reassuring, isn't it? Not only can you get a job, your job can be directly related to your major.

There's only one problem with the list: *it's all wrong*. These are the *actual* careers of graduates with those majors:

MAJOR	JOB
Art	Special prosecutor, district attorney's office
Asian American Studies	Bond trader on Wall Street
Chemistry	Teaching English as a second language in Korea
Classics/Archaeology	Foreign service officer
Dramatic Arts	Republican National Committee PR staff
Economics	Veterinarian
English	Psychotherapist
French and Spanish	Latin teacher
Geography	Editor, major publishing house
Government	Minister, single odults program
Government	High school geography teacher
Psychology	Cartoonist
Religion	MTV program developer

Oops.

Is something wrong here? No, something's actually right. Clearly, reality doesn't always match up to that traditional linear career path. These graduates, whether by design or by accident, have channeled the real, deep value of their academic and life experiences, and taken them beyond traditional thinking.

The linear career path hasn't disappeared. Some psychology majors do become psychologists and some English majors become English professors. But linear thinking can keep you from thinking broadly about your options and being open-minded to new opportunities.

Linear Thinking About Careers

Right about now you're probably thinking that pursuing an education that directly relates to a career, and vice versa, seems so stable and easy. Wouldn't it make more sense to follow a more direct path? After all, if you try to use that second chart as a guide, you really have no idea where you might end up. And doesn't most of the advice out there on career planning focus on that direct path?

As we saw earlier, the roots of modern-day career counseling lie in the early twentieth century, 1909 to be exact, when Frank Parsons, an engineering professor, developed his trait-and-factor approach to making career decisions. Parsons defined a *trait* as a characteristic of a person that could be discovered by testing, and a *factor* as a characteristic of a job. He described his approach as "matching men to jobs" and believed there was one right career for each worker.

This approach to career analysis was designed to reduce any elements of chance or uncertainty in the process, just like those books and Web sites that neatly outline the "five steps to your career" and ask you to quickly set a goal and move toward it. Career assessments are integral to this method to further eliminate the element of chance, on the assumption that a test will help you determine the exact fit between your traits and the workplace factors.

Now, any theory that has hung around for a hundred years can't be all bad, and it *is* important to know how your strengths and skills fit into the workplace (and you'll explore these in the next few chapters), but many career systems and assessment instruments follow the trait-and-factor approach too literally, leading you down the linear path using traditional linear thinking and reasoning. They are too simplistic for twenty-first-century career planning.

For instance, if you use traditional deductive reasoning, where you start with one personal trait and expand it to a career factor, you might follow this logical train of thought:

- Pilots must have strong attention to detail.
- I have strong attention to detail.
- I should be a pilot.

Or

- The Peace Corps helps people.
- I want to help people.
- I should work for the Peace Corps.

One particular challenge with deductive reasoning is that it assumes the first statement is true. If the first statement is inaccurate, then the reasoning quickly falls apart. On the other hand, if you rely on traditional inductive reasoning, where you start with a large factor like a field of employment and reduce it to a simple trait, you might follow this train of thought:

- Every lawyer I've met has been untrustworthy.
- Therefore all lawyers are untrustworthy.
- I can't be a lawyer.

Or

- My insurance salesperson is boring.
- Therefore the insurance industry is boring.
- I won't look at careers at an insurance company.

While these traditional reasoning methods are simple and (on the surface) logical, they could actually impede your career planning. You might choose a career field or employer based on one arbitrary skill or characteristic (trait) you possess, which might ultimately not work for you, or conversely, you might completely avoid a career field because you have developed a global perception of it (factor) based on your limited personal experience.

For instance, if you speak with Peace Corps recruiters, they will tell you that the Peace Corps volunteer position is extremely tough, demanding, and often frustrating. They don't want people who just want to "help." They need practical people with their heads on their shoulders who see the big picture of providing service but aren't there to save the world.

And did you know that the insurance industry offers fascinating positions for people with all sorts of interests? In the field of underwriting, for example, special knowledge or expertise is often called for to make important judgments about the value of property. An art history major, for example, works with a major insurance firm valuing the oriental carpets and art holdings of major corporations. A geology major evaluates beach properties for an insurance company, determining the odds of hurricanes or other natural phenomena destroying them. She spends much of her time traveling to beachfront communities, sometimes to review new developments and other times to assess damage after a hurricane or other tragic event. Is that a "boring" job?

WANDERING OFF
My Degree Equals My Earning Power

Want to know the number one most requested piece of information from college career centers? The employment figures from alumni surveys. Everyone, from students to parents to government agencies, wants to know what percentage of students found jobs by graduation. And how much were they earning. And their major. There seems to be a theory that if sociology majors found jobs in X field, making X dollars, then I, a sociology major, can find a job in X field making X dollars. While there's some truth to that theory, there's less truth than you might imagine.

Study after study show poor correlations between students' undergraduate majors and their income. Get that? *Weak* correlation. You're working off a common myth that your degree equals your earning power.

Your earning power is much more affected by where you live, your field of work, and your job title. An accounting major working for a small nonprofit organization in the Midwest will likely earn less than on English major working as an investment banker in New York City. Get the point?

Is it true that engineers generally make higher salaries than liberal arts majors? Yes. But—hello—they're *engineers. Do you want to be an engineer? Then go to engineering school and be one. Problem solved.*

So take a minute to think about what you've said and heard about career planning. You can catch yourself (or your parents) thinking linearly about careers if you're harboring any of these thoughts:

- "My major equals my career."
- "If I can just combine the right skills and the right values, I'll know what I want to do."

- "I can't do much with a liberal arts degree."
- "I guess I should go to grad school."
- "I guess I should go to law school."
- "Career tests will tell me what to do"
- "Career counselors can tell me what to do"
- "I should wait until I know what I want to do before starting my job search."
- "I should wait until I graduate to start my job search."

So if this linear approach doesn't really work all that well in the twenty-first century, what model do you turn to if you're multitalented, multifaceted, or just not sure?

How College Students *Really* Find Jobs

It's ridiculous to ask liberal arts students what they plan to do in five years. They don't even know what they plan to have for dinner.

—*ANONYMOUS COLLEGE CAREER COUNSELOR*

As we've noted, if you listen to most people and read most career books or Web sites, you might assume that the job search is a linear logical process: you set a specific career goal, follow clearly outlined steps, and arrive at the perfect job. But try asking graduates how they actually arrived at their current jobs. You'll get replies like this one:

> I don't know exactly. I majored in psychology and thought I'd pursue a Ph.D. and maybe become a professor. But I also liked my anthropology classes, and a professor told me about a summer internship in a museum. I helped create an exhibit an Native American art and I really enjoyed the work. Then an alumna spoke at a career program on her work at the Smithsonian Institution. It sounded interesting so I went up and introduced myself to her. We kept in touch and she called me during my senior year to see if I would be interested in a fund-raising position for the Smithsonian's new Native American exhibit, So here I am using my psychology skills to ask important business and community leaders to fund our research and exhibits. And I love it. And now that I know how museums work and how to raise money, my goal is to open an art gallery/museum on a Native American reservation.

Notice how this story starts out in a linear way: the student was studying psychology so she could become a psychology professor. But then a totally unpredictable event occurred: her internship at a museum caused her to start thinking about other choices. And then a chance meeting with an alumna resulted in a job opportunity. If you had asked her at age eighteen, "What are you going to do with that psychology major?" do you think she would have said, "I'm going to open an art gallery/museum in New Mexico"?

Clearly the linear approach isn't at work here. Unplanned events and emerging conditions changed this individual's circumstances. We need a theory that fits this more typical situation, a theory that recognizes that just like the life of the psychology major above, yours isn't unfolding in a straight line either, and the job search seems chaotic and messy at best. Enter chaos theory—a nonlinear and much more relevant career theory for you. Now, that sounds daunting and complicated, not to mention, well, chaotic. But it's really rather simple. And believe it or not, once you learn the key elements of chaos theory, which form the basis of the Wise Wanderings system you will learn in this book, you'll find you can relax and go with the flow of your job search instead of wanting to force and control everything.

In fact, you have just witnessed a key element of chaos theory: the butterfly effect. The butterfly effect states that a small incident at the beginning of a process (such as a butterfly flapping its wings or a graduate speaking at a career event) can produce a large variation in the long-term outcome (ultimately causing a tornado or a new career). A chaos-based career system allows for change and the unexpected. It takes into account your diverse interests and broad scope of knowledge, and takes advantage of how the job search really works today. You might be surprised to learn that in one study of university graduates almost 70 percent reported that their careers were significantly influenced by unplanned events–in other words, the butterfly effect (Krumboltz and Levin, 2004).

What if you could actually harness the power of the butterfly?

You can. Let's start by learning more about chaos theory.

ENGLISH LITERATURE AT WORK

Charles Dickens Explains the Butterfly Effect

In Charles Dickens's book *Great Expectations*, the lead character Pip makes the following observation:

> *"That was a memorable day to me, for it made great changes in me. But, it is the same with any life. Imagine one selected day struck out of it, and think how different its course would have been. Pause you who read this, and think for a moment of the long chain of iron or gold, of thorns or flowers, that would never have bound you, but for the formation of the first link on one memorable day."*

Sounds a lot like the butterfly effect doesn't it? With a twist though: instead of thinking about an event that happened, Dickens is asking you to think about something that didn't happen. How would your life be different if a particular event had not occurred?

Chaos Theory

People usually smile when you tell them that careers follow chaos theory rather than linear theory. Chaos theory conjures up thoughts of craziness and being out of control: the notion that there is no rhyme or reason to one's career path. The irony is that despite its name, chaos theory is anything but chaotic. It's just complex—as you and you career can be. The order is there, but it's just not immediately visible on the surface.

Chaos theory is based on mathematical formulas originally designed to develop a better weather prediction model. Think about it: how successful are we at predicting the weather? Sometimes we're pretty good. When the conditions are foreseen, when nothing changes, and when we know certain physical laws are being followed, we can predict the weather. If we see a front moving across the map, we know a storm is coming. But what happens when something interrupts the pattern? What if the front coming from the west suddenly encounters another storm coming up the East Coast? When and where will they meet? How well can we predict a tornado's path? Not too well generally. We know it's coming (sometimes) but we can't tell where it's going. Chaos theory helps us understand that too many variables in a complex system make it hard to predict the outcome.

We also know from chaos theory that the greater the distance between now and the future, the weaker our prediction will be. For instance, we're pretty good at predicting the weather today. Maybe even tomorrow or within the next week. But after that our predictions get shaky. We may notice trends, or make logical inferences such as if it's August, it will be hot (at least in most of the United States), but chaos theory helps us understand we can't predict the future in greater detail.

Chaos Theory and Your Career

Just as complex factors influence the weather, the path to a career can be complex with all sorts of intervening variables, including family origin, level of education, individual skills and talents, the job market, and so on. And just like weather fore-casting, career planning is a form of prediction, right? Aren't you trying to guess the career path you'll pursue in the future based on the degree you're pursuing, the experiences you've had, or what you like or dislike? And isn't it easier to predict what you'll do this evening (or even this semester) than what you'll be doing in two years?

Traditional chaos theory is a mathematical model that serves as an excellent basis and metaphor for the Wise Wanderings system. To see how this works, let's consider five basic tenets of chaos theory and how they apply to career planning:

1. Chaos theory helps us predict the outcome of complex situations by asking us to *assess what we currently know, what we cannot know, and what we can learn.* Then we can make reasonable choices based on that information. So instead of trying to predict a future you can't see, you can start your career planning by focusing on what you know right now, what you don't know, and what you can learn. What you probably know right now is that you have a variety of interests and talents and you aren't ready to make a decision. You aren't ready to—and cannot—predict the future, but you can also see that it's not total anarchy: you do have some ideas and interests you could pursue if you wanted to. So instead of having to make a career choice right now, consider yourself in an information-gathering phase. Is the pressure lessening already?

2. Chaos theory relies on abductive reasoning (as opposed to simple deductive and inductive reasoning of linear theory), which says *we can't base decisions on single factors or traits.* We make better decisions when we look at the big picture, stay open-minded, and consider a variety of perspectives. And chaos theory even has a nice term for changing your mind: it's called phase shifting. So you don't need to base your career plans on one piece of information, such as your major, or find the simple answer to **THE QUESTION.** You can find the

patterns and connections between your interests, knowledge, and experiences and know that a variety of career choices are available to you—and during your lifetime you may try them all! You will not only tolerate but also welcome the ambiguity, recognizing that what others might call cluelessness you can call open-mindedness, because you know lots of unexpected opportunities await and you're not ready to limit yourself.

3. Chaos theory assumes that change occurs constantly and that the unexpected and unpredicted will occur. As you develop your career plans, you'll encounter changes (or what chaos theory calls emergent variables) that will lead to new paths. Just think back to the psychology major who planned to teach psychology. She went through a series of events (what chaos theory calls recursive changes): an interesting class, internship, and job offer that resulted in her plans to open an art gallery. And who knows where she'll be in ten years? This is one of the most fun aspects of applying chaos theory to careers. All you have to do is pay attention and take advantage of those emerging variables. Isn't it great that something's coming up that will propel you forward in ways you haven't even considered yet?

4. Now, just in case you're getting a little nervous about all these changes that seem out of your control, chaos theory comes to the rescue because it holds that *systems will ultimately reveal an order.* This is a key piece of knowledge: what looks like chaos isn't always chaotic. You may just be too close to it to see the organizing patterns. Chaos looks orderly from afar and so will your career. By using the Wise Wanderings system, you'll begin to see the order to your seeming career chaos. And while you may not see a coherent pattern in what you're doing right now, you'll learn to think about the connections you're building between your classes, your experiences, and so on. You get to create your future, and suddenly the major that seemed to be a problem and a source of concern might actually be a part of the solution. You will start to see this more clearly when you create the Wandering Map in Chapter 2 and perform other exercises in this book.

5. Finally, chaos theory describes several attractors that grab our attention and control our behavior. *Point attractors* move us toward or away from something; for instance, a party is usually a point attractor for college students and a raise or promotion is a point attractor for someone at work. Point attractors cut through the chaos because they keep you focused on one specific item and not the whole chaotic scene. Later in this book you'll learn to analyze your point attractors and develop new ones that will help you move forward without the stress. *Pendulum attractors* are two or more points that we move between. Attending graduate school or working after graduation might be two pendulum attractors that you move between. Or perhaps you are stuck between two seemingly opposing goals, such as "I want to help people but I want to make money" or "I should start a career but I'd really like to take a year off." The Wise Wanderings system will help you look for creative ways to resolve the tension that keeps you from making a choice or, for that matter, feeling as if you to have to choose. (You don't, by the way.) *Strange attractors* are unpredictable or random events that don't repeat. Later, you'll identify your strange attractors and use them to your advantage or keep them from distracting you. Finally, *torus attractors* represent cycles of behavior we repeat. By analyzing your torus attractors you'll be able to break cycles of behavior (like procrastination) that might impede your job search or career plans.

On the surface, chaos theory seems more complicated than linear theory. And perhaps it is. Life is more complicated now than in 1909. But you're smart and, as you've already discovered, applying linear theory to your future is a joke—and a bad one at that. The chaos theory tenets behind the Wise Wanderings system give you the confidence to welcome the seeming chaos of your future as you learn that what appears chaotic is actually well organized and ordered. Linear approaches get thrown off by change; chaos theory harnesses the power of change. Linear approaches can make you nervous: Are you limited by your choice of major? Do you have to have a career goal? And what do you do if you don't have one? Chaos theory says, "Relax." A world of possibilities is within your grasp and you don't need a specific goal. And you don't need to answer **THE QUESTION.** Chaos theory says, "Let's get going—a butterfly awaits."

Discussion Questions

How often have you been asked, "What are you going to do with that?" and what conclusions can you draw about why we ask that question?

What messages have received about career planning? Would you classify these as linear or chaotic? How do they affect your outlook on career planning?

Compare the Linear Model of choosing a career path to Chaos Theory. Which would you recommend to your peers and why?

IT'S NOT JUST THE MONEY

THE BENEFITS OF COLLEGE EDUCATION TO INDIVIDUALS AND TO SOCIETY

Philip Trostel

Summary

In some contexts an issue basically boils down to the monetary bottom line. In other contexts, though, focusing just on the dollars is like throwing the baby out with the bathwater. Narrowly defined economics does not always capture all of the essential aspects of an issue. The value of a college education is one such example.

The value of a college education is often presented in purely monetary terms, probably because the average monetary payoff from a college degree is so high. The substantial financial rewards from obtaining college degrees are well known and documented. The link between college attainment and economic prosperity has been clearly demonstrated for individuals, as well as for cities, states and nations.

It is no secret that the financial payoff is only one of the benefits from a college education. But the other benefits, and particularly their magnitudes, are considerably less well known. These other benefits of college education are often difficult to quantify and harder to demonstrate. Consequently, these frequently unmeasured benefits are often ignored in policy discussions. It is sometimes joked that "if you can't measure it, it doesn't exist." Unfortunately, there is more than a grain of truth in this quip. But the lack of quantification does not make the benefits any less real or any less important, except for perhaps in policy discussions. Moreover, the "other" benefits of college education appear to be at least as important as the well-known effect on earnings. Thus, public policy debates about postsecondary education frequently omit more than half of the story.

This report provides a more complete picture by highlighting many of the frequently unmeasured and ignored benefits of college attendance. Education has numerous beneficial effects, and many of these have been estimated in large academic literatures. But research articles typically carefully examine just one effect. This report organizes and compiles the evidence from several different literatures into one easily accessible place.

From "It's Not Just the Money: The Benefits of College Education to Individuals and to Society." by Philip Trostel, Margaret Chase Smith Policy Center & School of Economics Luumina Issue Paper, October 14, 2015, https://www.luminafoundation.org/resources/its-not-just-the-money.pdf.

On average in 2012, Americans with bachelor's degrees (and without graduate degrees) receive the following benefits in comparison to high school graduates never attending college:

- Annual earnings are about $32,000 (134 percent) higher. Moreover, there is no evidence that the college earnings premium is declining. Indeed, it has been increasing.
- Lifetime earnings are, conservatively, about $625,000 (114 percent) greater in present discounted value (using a 3 percent real interest rate and taking forgone earnings while in college into account).
- The incidence of poverty is 3.5 times lower.
- The likelihood of having health insurance through employment is 47 percent higher. Annual additional compensation in the form of employer contributions for health insurance is $1,400 (74 percent greater).
- The likelihood of having a retirement plan through employment is 72 percent greater. Retirement income is 2.4 times higher.
- Job safety is greater. The incidence of receiving workers' compensation is 2.4 times lower.
- Measures of occupational prestige are significantly higher.
- The probability of being employed is 24 percent higher.
- The likelihood of being unemployed is 2.2 times lower.
- The likelihood of being out of the labor force (neither employed nor unemployed) is 74 percent less.
- Age at retirement is higher. The probability of being retired between the ages 62 through 69 is about 25 percent lower.
- The likelihood of reporting health to be very good or excellent is 44 percent greater.
- The likelihood of being a regular smoker is 3.9 times lower. The incidence of obesity and heavy drinking are significantly lower. The likelihood of exercising, having a healthy diet, wearing seat belts and seeking preventative medical care are significantly higher.
- The incidence of a disability making it difficult to live independently is 3.6 times lower.
- Life expectancy at age 25 is seven years longer (for those having at least some college compared to those never having gone to college).
- Asset income is 4.9 times greater ($1,900 more per year).
- The likelihood of not having a bank account is 8.1 times lower. Reliance on expensive forms of banking and credit is significantly lower.
- The probability of being in prison or jail is 4.9 times lower.
- The probability of being married is 21 percent higher and the probability of being divorced or separated is 61 percent lower.
- The likelihood of being happy is significantly higher.

The total value of a college education is thus considerably greater than just the higher earnings. But the catalog of benefits above lists only those accruing to the degree holder. There are also substantial benefits accruing to the rest of society. On average in 2012, the rest of American society receives the following benefits from those with bachelor's degrees (and without graduate degrees) in comparison to high school graduates never attending college:

- Although the evidence is not completely conclusive, the positive effect on the aggregate earnings of others appears to be roughly similar to the effect on own earnings.

- Lifetime taxes are, conservatively, $273,000 (215 percent) greater in present discounted value (using a 3 percent real interest rate and taking into account forgone taxes while in college).

     That is, college graduates contribute hundreds of thousands of dollars more toward government services and social insurance programs.
- Lifetime government expenditures are about $81,000 (39 percent) lower in present value. College graduates rely much less on other taxpayers.
- The lifetime total fiscal effect is roughly $355,000 in present value.
- Crime is significantly lower.
- Volunteering is 2.3 times more likely. The estimated value of volunteer labor is 4.1 times ($1,300 annually) greater.
- Employment in the nonprofit sector is twice as likely. The estimated value of the implicit wage contribution to nonprofits is 8.7 times ($1,500 annually) greater.
- Annual cash donations to charities are $900 (3.4 times) higher.
- Total philanthropic contributions (i.e., the value of volunteer labor plus the value of the implicit contribution to nonprofits plus cash donations) are $3,600 (4.7 times) higher.
- Voting and political involvement are significantly higher.
- Participation in school, community, service, civic and religious organizations is substantially (1.9 times) higher. Leadership in these organizations is particularly (3.2 times) greater.
- Community involvement is significantly greater. For example, attendance at community meetings is 2.6 times greater.
- Neighborhood interactions and trust are significantly higher.

The magnitude of the total benefits to the rest of society is comparable to the substantial total benefits to college graduates. Moreover, these long lists represent just the (imperfectly) measurable benefits of college attainment. There are numerous vitally important effects that are almost impossible to quantify such as the positive influences on innovation, arts, culture, diversity, tolerance and compassion.

The evidence is overwhelming that investment in college education pays in a big way both for individuals and for society. But the typically emphasized financial payoff is only small part of the story. It is not overstatement to call the effect on earnings just the tip of the college-payoff iceberg. There are more benefits to college education beneath the surface than above it.

GREATER EARNINGS
OTHER BENEFITS

Discussion Questions

According to this article, those who attend college are significantly happier than those who do not. Using what you learned in the Happiness article read early, how would you explain the relationship between education and happiness?

Which three benefits of a college education are most significant for you personally? Why? Which three benefits are most significant for society? Why?

What examples of unquantifiable benefits of college education can you think of for yourself and society?

Chapter 7

How can you be successful?

FAKE OR REAL? HOW TO SELF-CHECK THE NEWS AND GET THE FACTS

Wynne Davis

Fake news stories can have real-life consequences. On Sunday, police said a man with a rifle who claimed to be "self-investigating" a baseless online conspiracy theory entered a Washington, D.C., pizzeria and fired the weapon inside the restaurant.

So, yes, fake news is a big problem.

These stories have gotten a lot of attention, with headlines claiming Pope Francis endorsed Donald Trump in November's election and sites like American News sharing misleading stories or taking quotes out of context. And when sites like DC Gazette share stories about people who allegedly investigated the Clinton family being found dead, the stories go viral and some people believe them. Again, these stories are not true in any way.

ALL TECH CONSIDERED

We Tracked Down A Fake-News Creator In The Suburbs. Here's What We Learned

---

THE TWO-WAY

Man Fires Rifle Inside D.C. Pizzeria, Cites Fictitious Conspiracy Theories

---

Stopping the proliferation of fake news isn't just the responsibility of the platforms used to spread it. Those who consume news also need to find ways of determining if what they're reading is true. We offer several tips below.

The idea is that people should have a fundamental sense of media literacy. And based on a study recently released by Stanford University researchers, many people don't.

Sam Wineburg, a professor of education and history at Stanford and the lead author of the study, said a solution is for all readers to read like fact checkers. But how do fact checkers do their job?

Alexios Mantzarlis, director of the International Fact-Checking Network at Poynter, says fact checkers have a process for each claim they deal with.

POLITICS

*Trump Makes Unfounded Claim That 'Millions' Voted Illegally
For Clinton*

"You'll isolate a claim that has something that can be objectively verified, you will seek the best primary sources in that topic. Find whether they match or refute or prove the claim being made, and then present with all limitations the data and what the data says about the claim being made," Mantzarlis says.

That's the framework for professionals, but there are ways for everyone to do a bit of fact checking themselves.

Melissa Zimdars is an assistant professor of communication and media at Merrimack College in North Andover, Mass. When she saw her students referencing questionable sources, she created and shared a document with them of how to think about sources, as well as a list of misleading, satirical and fake sites.

Both Mantzarlis and Zimdars agreed there are a few best practices people can use when reading articles online.

Pay attention to the domain and URL

ALL TECH CONSIDERED

TFor Advertisers, Fake News IS Not The Biggest Problem

Established news organizations usually own their domains and they have a standard look that you are probably familiar with. Sites with such endings like.com.co should make you raise your eyebrows and tip you off that you need to dig around more to see if they can be trusted. This is true even when the site looks professional and has semi-recognizable logos. For example, abcnews.com is a legitimate news source, but abcnews.com.co is not, despite its similar appearance.

Read the "About Us" section

Most sites will have a lot of information about the news outlet, the company that runs it, members of leadership, and the mission and ethics statement behind an organization. The language used here is straightforward. If it's melodramatic and seems overblown, you should be skeptical. Also, you should be able to find out more information about the organization's leaders in places other than that site.

Look at the quotes in a story

Or rather, look at the lack of quotes. Most publications have multiple sources in each story who are professionals and have expertise in the fields they talk about. If it's a serious or controversial issue, there are more likely to be quotes – and lots of them. Look for professors or other academics who can speak to the research they've done. And if they are talking about research, look up those studies.

Look at who said them

Then, see who said the quotes, and what they said. Are they a reputable source with a title that you can verify through a quick Google search? Say you're looking at a story and it says President Obama said he wanted to take everyone's guns away. And then there's a quote. Obama is an official who has almost everything he says recorded and archived. There are transcripts for pretty much any address or speech he has given. Google those quotes. See what the speech was about, who he was addressing and when it happened. Even if he did an exclusive interview with a publication, that same quote will be referenced in other stories, saying he said it while talking to the original publication.

THE TWO-WAY

Students Have 'Dismaying Inability To Tell Fake News From Real, Study Finds

---

Check the comments

A lot of these fake and misleading stories are shared on social media platforms. Headlines are meant to get the reader's attention, but they're also supposed to accurately reflect what the story is about. Lately, that hasn't been the case. Headlines often will be written in exaggerated language with the intention of being misleading and then attached to stories that are about a completely different topic or just not true. These stories usually generate a lot of comments on Facebook or Twitter. If a lot of these comments call out the article for being fake or misleading, it probably is.

Reverse image search

A picture should be accurate in illustrating what the story is about. This often doesn't happen. If people who write these fake news stories don't even leave their homes or interview anyone for the stories, it's unlikely they take their own pictures. Do a little detective work and reverse search for the image on Google. You can do this by right-clicking on the image and choosing to search Google for it. If the image is appearing on a lot of stories about many different topics, there's a good chance it's not actually an image of what it says it was on the first story.

These tips are just a start at determining what type of news an article is. Zimdars outlined these and others in a guide for her students.

If you do these steps, you're helping yourself and you're helping others by not increasing the circulation of these stories.

And you won't be the only one trying to stop the spread of this false content. The company leaders behind the platforms these stories are shared on are trying to figure out how to fix the issue from their side, but they are also trying to make sure not to limit anyone's right to freedom of speech. It's a tricky position to be in, but they've said they'll try. In the end, it really does depend on taking responsibility and being an engaged consumer of news.

Here's one last thing. Satirical publications exist and serve a purpose, but are clearly labeled as exaggerated and humorous by the writers and owners. Some of the more well-known ones like The Onion and ClickHole use satire to talk about current events. If people don't understand that, they might share these articles after reading them in the literal sense.

If this happens or if you see your friends sharing blatantly fake news, be a friend and kindly tell them it's not real. Don't shy away from these conversations even if they might be uncomfortable. As said, everyone has to help fix the fake news problem.

Wynne Davis is a Digital News intern.

Discussion Questions

Where do you think people see/hear/read the most fake news stories?

What do you believe is your responsibility, if any, in stopping the spread of fake news?

Davis suggests the proliferation of fake news is a direct result of society's lack of truth seeking. Why do you think we shy away from fact checking the information we receive?

LEARNING IS MISUNDERSTOOD

Peter C. Brown, Henry L. Roediger III and Mark A. McDaniel

EARLY IN HIS CAREER as a pilot, Matt Brown was flying a twin-engine Cessna northeast out of Harlingen, Texas, when he noticed a drop in oil pressure in his right engine. He was alone, flying through the night at eleven thousand feet, making a hotshot freight run to a plant in Kentucky that had shut down its manufacturing line awaiting product parts for assembly.

He reduced altitude and kept an eye on the oil gauge, hoping to fly as far as a planned fuel stop in Louisiana, where he could service the plane, but the pressure kept falling. Matt has been messing around with piston engines since he was old enough to hold a wrench, and he knew he had a problem. He ran a mental checklist, figuring his options. If he let the oil pressure get too low he risked the engine's seizing up. How much further could he fly before shutting it down? What would happen when he did? He'd lose lift on the right side, but could he stay aloft? He reviewed the tolerances he'd memorized for the Cessna 401. Loaded, the best you could do on one engine was slow your descent. But he had a light load, and he'd burned through most of his fuel. So he shut down the ailing right engine, feathered the prop to reduce drag, increased power on the left, flew with opposite rudder, and limped another ten miles toward his intended stop. There, he made his approach in a wide left-hand turn, for the simple but critical reason that without power on his right side it was only from a left-hand turn that he still had the lift needed to level out for a touchdown.

While we don't need to understand each of the actions Matt took, *he* certainly needed to, and his ability to work himself out of a jam illustrates what we mean in this book when we talk about learning: we mean acquiring knowledge and skills and having them readily available from memory so you can make sense of future problems and opportunities.

There are some immutable aspects of learning that we can probably all agree on:

First, to be useful, learning requires memory, so what we've learned is still there later when we need it.

Second, we need to keep learning and remembering all our lives. We can't advance through middle school without some mastery of language arts, math, science, and social studies. Getting ahead at work takes mastery of job skills and difficult colleagues. In retirement, we pick up new interests. In our dotage, we move into simpler housing while we're still able to adapt. If you're good at learning, you have an advantage in life.

Third, learning is an acquired skill, and the most effective strategies are often counterintuitive.

Claims We Make in This Book

You may not agree with the last point, but we hope to persuade you of it. Here, more or less unadorned in list form, are some of the principal claims we make in support of our argument. We set them forth more fully in the chapters that follow.

Learning is deeper and more durable when it's *effortful*. Learning that's easy is like writing in sand, here today and gone tomorrow.

We are *poor judges* of when we are learning well and when we're not. When the going is harder and slower and it doesn't feel productive, we are drawn to strategies that feel more fruitful, unaware that the gains from these strategies are often temporary.

Rereading text and *massed practice* of a skill or new knowledge are by far the preferred study strategies of learners of all stripes, but they're also among the *least productive*. By massed practice we mean the single-minded, rapid-fire repetition of something you're trying to burn into memory, the "practice-practice-practice" of conventional wisdom. Cramming for exams is an example. Rereading and massed practice give rise to feelings of fluency that are taken to be signs of mastery, but for true mastery or durability these strategies are largely a waste of time.

Retrieval practice—recalling facts or concepts or events from memory—is a more effective learning strategy than review by rereading. Flashcards are a simple example. Retrieval strengthens the memory and interrupts forgetting. A single, simple quiz after reading a text or hearing a lecture produces better learning and remembering than rereading the text or reviewing lecture notes. While the brain is not a muscle that gets stronger with exercise, the neural pathways that make up a body of learning do get stronger, when the memory is retrieved and the learning is practiced. Periodic practice arrests forgetting, strengthens retrieval routes, and is essential for hanging onto the knowledge you want to gain.

When you *space out practice* at a task and get a little rusty between sessions, or you interleave the practice of two or more subjects, retrieval is harder and feels less productive, but the effort produces longer lasting learning and enables more versatile application of it in later settings.

Trying to solve a problem *before being taught the solution* leads to better learning, even when errors are made in the attempt.

The popular notion that you learn better when you receive instruction in a form consistent with your preferred *learning style,* for example as an auditory or visual learner, is *not supported by the empirical research*. People do have multiple forms of intelligence to bring to bear on learning, and you learn better when you "go wide," drawing on all of your aptitudes and resourcefulness, than when you limit instruction or experience to the style you find most amenable.

When you're adept at extracting the *underlying principles or "rules"* that differentiate types of problems, you're more successful at picking the right solutions in unfamiliar situations. This skill is better acquired through *interleaved and varied practice* than massed practice. For instance, interleaving practice at computing the volumes of different kinds of geometric solids makes you more skilled at picking the right solution when a later test presents a random solid. Interleaving the identification of bird types or the works of oil painters improves your ability both to learn the unifying attributes within a type and to differentiate between types, improving your skill at categorizing new specimens you encounter later.

We're all *susceptible to illusions* that can hijack our judgment of what we know and can do. Testing helps calibrate our judgments of what we've learned. A pilot who is responding to a failure of hydraulic systems in a flight simulator discovers quickly whether he's on top of the corrective procedures or not. In virtually all areas of learning, you build better mastery when you use testing as a tool to identify and bring up your areas of weakness.

All new learning requires a *foundation of prior knowledge.* You need to know how to land a twin engine plane on two engines before you can learn to land it on one. To learn trigonometry, you need to remember your algebra and geometry. To learn cabinetmaking, you need to have mastered the properties of wood and composite materials, how to join boards, cut rabbets, rout edges, and miter corners.

In a cartoon by the *Far Side* cartoonist Gary Larson, a bugeyed school kid asks his teacher, "Mr. Osborne, can I be excused? My brain is full!" If you're just engaging in mechanical repetition, it's true, you quickly hit the limit of what you can keep in mind. However, if you practice *elaboration,* there's no known limit to how much you can learn. Elaboration is the process of giving new material meaning by expressing it in your own words and connecting it with what you already know. The more you can explain about the way your new learning relates to your prior knowledge, the stronger your grasp of the new learning will be, and the more connections you create that will help you remember it later. Warm air can hold more moisture than cold air; to know that this is true in your own experience, you can think of the drip of water from the back of an air conditioner or the way a stifling summer day turns cooler out the back side of a sudden thunderstorm. Evaporation has a cooling effect: you know this because a humid day at your uncle's in Atlanta feels hotter than a dry one at your cousin's in Phoenix, where your sweat disappears even before your skin feels damp. When you study the principles of heat transfer, you understand conduction from warming your hands around a hot cup of cocoa; radiation from the way the sun pools in the den on a wintry day; convection from the life-saving blast of A/C as your uncle squires you slowly through his favorite back alley haunts of Atlanta.

Putting new knowledge into a *larger context* helps learning. For example, the more of the unfolding story of history you know, the more of it you can learn. And the more ways you give that story meaning, say by connecting it to your understanding of human ambition and the untidiness of fate, the better the story stays with you. Likewise, if you're trying to learn an abstraction, like the principle of angular momentum, it's easier when you ground it in something concrete that you already know, like the way a figure skater's rotation speeds up as she draws her arms to her chest.

People who learn to *extract the key ideas from new material and organize them into a mental model* and connect that model to prior knowledge show an advantage in learning complex mastery. A mental model is a mental representation of some external reality.[1] Think of a baseball batter waiting for a pitch. He has less than an instant to decipher whether it's a curveball, a changeup, or something else. How does he do it? There are a few subtle signals that help: the way the pitcher winds up, the way he throws, the spin of the ball's seams. A great batter winnows out all the extraneous perceptual distractions, seeing only these variations in pitches, and through practice he forms distinct mental models based on a different set of cues for each kind of pitch. He connects these models to what he knows about batting stance, strike zone, and swinging so as to stay on top of the ball. These he connects to mental models of player positions: if he's got guys on first and second, maybe he'll sacrifice to move the runners ahead. If he's got men on first and third and there is one out, he's got to keep from hitting into a double play while still hitting to score the runner. His mental models of player positions connect to his models of the opposition (are they playing deep or shallow?) and to the signals flying around from the dugout to the base coaches to him. In a great at-bat, all these pieces come together seamlessly: the batter connects with the ball and drives it through a hole in the outfield, buying the time to get on first and advance his men. Because he has culled out all but the most important elements for identifying and responding to each kind of pitch, constructed mental models out of that learning, and connected those models to his mastery of the other essential elements of this complex game, an expert player has a better chance of scoring runs than a less experienced one who cannot make sense of the vast and changeable information he faces every time he steps up to the plate.

Many people believe that their intellectual ability is hardwired from birth, and that failure to meet a learning challenge is an indictment of their native ability. But every time you learn something new, *you change the brain*—the residue of your experiences is stored. It's true that we start life with the gift of our genes, but it's also true that we become capable through the learning and development of mental models that enable us to reason, solve, and create. In other words, the elements that shape your intellectual abilities lie to a surprising extent within your own control. Understanding that this is so enables you to see failure as a badge of effort and a source of useful information—the need to dig deeper or to try a different strategy. The need to understand that when learning is hard, you're doing important work. To understand that striving and setbacks, as in any action video game or new BMX bike stunt, are essential if you are to surpass your current level of performance toward true expertise. Making mistakes and correcting them builds the bridges to advanced learning.

Empirical Evidence versus Theory, Lore, and Intuition

Much of how we structure training and schooling is based on learning theories that have been handed down to us, and these are shaped by our own sense of what works, a sensibility drawn from our personal experiences as teachers, coaches, students, and mere humans at large on the earth. How we teach and study is largely a mix of theory, lore, and intuition. But over the last forty years and more, cognitive psychologists have been working to build a body of evidence to clarify what works and to discover the strategies that get results.

Cognitive psychology is the basic science of understanding how the mind works, conducting empirical research into how people perceive, remember, and think. Many others have their hands in the puzzle of learning as well. Developmental and educational psychologists are concerned with theories of human development and how they can be used to shape the tools of education—such as testing regimes, instructional organizers (for example topic outlines and schematic illustrations), and resources for special groups like those in remedial and gifted education. Neuroscientists, using new imaging techniques and other tools, are advancing our understanding of brain mechanisms that underlie learning, but we're still a very long way from knowing what neuroscience will tell us about how to improve education.

How is one to know whose advice to take on how best to go about learning?

It's wise to be skeptical. Advice is easy to find, only a few mouse-clicks away. Yet not all advice is grounded in research—far from it. Nor does all that passes as research meet the standards of science, such as having appropriate control conditions to assure that the results of an investigation are objective and generalizable. The best empirical studies are experimental in nature: the researcher develops a hypothesis and then tests it through a set of experiments that must meet rigorous criteria for design and objectivity. In the chapters that follow, we have distilled the findings of a large body of such studies that have stood up under review by the scientific community before being published in professional journals. We are collaborators in some of these studies, but not the lion's share. Where we're offering theory rather than scientifically validated results, we say so. To make our points we use, in addition to tested science, anecdotes from people like Matt Brown whose work requires mastery of complex knowledge and skills, stories that illustrate the underlying principles of how we learn and remember. Discussion of the research studies themselves is kept to a minimum, but you will find many of them cited in the notes at the end of the book if you care to dig further.

People Misunderstand Learning

It turns out that much of what we've been doing as teachers and students isn't serving us well, but some comparatively simple changes could make a big difference. People commonly believe that if you expose yourself to something enough times—say, a textbook passage or a set of terms from an eighth grade biology class—you can burn it into memory. Not so. Many teachers believe that if they can make learning easier and faster, the learning will be better. Much research turns this belief on its head: when learning is harder, it's stronger and lasts longer. It's widely believed by teachers, trainers, and coaches that the most effective way to master a new skill is to give it dogged, single-minded focus, practicing over and over until you've got it down. Our faith in this runs deep, because most of us see fast gains during the learning phase of massed practice. What's apparent from the research is that gains achieved during massed practice are transitory and melt away quickly.

The finding that rereading textbooks is often labor in vain ought to send a chill up the spines of educators and learners, because it's the number one study strategy of most people—including more than 80 percent of college students in some surveys—and is central in what we tell ourselves to do during the hours we dedicate to learning. Rereading has three strikes against it. It is time consuming. It doesn't result in durable memory. And it often involves a kind of unwitting self-deception, as growing familiarity with the text comes to feel like mastery of the content. The hours immersed in rereading can seem like due diligence, but the amount of study time is no measure of mastery.[2]

You needn't look far to find training systems that lean heavily on the conviction that mere exposure leads to learning. Consider Matt Brown, the pilot. When Matt was ready to advance from piston planes, he had a whole new body of knowledge to master in order to get certified for the business jet he was hired to pilot. We asked him to describe this process. His employer sent him to eighteen days of training, ten hours a day, in what Matt called the "fire hose" method of instruction. The first seven days straight were spent in the classroom being instructed in all the plane's systems: electrical, fuel, pneumatics, and so on, how these systems operated and interacted, and all their fail-safe tolerances like pressures, weights, temperatures, and speeds. Matt is required to have at his immediate command about eighty different "memory action items"—actions to take without hesitation or thought in order to stabilize the plane the moment any one of a dozen or so unexpected events occur. It might be a sudden decompression, a thrust reverser coming unlocked in flight, an engine failure, an electrical fire.

Matt and his fellow pilots gazed for hours at mindnumbing PowerPoint illustrations of their airplane's principal systems. Then something interesting happened.

"About the middle of day five," Matt said, "they flash a schematic of the fuel system on the screen, with its pressure sensors, shutoff valves, ejector pumps, bypass lines, and on and on, and you're struggling to stay focused. Then this one instructor asks us, 'Has anybody here had the fuel filter bypass light go on in flight?' This pilot across the room raises his hand. So the instructor says, 'Tell us what happened,' and suddenly you're thinking, Whoa, what if that was me?

"So, this guy was at 33,000 feet or something and he's about to lose both engines because he got fuel without anti-freeze in it and his filters are clogging with ice. You hear that story and, believe me, that schematic comes to life and sticks with you. Jet fuel can commonly have a little water in it, and when it gets cold at high altitude, the water will condense out, and it can freeze and block the line. So whenever you refuel, you make good and sure to look for a sign on the fuel truck saying the fuel has Prist in it, which is an antifreeze. And if you ever see that light go on in flight, you're going to get yourself down to some warmer air in a hurry."[3] Learning is stronger when it matters, when the abstract is made concrete and personal.

Then the nature of Matt's instruction shifted. The next eleven days were spent in a mix of classroom and flight simulator training. Here, Matt described the kind of active engagement that leads to durable learning, as the pilots had to grapple with their aircraft to demonstrate mastery of standard operating procedures, respond to unexpected situations, and drill on the rhythm and physical memory of the movements that are required in the cockpit for dealing with them. A flight simulator provides retrieval practice, and the practice is spaced, interleaved, and varied and involves as far as possible the same mental processes Matt will invoke when he's at altitude. In a simulator, the abstract is made concrete and personal. A simulator is also a series of tests, in that it helps Matt and his instructors calibrate their judgment of where he needs to focus to bring up his mastery.

In some places, like Matt Brown's flight simulator, teachers and trainers have found their way to highly effective learning techniques, yet in virtually any field, these techniques tend to be the exception, and "fire hose" lectures (or their equivalent) are too often the norm.

In fact, what students are advised to do is often plain wrong. For instance, study tips published on a website at George Mason University include this advice: "The key to learning something well is repetition; the more times you go over the material the better chance you have of storing it permanently."[4] Another, from a Dartmouth College website, suggests: "If you intend to remember something, you probably will."[5] A public service piece that runs occasionally in the *St. Louis Post-Dispatch* offering study advice shows a kid with his nose buried in a book. "Concentrate," the caption reads. "Focus on one thing and one thing only. Repeat, repeat, repeat! Repeating what you have to remember can help burn it into your memory."[6] Belief in the power of rereading, intentionality, and repetition is pervasive, but the truth is you usually can't embed something in memory simply by repeating it over and over. This tactic might work when looking up a phone number and holding it in your mind while punching it into your phone, but it doesn't work for durable learning.

A simple example, reproduced on the Internet (search "penny memory test"), presents a dozen different images of a common penny, only one of which is correct. As many times as you've seen a penny, you're hard pressed to say with confidence which one it is. Similarly, a recent study asked faculty and students who worked in the Psychology Building at UCLA to identify the fire extinguisher closest to their office. Most failed the test. One professor, who had been at UCLA for twenty-five years, left his safety class and decided to look for the fire extinguisher closest to his office. He discovered that it was actually right next to his office door, just inches from the doorknob he turned every time he went into his office. Thus, in this case, even years of repetitive exposure did not result in his learning where to grab the closest extinguisher if his waste-basket caught fire.[7]

Early Evidence

The fallacy in thinking that repetitive exposure builds memory has been well established through a series of investigations going back to the mid-1960s, when the psychologist Endel Tulving at the University of Toronto began testing people on their ability to remember lists of common English nouns. In a first phase of the experiment, the participants simply read a list of paired items six times (for example, a pair on the list might be "chair—9"); they did not expect a memory test. The first item in each pair was always a noun. After reading the listed pairs six times, participants were then told that they would be getting a list of nouns that they would be asked to remember. For one group of people, the nouns were the same ones they had just read six times in the prior reading phase; for another group, the nouns to be learned were different from those they had previously read. Remarkably, Tulving found that the two groups' learning of the nouns did not differ—the learning curves were statistically indistinguishable. Intuition would suggest otherwise, but prior exposure did not aid later recall. Mere repetition did not enhance learning. Subsequent studies by many researchers have pressed further into questions of whether repeated exposure or longer periods of holding an idea in mind contribute to later recall, and these studies have confirmed and elaborated on the findings that repetition by itself does not lead to good long-term memory.[8]

These results led researchers to investigate the benefits of rereading texts. In a 2008 article in *Contemporary Educational Psychology*, Washington University scientists reported on a series of studies they conducted at their own school and at the University of New Mexico to shed light on rereading as a strategy to improve understanding and memory of prose. Like most research, these studies stood on the shoulders of earlier work by others; some showed that when the same text is read multiple times the same inferences are made and the same connections between topics are formed, and others suggested modest benefits from rereading. These benefits had been found in two different situations. In the first, some students read and immediately reread study material, whereas other students read the material only once. Both groups took an immediate test after reading, and the group who had read twice performed a bit better than the group who had read once. However, on a delayed test the benefit of immediate rereading had worn off, and the rereaders performed at the same level as the one-time readers. In the other situation, students read the material the first time and then waited some days before they reread it. This group, having done spaced readings of the text, performed better on the test than the group who did not reread the material.[9]

Subsequent experiments at Washington University, aimed at teasing apart some of the questions the earlier studies had raised, assessed the benefits of rereading among students of differing abilities, in a learning situation paralleling that faced by students in classes. A total of 148 students read five different passages taken from textbooks and *Scientific American.* The students were at two different universities; some were high-ability readers, and others were low-ability; some students read the material only once, and others read it twice in succession. Then all of them responded to questions to demonstrate what they had learned and remembered.

In these experiments, multiple readings in close succession did not prove to be a potent study method for either group, at either school, in any of the conditions tested. In fact, the researchers found no rereading benefit at all under these conditions.

What's the conclusion? It makes sense to reread a text once if there's been a meaningful lapse of time since the first reading, but doing multiple readings in close succession is a time-consuming study strategy that yields negligible benefits at the expense of much more effective strategies that take less time. Yet surveys of college students confirm what professors have long known: highlighting, underlining, and sustained poring over notes and texts are the most-used study strategies, by far.[10]

Illusions of Knowing

If rereading is largely ineffective, why do students favor it? One reason may be that they're getting bad study advice. But there's another, subtler way they're pushed toward this method of review, the phenomenon mentioned earlier: rising familiarity with a text and fluency in reading it can create an illusion of mastery. As any professor will attest, students work hard to capture the precise wording of phrases they hear in class lectures, laboring under the misapprehension that the essence of the subject lies in the syntax in which it's described. Mastering the lecture or the text is not the same as mastering the ideas behind them. However, repeated reading provides the illusion of mastery of the underlying ideas. Don't let yourself be fooled. The fact that you can repeat the phrases in a text or your lecture notes is no indication that you understand the significance of the precepts they describe, their application, or how they relate to what you already know about the subject.

Too common is the experience of a college professor answering a knock on her office door only to find a first-year student in distress, asking to discuss his low grade on the first test in introductory psychology. How is it possible? He attended all the lectures and took diligent notes on them. He read the text and highlighted the critical passages.

How did he study for the test? she asks.

Well, he'd gone back and highlighted his notes, and then reviewed the highlighted notes and his highlighted text material several times until he felt he was thoroughly familiar with all of it. How could it be that he had pulled a D on the exam?

Had he used the set of key concepts in the back of each chapter to test himself? Could he look at a concept like "conditioned stimulus," define it, and use it in a paragraph? While he was reading, had he thought of converting the main points of the text into a series of questions and then later tried to answer them while he was studying? Had he at least rephrased the main ideas in his own words as he read?

Had he tried to relate them to what he already knew? Had he looked for examples outside the text? The answer was no in every case.

He sees himself as the model student, diligent to a fault, but the truth is he doesn't know how to study effectively.

The illusion of mastery is an example of poor metacognition: what we know about what we know. Being accurate in your judgment of what you know and don't know is critical for decision making. The problem was famously (and prophetically) summed up by Secretary of State Donald Rumsfeld in a 2002 press briefing about US intelligence on Iraq's possible possession of weapons of mass destruction: "There are known knowns; there are things we know that we know. There are known unknowns; that is to say, there are things that we now know we don't know. But there are also unknown unknowns—*there are things we do not know we don't know.*"

The emphasis here is ours. We make it to drive home the point that students who don't quiz themselves (and most do not) tend to overestimate how well they have mastered class material. Why? When they hear a lecture or read a text that is a paragon of clarity, the ease with which they follow the argument gives them the feeling that they already know it and don't need to study it. In other words, they tend not to know what they don't know; when put to the test, they find they cannot recall the critical ideas or apply them in a new context. Likewise, when they've reread their lecture notes and texts to the point of fluency, their fluency gives them the false sense that they're in possession of the underlying content, principles, and implications that constitute real learning, confident that they can recall them at a moment's notice. The upshot is that even the most diligent students are often hobbled by two liabilities: a failure to know the areas where their learning is weak—that is, where they need to do more work to bring up their knowledge—and a preference for study methods that create a false sense of mastery.[11]

Knowledge: Not Sufficient, but Necessary

Albert Einstein declared "creativity is more important than knowledge," and the sentiment appears to be widely shared by college students, if their choice in t-shirt proclamations is any indication. And why wouldn't they seize on the sentiment? It embodies an obvious and profound truth, for without creativity where would our scientific, social, or economic breakthroughs come from? Besides which, accumulating knowledge can feel like a grind, while creativity sounds like a lot more fun. But of course the dichotomy is false. You wouldn't want to see that t-shirt on your neurosurgeon or on the captain who's flying your plane across the Pacific. But the sentiment has gained some currency as a reaction to standardized testing, fearing that this kind of testing leads to an emphasis on memorization at the expense of high-level skills. Notwithstanding the pitfalls of standardized testing, what we really ought to ask is how to do better at building knowledge *and* creativity, for without knowledge you don't have the foundation for the higher-level skills of analysis, synthesis, and creative problem solving. As the psychologist Robert Sternberg and two colleagues put it, "one cannot apply what one knows in a practical manner if one does not know anything to apply."[12]

Mastery in any field, from cooking to chess to brain surgery, is a gradual accretion of knowledge, conceptual understanding, judgment, and skill. These are the fruits of variety in the practice of new skills, and of striving, reflection, and mental rehearsal. Memorizing facts is like stocking a construction site with the supplies to put up a house. Building the house requires not only knowledge of countless different fittings and materials but conceptual understanding, too, of aspects like the load-bearing properties of a header or roof truss system, or the principles of energy transfer and conservation that will keep the house warm but the roof deck cold so the owner doesn't call six months later with ice dam problems. Mastery requires both the possession of ready knowledge and the conceptual understanding of how to use it.

When Matt Brown had to decide whether or not to kill his right engine he was problem solving, and he needed to know from memory the procedures for flying with a dead engine and the tolerances of his plane in order to predict whether he would fall out of the air or be unable to straighten up for landing. The would-be neurosurgeon in her first year of med school has to memorize the whole nervous system, the whole skeletal system, the whole muscular system, the humeral system. If she can't, she's not going to be a neurosurgeon. Her success will depend on diligence, of course, but also on finding study strategies that will enable her to learn the sheer volume of material required in the limited hours available.

Testing: Dipstick versus Learning Tool

There are few surer ways to raise the hackles of many students and educators than talking about testing. The growing focus over recent years on standardized assessment, in particular, has turned testing into a lightning rod for frustration over how to achieve the country's education goals. Online forums and news articles are besieged by readers who charge that emphasis on testing favors memorization at the expense of a larger grasp of context or creative ability; that testing creates extra stress for students and gives a false measure of ability; and so on. But if we stop thinking of testing as a dipstick to measure learning—if we think of it as practicing retrieval of learning from memory rather than "testing," we open ourselves to another possibility: *the use of testing as a tool for learning.*

One of the most striking research findings is the power of active retrieval—testing—to strengthen memory, and that the more effortful the retrieval, the stronger the benefit. Think flight simulator versus PowerPoint lecture. Think quiz versus rereading. The act of retrieving learning from memory has two profound benefits. One, it tells you what you know and don't know, and therefore where to focus further study to improve the areas where you're weak. Two, recalling what you have learned causes your brain to reconsolidate the memory, which strengthens its connections to what you already know and makes it easier for you to recall in the future. In effect, retrieval—testing—interrupts forgetting. Consider an eighth grade science class. For the class in question, at a middle school in Columbia, Illinois, researchers arranged for part of the material covered during the course to be the subject of low-stakes quizzing (with feedback) at three points in the semester. Another part of the material was never quizzed but was studied three times in review. In a test a month later, which material was better recalled? The students averaged A- on the material that was quizzed and C+ on the material that was not quizzed but reviewed.[13]

In Matt Brown's case, even after ten years piloting the same business jet, his employer reinforces his mastery every six months in a battery of tests and flight simulations that require him to retrieve the information and maneuvers that are essential to stay in control of his plane. As Matt points out, you hardly ever have an emergency, so if you don't practice what to do, there's no way to keep it fresh.

Both of these cases—the research in the classroom and the experience of Matt Brown in updating his knowledge—point to the critical role of retrieval practice in keeping our knowledge accessible to us when we need it. The power of active retrieval is the topic of Chapter 2.[14]

The Takeaway

For the most part, we are going about learning in the wrong ways, and we are giving poor advice to those who are coming up behind us. A great deal of what we think we know about how to learn is taken on faith and based on intuition but does not hold up under empirical research. Persistent illusions of knowing lead us to labor at unproductive strategies; as recounted in Chapter 3, this is true even of people who have participated in empirical studies and seen the evidence for themselves, firsthand. Illusions are potent persuaders. One of the best habits a learner can instill in herself is regular self-quizzing to recalibrate her understanding of what she does and does not know. Second Lieutenant Kiley Hunkler, a 2013 graduate of West Point and winner of a Rhodes Scholarship, whom we write about in Chapter 8, uses the phrase "shooting an azimuth" to describe how she takes practice tests to help refocus her studying. In overland navigation, shooting an azimuth means climbing to a height, sighting an object on the horizon in the direction you're traveling, and adjusting your compass heading to make sure you're still gaining on your objective as you beat through the forest below.

The good news is that we now know of simple and practical strategies that any-body can use, at any point in life, to learn better and remember longer: various forms of retrieval practice, such as low-stakes quizzing and self-testing, spacing out practice, interleaving the practice of different but related topics or skills, try-ing to solve a problem before being taught the solution, distilling the underlying principles or rules that differentiate types of problems, and so on. In the chapters that follow we describe these in depth. And because learning is an iterative process that requires that you revisit what you have learned earlier and continually update it and connect it with new knowledge, we circle through these topics several times along the way. At the end, in Chapter 8, we pull it all together with specific tips and examples for putting these tools to work.

Discussion Questions

Think of a class you are having difficulty in and pick one concept you are currently discussing. How can you connect this concept to something that is important to you?

What have you been told about learning prior to entering college and once you arrived at UNCW?

What did you do to prepare for your first test? What can you do in the future to increase your chances of earning a better grade?

Chapter 8

How do you find balance?

BRAIN RULES

John Medina

SUMMARY

Rule #7

Sleep well, think well.

○ The brain is in a constant state of tension between cells and chemicals that try to put you to sleep and cells and chemicals that try to keep you awake.

○ The neurons of your brain show vigorous rhythmical activity when you're asleep—perhaps replaying what you learned that day.

○ People vary in how much sleep they need and when they prefer to get it, but the biological drive for an afternoon nap is universal.

○ Loss of sleep hurts attention, executive function, working memory, mood, quantitative skills, logical reasoning, and even motor dexterity.

Get more at www.brainrules.net

Medina, J. (2014). *Brain rules: 12 principles for surviving and thriving at work, home, and school.* Seattle, WA: Pear Press (www.brainrules.net). (Rule 4 Stress: pp. 58-81). Reprinted by permission of Pear Press.

STRESS

Rule #8

Stressed brains don't learn the same way.

IT IS, BY ANY measure, a thoroughly rotten experiment.

Here is this beautiful German shepherd, lying in one corner of a metal box, whimpering. He is receiving painful electric shocks, stimuli that should leave him howling in pain. Oddly enough, the dog could easily get out. The other side of the box is perfectly insulated from shocks, and only a low barrier separates the two sides. Though the dog could jump over to safety when the whim strikes him, the whim doesn't strike him. Ever. He just lies down in the corner of the electric side, whimpering with each jarring jolt. He must be physically removed by the experimenter to be relieved of the experience.

What has happened to that dog?

A few days before entering the box, the animal was strapped to a restraining harness rigged with electric wires, inescapably receiving the same painful shock day and night. And at first he didn't just stand there taking it, he *reacted*. He howled in pain. He urinated. He strained mightily against his harness in an increasingly desperate attempt to link some behavior of his with the cessation of the pain. But it was no use. As the hours and even days ticked by, his resistance eventually subsided. Why? The dog began to receive a very clear message: The pain was not going to stop; the shocks were going to be forever. *There was no way out.* Even after the dog had been released from the harness and placed into the metal box with the escape route, he could no longer understand his options. Indeed, most learning had been shut down, and that's probably the worst part of all.

Those of you familiar with psychology already know I am describing a famous set of experiments begun in the late 1960s by legendary psychologist Martin Seligman. He coined the term "learned helplessness" to describe both the perception of inescapability and its associated cognitive collapse. Many animals behave in a similar fashion where punishment is unavoidable, and that includes humans. Inmates in concentration camps routinely experienced these symptoms in response to the horrid conditions of the internment, and some camps even gave it the name *Gamel,* derived from the colloquial German word *Gameln,* which literally means "rotting." Perhaps not surprisingly, Seligman has spent the balance of his career studying how humans respond to optimism.

What is so awful about severe, chronic stress that it can wreak such extraordinary changes in behavior? Why is learning so radically altered? Let's begin with a definition of stress, talk about biological responses, and then move to the relationship between stress and learning. Along the way, we will talk about marriage and parenting, about the workplace, and about the first and only time I ever heard my mother, a fourth-grade teacher, swear. It was her first real encounter with learned helplessness.

Terror and Titillation

We begin with an attempt at definitions, and, as is true of all things cognitive, we suddenly run into turbulence. First, not all stress is the same. Certain types of stress really hurt learning, but some types of stress *boost* learning. Second, it's difficult to detect when someone is experiencing stress. Some people love skydiving for recreation; it's others' worst nightmare. Is jumping out of an airplane inherently stressful? The answer is no, and that highlights the subjective nature of stress.

The body isn't of much help in providing a definition, either. There is no unique grouping of physiological responses capable of telling a scientist whether or not you are experiencing stress. The reason? Many of the same mechanisms that cause you to shrink in horror from a predator are also used when you are having sex—or even while you are consuming your Thanksgiving dinner. To your body, saber-toothed tigers and orgasms and turkey gravy look remarkably similar. An aroused physiological state is characteristic of both stress and pleasure.

So what's a scientist to do? A few years ago, gifted researcher Jeansok Kim and David Diamond came up with a three-part definition that covers many of the bases. In their view, if all three are happening simultaneously, a person is stressed.

Part one: There must be an aroused physiological response to the stress, and it must be measurable by an outside party. I saw this in obvious fashion the first time my then 18-month-old son encountered a carrot on his plate at dinner. He promptly went ballistic: He screamed and cried and peed in his diaper. His aroused physiological state was immediately measurable by his dad, and probably by anyone else within a half mile of our kitchen table.

Part two: The stressor must be perceived as aversive. This can be assessed by a simple question: "If you had the ability to turn down the severity of this experience, or avoid it altogether, would you?" he was obvious where my son stood on the matter. Within seconds, he took the carrot off his plate and threw it on the floor. Then he deftly got down off his chair and tried to stomp on the predatory vegetable. The avoidance question was answered in full.

Part three. The person must not feel in control of the stressor. Like a volume knob on some emotional radio, the more the loss of control, the more severe the stress is perceived to be. This element of control and its closely related twin, predictability, lie at the heart of learned helplessness. My son reacted as strongly as he did in part because he knew I wanted him to eat the carrot, and he was used to doing what I told him to do. Control was the issue. Despite my picking up the carrot, washing it, then rubbing my tummy while enthusiastically saying "yum, yum," he was having none of it. Or, more important, he was wanting to have none of it, and he thought I was going to make him have all of it. Out-of-control carrot equaled out-of-control behavior.

When you find this trinity of components working together, you have the type of stress easily measurable in a laboratory setting. When I talk about stress, I am usually referring to situations like these.

Flooding the System

You can feel your body responding to stress: Your pulse races, your blood pressure rises, and you feel a massive release of energy. That's the famous hormone adrenaline at work. It's spurred into action by your brain's hypothalamus, that pea-size organ sitting almost in the middle of your head. When your sensory systems detect stress, the hypothalamus reacts by sending a signal to your adrenal glands, lying far away on the roof of your kidneys. The glands immediately dump bucketloads of adrenaline into your bloodstream. The overall effect is called the fight or flight response.

But there's a less famous hormone at work, too—also released by the adrenals, and just as powerful as adrenalin. It's called cortisol. You can think of it as the "elite strike force" of the human stress response. It's the second wave of our defensive reaction to stressors, and, in small doses, it wipes out most unpleasant aspects of stress, returning us to normalcy.

Why do our bodies need to go through all this trouble? The answer is very simple. Without a flexible, immediately available, highly regulated stress response, we would die. Remember, the brain is the world's most sophisticated survival organ. All of its many complexities are built toward a mildly erotic, singularly selfish goal: to live long enough to thrust our genes on to the next generation. Our reactions to stress serve the live-long-enough part of that goal. Stress helps us manage the threats that could keep us from procreating.

And what kinds of sex-inhibiting threats did we experience in our evolutionary toddlerhood? It's a safe bet they didn't involve worrying about retirement. Imagine you were a cave person roaming around the east African savannah. What kinds of concerns would occupy your waking hours? Predators would make it into your top 10 list. So would physical injury, which might very well come from those predators. In modern times, a broken leg means a trip to the doctor. In our distant past, a broken leg often meant a death sentence. The day's climate might also be a concern, the day's offering of food another. A lot of very *immediate* needs rise to the surface, needs that have nothing to do with old age.

Why immediate? Most of the survival issues we faced in our first few million years did not take hours, or even minutes, to settle. The saber-toothed tiger either ate us or we ran away from it—or lucky few might stab it, but the whole thing was usually over in less than half a minute. Consequently, our stress responses were shaped to solve problems that lasted not for years, but for seconds. They were primarily designed to get our muscles moving us as quickly as possible, usually out of harm's way. You can see the importance on this immediate reaction by observing people who cannot mount thorough and sudden stress response. If you had Addison's disease for example, you would be unable to raise your blood pressure in response to severe stress, such as being attacked by a mountain lion. Your blood pressure would drop catastrophically, probably putting you into a state of debilitating shock. You would become limp. Then you would become lunch.

These days, our stresses are measured not in moments with mountain lions, but in hours, days, and sometimes months with hectic workplaces, screaming toddlers, and money problems. Our system isn't built for that. And when moderate amounts of hormone build up to large amounts, or when moderate amounts of hormone hang around too long, they become quite harmful. That's how an exquisitely tuned system can become deregulated enough to affect a dog in a metal crate—or a report card, or a performance review.

From Sniffles to Forgetfulness

Stress can hurt more than our brains. In the short term, acute stress can boost cardiovascular performance—the probable source of those urban legends about grandmothers lifting one end of a car to rescue their grandchildren stuck under the wheels. Over the long term, however, too much adrenaline stops regulating surges in your blood pressure. These unregulated surges create sandpaper-like rough spots on the insides of your blood vessels. The spots turn into scars, which allow sticky substances in the blood to build up there, clogging your arteries. If it happens in the blood vessels of your heart, you get a heart attack; in your brain, you get a stroke. Not surprisingly, people who experience chronic stress have an elevated risk of heart attacks and strokes.

Stress also affects our immune response. At first, the stress response helps equip your white blood cells, sending them off to fight on the body's most vulnerable fronts, such as the skin. Acute stress can even make you respond better to a flu shot. But chronic stress reverses these effects, decreasing your number of heroic white-blood-cell soldiers, stripping them of their weapons, even killing them outright. Over the long term, stress ravages parts of the immune system involved in producing antibodies. Together, these can cripple your ability to fight infection. Chronic stress also can coax your immune system to fire indiscriminately, even at targets that aren't hooting back—like your own body.

Not surprisingly, people who experience chronic stress are sick more often. A *lot* more often. One study showed that stressed individuals were three times as likely to suffer from the common cold. People were especially vulnerable to the cold-producing virus if the stressors were social in nature and lasted more than a month. They also are more likely to suffer from autoimmune disorders, such as asthma and diabetes.

To show how sensitive the immune system can be to stress, you need look no further than an experiment done with the drama department at UCLA. If you can imagine having to think all day of the most depressing things that have ever happened in your life, then acting out these feelings in front of scientists *while they are taking your blood,* you will have a pretty good idea of this Transylvanian research exercise. During the experiment, the actors practiced method acting (which asks you, if the scene calls for you to be scared, to think of something frightening, then recite your lines while plumbing those memories). One group performed using only happy memories, the other only sad. The researchers monitored their blood samples, continually looking for immune "competence." Those people who had been working with uplifting scripts all day long had healthy immune systems. Their immune cells were plentiful, happy, readily available for work. Those people who had been working with depressing scripts all day long showed something unexpected: a marked decrease in immune responsiveness. Their immune cells were not plentiful, not as robust, not as available for work. These actors were much more vulnerable to infection.

The brain is just as influenced by stress as the immune system is. The hippocampus, that fortress of human memory, is studded with cortisol receptors like cloves in a ham. This makes it *very* responsive to stress signals. If the stress is not too severe, the brain performs better. Its owner can solve problems more effectively and is more likely to retain information. There's an evolutionary reason for this. Life-threatening events are some of the most important experiences we can remember. They happened with lightning speed in the savannah, and those who could commit those experiences to memory the fastest (and recall them accurately with equal speed) were more apt to survive than those who couldn't. Indeed, research shows that memories of stressful experiences are formed almost instantaneously in the human brain, and they can be recalled very quickly during times of crises.

If the stress is too severe or too prolonged, however, stress begins to harm learning. The influence can be devastating. You can see the effects of stress on learning in everyday life. Stressed people don't do math very well. They don't process language very efficiently. They have poorer memories, both short and long forms. Stressed individuals do not generalize or adapt old pieces of information to new scenarios as well as non-stressed individuals. They can't concentrate. In almost every way it can be tested, chronic stress hurts our ability to learn. One study showed that adults with high stress levels performed 50 percent worse on certain cognitive tests than adults with low stress. Specifically, stress hurts declarative memory (things you can declare) and executive function (the type of thinking that involves problem-solving). Those, of course, are the skills needed to excel in school and business.

The Villain, the Hero

The biology behind this obvious assault on our intelligences can be described as a tale of two molecules, one a villain, the other a hero. The villain is the previously discussed cortisol, part of a motley crew of hormones going by the tongue-twisting name of glucocorticoids (I'll call them stress hormones). These hormones are secreted by the adrenal glands, which lie like a roof on top of your kidneys. The adrenal glands are so exquisitely responsive to neural signals, they appear to have once been a part of your brain that somehow fell off and landed in your mid-abdomen.

Stress hormones can do some truly nasty things to your brain if boatloads of the stuff are given free access to your central nervous system. That's what's going on when you experience chronic stress. Stress hormones seem to have a particular liking for cells in the hippocampus, and that's a problem, because the hippocampus is deeply involved in many aspects of human learning. Stress hormones can make cells in the hippocampus more vulnerable to other stresses Stress hormones can disconnect neural networks, the webbing of brain cells that act like a safety deposit vault, storing your most precious memories. They can stop the hippocampus from giving birth to brand-new baby neurons. Under extreme conditions, stress hormones can even kill hippocampal cells. Quite literally, severe stress can cause brain damage in the very tissues most likely to help your children pass their SATs.

The brain seems to be aware of all this and has supplied our story not only with a villain but also with a hero. We met this champion back in the Exercise chapter. It's the Brain Derived Neurotrophic Factor. BDNF is the premier member of the powerful group of proteins called neurotrophins. BDNF in the hippocampus acts like a standing military armed with bags of Miracle Gro, keeping neuron alive and growing in the presence of hostile action. As long as there is enough BDNF around, stress hormones cannot do their damage. As I said, BDNF is a hero. How, then, does the system break down?

The problem begins when too many stress hormones hang around in the brain too long, a situation you find in chronic stress especially of the learned helplessness variety. As wonderful as the BDNF fertilizer armies are, it is possible to overwhelm them if they are assaulted with a sufficiently strong (and sufficiently lengthy glucocorticoid siege. Like a fortress overrun by invaders, enough stress hormones will eventually overwhelm the brain's natural defenses and wreak their havoc. In sufficient quantities, stress hormones are fully capable of turning off the gene that makes BDNF in hippocampal cells. You read that right: Not only can they overwhelm our natural defenses, but they can actually turn them *off.* The damaging effects can be long-lasting, a fact easily observed when people experience catastrophic stress.

You might recall the bodyguard who was in the car with Princess Diana on the night of her death. To this day, he cannot remember the events several hours before or after the crash. That is a typical response to severe trauma. Its lighter cousin, forgetfulness, is quite common when the stress is perhaps less severe but more pervasive.

One of the most insidious effects of prolonged stress is that it pushes people into depression. I don't mean the type of "blues" people can experience as a normal part of daily living. Nor do I mean the type resulting from tragic circumstance, such as the death of a relative. I am talking about the kind of depression that causes as many as 800,000 people a year to attempt suicide. It is a disease every bit as organic as diabetes, and often deadlier. Chronic exposure to stress can lead you to depression's doorstep, then push you through. Depression is a deregulation of thought processes, including memory, language, quantitative reasoning, fluid intelligence, and spatial perception. The list is long and familiar. But one of its hallmarks may not be as familiar, unless you are in depression. Many people who feel depressed also feel there is no way out of their depression. They feel that life's shocks are permanent and things will never get better. Even when there is a way out—treatment is often very successful—there is no perception of it. They can no more argue their way out of a depression than they could argue their way out of a heart attack.

Clearly, stress hurts learning. Most important, however, stress hurts *people*.

A Genetic Buffer

In a world as complex as the brain, is the relationship between stress and learning that straightforward? For once, the answer is yes. Out-of-control stress is bad news for the brains of most people. Of course, most doesn't mean all. Like oddly placed candles in a dark room, some people illuminate corners of human behavior with unexpected clarity. They illustrate the complexity of environmental and genetic factors.

Jill was born into an inner-city home. Her father began having sex with Jill and her sister during their preschool years. Her mother was institutionalized twice because of what used to be termed "nervous breakdowns." When Jill was 7 years old, her agitated dad called a family meeting in the living room. In front of the whole clan, he put a handgun to his head, said, "You drove me to this," then blew his brains out. The mother's mental condition continued to deteriorate, and she revolved in and out of mental hospitals for years. When Mom was home, she would beat Jill. Beginning in her early teens, Jill was forced to work outside the home to help make ends meet. As Jill got older, we would have expected to see deep psychiatric scars, severe emotional damage, drugs, maybe even a pregnancy or two. Instead, Jill developed into a charming and quite popular young woman at school. She became a talented singer, an honor student, and president of her high school class. By every measure, she was emotionally well-adjusted and seemingly unscathed by the awful circumstances of her childhood.

Her story, published in a leading psychiatric journal, illustrates the unevenness of the human response to stress. Psychiatrists long have observed that some people are more tolerant of stress than others. Molecular geneticists are beginning to shed light on the reasons. Some people's genetic complement naturally buffers them against the effects of stress, even the chronic type. Scientists have isolated some of these genes. In the future, we may be able to tell stress-tolerant from stress-sensitive individuals with a simple blood test, looking for the presence of these genes.

The Tipping Point

How can we explain both the typical responses to stress, which can be quite debilitating, and the exceptions? For that, we turn to a senior scientist, Bruce McEwen, an elder statesman, smart, always in a suit and tie.

McEwen developed a powerful framework that allows us to understand all the various ways humans respond to stress. He gave it a name straight out of a *Star Trek* engineering manual: allostasis. Allo is from a Greek word meaning variable; stasis means a condition of balance. The idea is that there are systems that help keep the body stable by changing themselves. The stress system in the human body, and its many intricate subsystems, is one of those. The brain coordinates these body-wide changes—behavior included—in response to potential threats.

This model says that stress, left alone, is neither harmful nor toxic. Whether stress becomes damaging is the result of a complex interaction between the outside world and our physiological capacity to manage the stress. Your body's reaction to stress depends on the stress, on its length and severity, and on your body. There's a point where stress becomes toxic, and McEwen calls it the allostatic load. I know it as the first time, and only time, I ever heard my mother use profanity. I also know it as the time I got the worst grade in my academic career. We all have stories that illustrate the concrete effects of stress on real life.

As you may recall, my mother was a fourth-grade teacher. I was upstairs in my room, unbeknownst to my mother, who was upstairs in her room grading papers. She was grading one of her favorite students, a sweet, brown-haired little wisp of a girl I will call Kelly. Kelly was every teacher's dream kid: smart, socially poised, blessed with a wealth of friends. Kelly had done very well in the first half of the school year.

The second half of the school year was another story, however. My mother sensed something was very wrong the moment Kelly walked into class after Christmas break. Her eyes were mostly downcast, and within a week she had gotten into her first fight. In another week, she got her first C on an exam, and that would prove to be the high point, as her grades for the rest of the year fluttered between D's and F's. She was sent to the principal's office numerous times, and my mother, exasperated, decided to find out what caused this meltdown. She learned that Kelly's parents had decided to get a divorce over Christmas and that the family conflicts, from which the parents valiantly had insulated Kelly, had begun spilling out into the open. As things unraveled at home, things also unraveled at school. And on that snowy day, when my mother gave Kelly her third straight D in spelling, my mother also swore:

"Dammit!" she said, nearly under her breath. I froze as she shouted, "THE ABILITY OF KELLY TO DO WELL IN MY CLASS HAS NOTHING TO DO WITH MY CLASS!"

She was, of course, describing the relationship between home life and school life, a link that has frustrated teachers for a long time. One of the greatest predictors of performance in school turns out to be the emotional stability of the home.

Stress in the Home

I want to focus on stress in the home because it is profoundly related to kids' ability to do well in the classroom and, when they grow up, in the workforce.

Consider the all-too common case of kids witnessing their parents fighting. The simple fact is that children find unresolved marital conflict deeply disturbing.

Kids cover their ears, stand motionless with clenched fists, cry, scowl, ask to leave, beg parents to stop. Study after study has shown that children—some as young as 6 months—react to adult arguments physiologically, such as with a faster heart rate and higher blood pressure. Kids of all ages who watch parents constantly fight have more stress hormones in their urine. They have more difficulty regulating their emotions, soothing themselves, focusing their attention on others. They are powerless to stop the conflict, and the loss of control is emotionally crippling. As you know, control is a powerful influence on the perception of stress. This loss can influence many things in their lives, including their schoolwork. They are experiencing allostatic load.

I have firsthand experience with the effects of stress on grades. I was a senior in high school when my mother was diagnosed with the disease that would eventually kill her. She had come home late from a doctor's visit and was attempting to fix the family dinner. But when I found her, she was just staring at the kitchen wall. She haltingly related the terminal nature of her medical condition and then, as if that weren't enough, unloaded another bombshell. My dad, who had some prior knowledge of Mom's condition, was not handling the news very well and had decided to file for divorce. I felt as if I had just been punched in the stomach. For a few seconds I could not move. School the next day, and for the next 13 weeks, was a disaster. I don't remember much of the lectures. I only remember staring at my textbooks, thinking that this amazing woman had taught me to read and love such books, that we used to have a happy family, and that all of this was coming to an end. What she must have been feeling, much worse than I could ever fathom, she never related. Not knowing how to react, my friends soon withdrew from me even as I withdrew from them. I lost the ability to concentrate, my mind wandering back to childhood. My academic effort became a train wreck. I got the only D I would ever get in my school career, and I couldn't have cared less.

Even after all these years, it is still tough to write about that high school moment. But it easily illustrates this second, very powerful consequence of stress, underscoring with sad vengeance our Brain Rule: Stressed brains do not learn the same way as non-stressed brains. My grief at least had an end-point. Imagine growing up in an emotionally unstable home, where the stress seems never-ending. Given that stress can powerfully affect learning, one might predict that children living in high-anxiety households would not perform as well academically as kids living in more nurturing households.

That is exactly what researchers have found. Marital stress at home can negatively affect academic performance in almost every way measurable, and at nearly any age. Initial studies focused on grade-point averages over time. They reveal striking disparities of achievement between divorce and control groups. Subsequent investigations showed that even when a couple stays together, children living in emotionally unstable homes get lower grades. (Careful subsequent investigations showed that it was the presence of overt conflict, not divorce, that predicted grade failure.) They also do worse on standardized math and reading tests.

The stronger the degree of conflict, the greater the effect on performance. Teachers typically report that children from disrupted homes rate lower in both aptitude and intelligence. Such children are three times as likely to be expelled from school or to become pregnant as teenagers, and five times as likely to live in poverty. As social activist Barbara Whitehead put it, writing for the *Atlantic Monthly:* "Teachers find many children emotionally distracted, so upset and preoccupied by the explosive drama of their own family lives that they are unable to concentrate on such mundane matters as multiplication tables."

Physical health deteriorates; absenteeism and truancy increase. The absenteeism may occur because stress is depleting the immune system, which increases the risk of infection. Though the evidence is not as conclusive, a growing body of data suggests that children living in hostile environments are at greater risk for certain psychiatric disorders, such as depression and anxiety disorders. Such disorders can wreak havoc on cognitive processes important to successful academic performance. As children grow up, the effects of childhood stress can stay with them. Indeed, performance can take a negative hit regardless of one's age, even if you were a previously high functioning and much admired employee, like Lisa Nowak.

Stress at Work

You may have heard of Lisa Nowak. She is a lethal combat pilot, decorated electronics warfare specialist, pretty, smart. The government spent millions of dollars training her to be an astronaut. She was also a mother with two kids on the verge of divorcing her husband one month before her biggest professional assignment: mission control specialist for a shuttle mission. Talk about built-up stress. She put some weapons in her automobile, grabbed a disguise, even packed up a bunch of adult diapers so she didn't have to stop to use a bathroom. She then drove virtually nonstop from Orlando to Houston, allegedly to kidnap her target, a woman she thought was a threat to a fellow astronaut to whom she had taken a fancy. Instead of serving as the lead for one of America's most technically challenging jobs, this highly skilled engineer is awaiting trial on attempted kidnapping and burglary charges. She will probably never fly again, which makes this sad story nearly heartbreaking. It also makes the money spent on her training a colossal waste. But those few million dollars are miniscule compared with the cost of stress on the workplace as a whole.

Stress attacks the immune system, increasing employees' chances of getting sick. Stress elevates blood pressure, increasing the risk of heart attack, stroke, and autoimmune diseases. That directly affects health-care and pension costs. Stress is behind more than half of the 550 million working days lost each year because of absenteeism. Stressed employees tend to avoid coming to work at the slightest excuse, and they often show up late. Yet executives often give stress the shortest shrift. The Centers for Disease Control and Prevention asserts that a full 80 percent of our medical expenditures are now stress-related. In a work force where 77 percent report being burned out, this translates into a lot of cortisol, a lot of missed meetings, and a lot of trips to the doctor. That's not all. Prolonged stress can cause depression, which alters the ability to think—a direct assault on a corporation's intellectual capital. This injury to business productivity is threefold.

First, depression hobbles the brain's natural improvisatory instincts the way arthritis hobbles a dancer. Fluid intelligence. problem-solving abilities (including quantitative reasoning), and memory formation are deeply affected by depression. The result is an erosion of innovation and creativity, just as biochemically real as if we were talking about joints and muscles. In a knowledge-based economy where intellectual dexterity is often *the* key to survival, that's bad news for competitiveness, shareholder value, and the bottom line. In fact, the cost of depression to the work force in 1990 was estimated to be $53 billion. The loss of productivity contributed the most, about $33 billion of the total.

Second, those same people who have lost their creativity incur more health-care expenses. Thus, not only does stress reduce the contributions valuable employees can make, but those same employees begin to cannibalize their company's internal resources. And it's not just mental-health expenditures. Depressed individuals are at increased risk for a number of other diseases.

Third, people who burn out are often fired, if they don't leave on their own. Turnover further disrupts productivity, plus sets off a costly recruiting and training effort. The ugly truth is that any assault on human brain cells is an assault on competitiveness. The final tab? Statistical analyses from many studies form the same dismal picture. Stress causes companies to lose between $200 billion and $300 billion a year—as much as $75 billion of red ink a quarter.

Three things matter in determining whether a workplace is stressful: the type of stress, a balance between occupational stimulation and boredom, and the condition of the employee's home life. Business professionals have spent a long time studying what types of stress make people less productive and, not surprisingly, have arrived at the same conclusion that Marty Seligman's German shepherds did: Control is critical. The perfect storm of occupational stress appears to be a combination of two malignant facts: a) a great deal is expected of you and b) you have no control over whether you will perform well. Sounds like a formula for learned helplessness to me.

On the positive side, restoration of control can return groups to productivity. In one instance, a for-profit consented to be studied after agreeing to institute a control-based stress management program. At the end of two years, the unit had saved almost $150,000 in workers' compensation costs alone. The cost of deploying the stress management program? About $6,000. And just 16 hours of the program reduced toxic blood pressure levels for employees diagnosed with hypertension.

Control isn't the only factor in productivity. Employees on an assembly line, doing the same tired thing day after day, are certainly in control of their work processes. But the tedium can be a source of brain-numbing stress. What spices things up? Studies show that a certain amount of uncertainty can be good for productivity, especially for bright, motivated employees. What they need is a balance between controllability and uncontrollability. Slight feelings of uncertainty may cause them to deploy unique problem-solving strategies.

The third characteristic, if you are a manager, is none of your business. I am talking about the effects of family life on business life. There's no such thing as a firewall between personal issues and work productivity. That's because we can't have two brains we can interchange depending upon whether we are in our office or in our bedroom. Stress in the workplace affects family life, causing more stress in the family. More stress in the family causes more stress at work, which in turn gets brought home again. It's a deadly, self-feeding spiral, and researchers call it "work-family conflict." So you may have the most wonderful feelings about autonomy at work, and you may have tremendous problem-solving opportunities with your colleagues. But if your home life is a wreck, you can still suffer the negative effects of stress, and so can your employer.

Whether we look at school performance or job performance, we keep running into the profound influence of the emotional stability of the home. Is there anything we can do about something so fundamentally personal, given that its influence can be so terribly public? The answer, surprisingly, may be yes.

Marriage Intervention

Famed marriage researcher John Gottman can predict the future of a relationship within three minutes of interacting with the couple. His ability to accurately forecast marital success or failure is close to 90 percent. His track record is confirmed by peer-reviewed publications. He may very well hold the future of the American education and business sectors in his hands.

How is he so successful? After years of careful observation, Gottman isolated specific marital behaviors—both positive and negative—that hold most of the predictive power. But this research was ultimately unsatisfying to a man like Gottman, akin to telling someone they have a life-threatening illness but not being able to cure them. And so the next step in his research was to try to harness some of that predictive knowledge to give a couple a better future. Gottman devised a marriage intervention strategy based on his decades of research. It focuses on improving the behaviors proven to predict marital success and eliminating the ones proven to predict failure. Even in its most modest forms, his intervention drops divorce rates by nearly 50 percent.

What do his interventions actually do? They drop both the frequency and severity of hostile interactions between husband and wife. This return to civility has many positive side effects besides marital reconstruction, especially if the couple has kids. The link is direct. These days, Gottman says, he can predict the quality of a relationship not only by examining the stress responses of the parents but also by taking a urine sample of their children.

That last statement deserves some unpacking. Gottman's marriage research invariably put him in touch with couples who were starting families. When these marriages started their transition to parenthood Gottman noticed that the couple's bostile interactions skyrocketed. There were many causes, ranging from chronic sleep deprivation to the increased demands of a helpless new family member (little ones typically require that an adult satisfy some demand of theirs about 3 times a minute). By the time the baby was 1 year old, marital satisfaction had plummeted 70 percent. At that same point, the risk for maternal depression went from 25 percent to a whopping 62 percent. The couples' risk for divorce increased, which meant American babies often were born into a turbulent emotional world.

That single observation gave Gottman and fellow researcher Alyson Shapiro an idea. What if he deployed his proven marital intervention strategies to married couples while the wife was pregnant? Before the hostility floodgates opened up? Before the depression rates went through the roof? Statistically, he already knew the marriage would significantly improve. The big question concerned the kids. What would an emotionally stabilized environment do to the baby's developing nervous system? He decided to find out.

The research investigation, deployed over several years, was called Bringing Baby Home. It consisted of exposing expectant couples to the marital interventions whether their marriages were in trouble or not, and then assessing the development of the child. Gottman and Shapiro uncovered a gold mine of information. They found that babies raised in the intervention households didn't look anything like the babies raised in the controls. Their nervous systems didn't develop the same way. Their behaviors weren't in the same emotional universe. Children in the intervention groups didn't cry as much. They had stronger attention-shifting behaviors and they responded to external stressors in remarkably stable ways. Physiologically, the intervention babies showed all the cardinal signs of healthy emotional regulation, while the controls showed all the signs of unhealthy, disorganized nervous systems. The differences were remarkable and revealed something hopeful and filled with common sense. By stabilizing the parents, Gottman and Shapiro were able to change not only the marriage; they also were able to change the child.

I think Gottman's findings can change the world, starting with report cards and performance evaluations.

Ideas

What people do in their private life is their own business, of course. Unfortunately, what people do in their private life often affects the public. Consider the criminal history of a fellow who had recently moved from Texas to a city in the Pacific Northwest. He absolutely *hated* his new home and decided to leave. Stealing the car of a neighbor (for the second time that month), he drove several miles to the airport and ditched the car. He then found a way to fool both the security officials and the gate managers and hopped a free ride back to Texas. He accomplished this feat a few months shy of his 10th birthday. Not surprisingly, this boy comes from a troubled home. This is a fairly recent event, but if something isn't done soon, the private issue of raising this child soon will become a very public problem. And he is hardly alone. How can we capture our Brain Rule, that stressed brains learn differently from non-stressed brains, and change the way we educate, parent, and do business? I have thought a lot about that.

Teach Parents First

The current education system starts in first grade, typically around age 6. The curriculum is a little writing, a little reading, a little math. The teacher is often a complete stranger. And there is something important missing. The stability of the home is completely ignored, even though it is one of the greatest predictors of future success at school. But what if we took its influence seriously?

My idea envisions an educational system where the first students are not the children. The first students are the parents. The curriculum? How to create a stable home life, using Gottman's powerful, baby-nervous-system changing protocols. The intervention could even start in a maternity ward, offered by a hospital (like a Lamaze class, which takes just about as much time). There would be a unique partnership between the health system and the education system. *And it makes education, from the beginning of a child's life, a family affair.*

First grade would begin a week after birth. The amazing cognitive abilities of infants, from language acquisition to the powerful need for luxurious amounts of active playtime, are fully unleashed in a curriculum designed just for them. (This is *not* a call to implement products in the strange industry that seeks to turn babies into Einsteins in the first year of life. Most of those products have not been tested, and some have been shown to be harmful to learning. My idea envisions a mature, rigorously tested pedagogy that does not yet exist—one more reason for educators and brain scientists to work together.) Along with this, parents would take an occasional series of marital refresher courses, just to ensure the stability of the home. Can you imagine what a child might look like academically after years of thriving in an emotionally stable environment? The child flourishes in this fantasy.

No hospitals or schools currently offer these interventions to the future students of America, and there is no formal curriculum for harnessing the cognitive horse-power of the under-solid-food crowd. But it could be developed and tested, beginning right this minute. The best shot would come from collaborative experiments between brain scientists and education scientists. All one needs is a cooperative educational will, and maybe a sense of adventure.

Free Family Counseling, Child Care

Historically, people have done their best work—sometimes world-changing work—in their first few years after joining the work force. In the field of economics, most Nobel Prize-winning research is done in the first 10 years of the recipient's career. Albert Einstein published most of his creative ideas at the ripe old age of 26. It's no wonder that companies want to recruit young intellectual talent.

The problem in today's economy is that people are typically starting a family at the very time they are also supposed to be doing their best work. They are trying to be productive at some of the most stressful times of their lives. What if companies took this unhappy collision of life events seriously? They could offer Gottman's intervention as a benefit for every newly married, or newly pregnant, employee. Would that reverse the negative flow of family stress that normally enters the workplace at this time in a person's life? Such an intervention might enhance productivity and perhaps even generate grateful, loyal employees.

Businesses also risk losing their best and brightest at this time, as talented people are forced to make a terrible decision between career and family. The decision is especially hard on women. In the 21st century, we have invented two economic classifications: the child-free class (people with no kids or without primary responsibility for them) and the child-bound class (people who act as a main caregiver). From a gender perspective, these categories have very little symmetry. According to Claudia Goldin, Henry Lee Professor of Economics at Harvard, women are over-represented in the child-bound category by nearly 9 to 1.

What if talented people didn't have to choose between career and family? What if businesses offered onsite child care just so they could retain employees at the very time they are most likely to be valuable? This obviously would affect women the most, which means businesses immediately achieve more gender balance. Would such an offering so affect productivity that the costs of providing child care become offset by the gains? That's a great research question. Not only might businesses create more stable employees in the current generation, they might be raising far healthier children for work in the next.

Power to the Workers

Plenty of books discuss how to manage stress; some are confusing, others extraordinarily insightful. The good ones all say one thing in common: The biggest part of successful stress management involves getting control back into your life. This means that a manager or human-resources professional has a powerful predictive insight at his or her disposal. To detect stress-related problems, one might simply examine the situations where an employee feels the most helpless. Questionnaires based on Jeansok Kim's and David Diamond's three-pronged definition of stress could be developed that routinely assess not the broad perception of aversion, but the narrower issue of powerlessness. The next step would be to change the situation.

These are only a few of the possibilities that could be realized if brain scientists and business professionals ever collaborated on the biology of stress in the work force. It is possible their findings would change the absentee rate of their employees, cut down on the number of trips to the doctor, and reduce their insurance overhead. As well as money saved, a great deal of creativity may be engendered simply by routinely giving employees a way out—not from their jobs but from the stress they experience in them.

It's no coincidence that stress researchers, education scientists, and business professionals come to similar conclusions about stress and people. What's astonishing is that we have known most of the salient points since Marty Seligman stopped shocking his dogs in the mid-1970s. It is time we made productive use of that horrible line of research.

SUMMARY

Rule #8

Stressed brains don't learn the same way.

○ Your body's defense system—the release of adrenaline and cortisol—is built for an immediate response to a serious but passing danger, such as a saber-toothed tiger. Chronic stress, such as hostility at home, dangerously deregulates a system built only to deal with short-term responses.

○ Under chronic stress, adrenaline creates scars in your blood vessels that can cause a heart attack or stroke, and cortisol damages the cells of the hippocampus, crippling your ability to learn and remember.

○ Individually, the worst kind of stress is the feeling that you have no control over the problem—you are helpless.

○ Emotional stress has huge impacts across society, on children's ability to learn in school and on employees' productivity at work.

Get more at www.brainrules.net

Discussion Questions

How much stress have you experienced in college and how has it affected you?

What elements of home stress, before coming to UNCW or since, impacted your academic performance?

Appendices

SECTION I
STUDENT ACADEMIC HONOR CODE POLICY 03.100

I-1 THE UNCW STUDENT ACADEMIC HONOR CODE

The University of North Carolina Wilmington is a community of high academic standards where academic integrity is valued. UNCW students are committed to honesty and truthfulness in academic inquiry and in the pursuit of knowledge. This commitment begins when new students matriculate at UNCW, continues as they create work of the highest quality while part of the university community, and endures as a core value throughout their lives.

1-2 THE UNCW HONOR PLEDGE

All students enrolled at UNCW are subject to the UNCW Student Academic Honor Code (hereafter referred to as the Honor Code), which is intended to help every member of the UNCW community appreciate the high value placed on academic integrity and the means that will be employed to ensure its preservation. Students are expected to perpetuate a campus culture where each student does his or her own work while relying on appropriate resources for assistance. In such a climate students enjoy a special trust that they are members of a unique community where one's thoughts and words are attributed correctly and with proper ownership, and where there is little need for systems to sanction those who cheat. As such, all UNCW students shall commit to the principles and spirit of the Honor Code by adhering to the following pledge:

> *"As a student at The University of North Carolina Wilmington, I am committed to honesty and truthfulness in academic inquiry and in the pursuit of knowledge. I pledge to uphold and promote the UNCW Student Academic Honor Code."*

1-3 GUIDELINES IN SUPPORT OF THE HONOR CODE

Disciplinary action will ensue when students fail to align themselves with the ideals and expectations outlined in the Honor Code. The following guidelines are designed to educate students about the types of academic dishonesty, the roles

---

that the university community has in upholding the Honor Code, the procedures used to report and adjudicate alleged offenses, and the limitations on withdrawals and repeating courses in the event of academic dishonesty. Because the university takes a holistic approach to addressing student misconduct, both of an academic and non-academic nature, incidents involving students with prior findings of responsibility for academic dishonesty or serious non-academic misconduct (typically denoted by the status of "disciplinary probation") will be referred to the Student Academic Honor Board.

A. ACADEMIC DISHONESTY OFFENSES

No form of academic dishonesty is tolerated in our community. Academic dishonesty is broadly defined as attaining academic goals by deception, and includes but is not limited to attempted or completed offenses as follows:

1. CHEATING

Cheating is deception implying that work in fulfillment of course or degree requirements represents a student's own level of knowledge when it actually does not. Common examples of cheating include:

a. Any conduct during a program, course, quiz or examination which involves the unauthorized use of written or oral information, or information obtained by any other means of communication. Students are expected to consult with their instructors for clarification on whether assignments may be conducted jointly with other students. In the absence of approval for joint work, the expectation is that students will conduct their own work and research both outside and within the classroom environment (not including authorized assistance and sanctioned university resources such as the University Learning Center). Students must receive approval by their instructor(s) in advance for submitting a paper previously written and submitted by them for another class.

b. The unauthorized acquisition, buying, selling, trading or theft of any examination, quiz, term paper or project.

c. The unauthorized use of any electronic or mechanical device during any program, course, quiz or examination, or in connection with laboratory reports or other materials related to academic performance.

d. The unauthorized use of laboratory reports, term reports, theses, or written materials in whole or in part.

e. The unauthorized assistance or collaboration on any test, assignment, or project.

f. The unauthorized use by a student of another person's work, or the falsification of any other person's work, or writing another person's work for them to submit.

g. Bribery, including but not limited to the offering, giving, receiving or soliciting of any consideration in order to obtain a grade or other treatment not otherwise earned by the student through his/her own academic performance.

h. Any form of lying or furnishing false information to a professor, administrator or staff member acting in performance of their duties (including taking an exam for another student).

2. PLAGIARISM

Plagiarism is the copying of language, phrasing, structure, or specific ideas of another and presenting any of these as one's own work, including information found on the Internet. Common examples of plagiarism include but are not limited to:

a. Reproducing someone else's work without quotation marks or proper attribution and submitting it as your own.
b. Paraphrasing or summarizing another's work without attribution or acknowledgement of the source and submitting it as your own.
c. Deliberate attribution to a source from which the referenced material was not in fact derived.
d. Failing to cite a source for ideas or information.

B. RESPONSIBILITY OF THE UNIVERSITY COMMUNITY

1. GENERAL RESPONSIBILITY

It is the responsibility of every faculty member, student, administrator and staff member of the university community to uphold and maintain the highest academic standards and integrity of the university. Any member of the university community who has reasonable grounds to believe that an infraction of the Honor Code has occurred has an obligation to report the alleged violation to the faculty member teaching the class who, in turn, must report the allegation to the Office of the Dean of Students. This obligation is a core value of the Honor Code, and must be fulfilled by each and every member of the university.

2. STUDENT RESPONSIBILITY

UNCW students affirm their adherence to the Honor Code by signing an Honor Pledge after enrolling at the university; thereafter, each student must conform to the Honor Code at all times. The absence of signing the pledge does not excuse students from their obligation to read, practice and be held accountable to the rules and spirit of the Honor Code. Students are responsible for seeking clarification from faculty whether and to what degree they are permitted to collaborate on assignments; use laptops, cell phones, and other electronic media in class; and submit papers that they have submitted or intend to submit for another course. It is the student's responsibility to receive approval in advance for conducting joint academic work (work which involves anyone other than the student him/herself) or when attempting to submit work that was previously written/conducted by the student (commonly known as "recycling" one's work). Students who observe or suspect an Honor Code violation are to notify the instructor in whose course the alleged infraction occurred.

3. RESPONSIBILITY OF INDIVIDUAL INSTRUCTORS

Instructors should remind their students of the Honor Code during the first week of classes and include Section I of the Honor Code and the Honor Pledge in their syllabi. In addition to discussing the Honor Code with students, instructors should clarify whether and to what degree students are permitted to collaborate on assignments; use laptops, cell phones, and other electronic media in class; and submit papers that they have submitted or intend to submit for another course. While faculty are encouraged to discuss these issues with students, it is the student's responsibility to receive approval in advance for conducting joint academic work (work which involves anyone other than the student him/herself) or when attempting to submit work that was previously written/conducted by the student (commonly known as "recycling" one's work). While all students are bound by the Honor Code through either a signed pledge or by virtue of enrollment at UNCW, instructors have the option of including the Honor Pledge on examinations and requiring students to include a signed pledge with submitted work. Each instructor is obligated to report allegations of academic dishonesty, upon discovery, to the Office of the Dean of Students.

4. RESPONSIBILITY OF ACADEMIC AFFAIRS

The Division of Academic Affairs is responsible for advising all new university faculty and academic administrative staff regarding the Honor Code. The provost or designee shall have the right to hear an expedited student case as requested by the Office of the Dean of Students, and to review appeals for students sanctioned as a result of Honor Code Infractions.

5. RESPONSIBILITY OF THE OFFICE OF THE DEAN OF STUDENTS

The Office of the Dean of Students is responsible for overall education of the university community on the Honor Code; for advising all current university faculty, administrative staff, personnel and students of the Honor Code; and for collecting signed Honor Pledges. In consultation with the Faculty Senate, the Office of the Dean of Students will see that the Honor Code and any amendments or changes approved by the Faculty Senate and the UNCW administration are published and promulgated annually. The Office of the Dean of Students shall also receive and maintain comprehensive records of all matters relating to violations of the Honor Code; therefore, faculty must consult with the Office of the Dean of Students upon making or receiving a complaint of any Honor Code infraction.

I-4 REPORTING PROCEDURES

A. FILING COMPLAINTS

An alleged infraction of the Honor Code observed by anyone other than the course instructor shall be reported, preferably in writing, to the instructor of the course in which it occurred. Such a report shall be made within five (5) business days from the time of discovery, unless extenuating circumstances prevent reporting. Faculty who observe, discover, or are informed of infractions should report them immediately to the Office of the Dean of Students. Faculty may report infractions at any point during the term of the class or at any point preceding the end of the tenth calendar day after grades are due for the final class of enrollment for the student in question.

A suspected infraction of the Honor Code may be reported by:

a. the student committing the infraction; or
b. any member of the university community observing the alleged infraction; or
c. any individual who has credible and reliable information that an infraction may have occurred.

B. CONSULTATION WITH THE OFFICE OF THE DEAN OF STUDENTS

Upon observing or discovering an alleged Honor Code infraction, or upon receiving a report of an infraction, the instructor shall consult with the Office of the Dean of Students to discuss appropriate procedures and protection of student rights, and to determine whether the case shall be heard by the faculty member, the Office of the Dean of Students or the Student Academic Honor Board. Any student with a prior finding of responsibility for an Honor Code offense or students with a history of serious non-academic misconduct (typically consistent with the status of "disciplinary probation") will be referred to the Student Academic Honor Board for resolution.

C. PRIOR OFFENSES

1. If the student has no prior Honor Code offenses and no history of serious non-academic misconduct, the faculty member will meet with the student to inform the student of the allegation of academic dishonesty and explain to the student their options, as follows:
    a. If the student admits the infraction, the faculty member must either propose a settlement by private resolution OR refer the case to the Office of the Dean of Students (without assigning a grade until after being informed of the final outcome of the case).
    b. If the faculty member decides on proposing a settlement by private resolution, proposed penalties should accord with the severity of the offense. Penalties can range from a failing grade on the work in question to a failing grade in the course.[1] The chairperson of the department in which the faculty member teaches may be consulted for assistance in reaching a settlement. If the penalty proposed by the instructor is acceptable to the student, the case can be resolved by providing notification to the department chair and to the dean of the college/school in which the faculty member teaches, and must be copied to the Office of the Dean of Students for inclusion in the student's disciplinary record.
    c. If the student does not admit the infraction, the faculty member must either:
        1. Refer the case to the Office of the Dean of Students (without assigning a grade). OR
        2. Decide not to pursue the accusation(s) due to lack of evidence, whereupon he/she shall inform the reporting party of this decision within five (5) business days and also inform the Office of the Dean of Students.

D. DISCIPLINARY CORRESPONDENCE

All disciplinary correspondence will be sent to the student's UNCW e-mail address. UNCW regards e-mail as an official method of communication with student, staff and faculty (UNCW Policy 07.100). The university reserves the right to use other reasonable means to notify students.

E. SUMMONING A STUDENT RESPONDENT FOR A CONFERENCE

Should a respondent not appear when requested by the dean of students/designee, the dean of students/designee may formally summon the respondent to appear for a meeting in connection with an alleged violation by sending him/her notification of this. This notification shall direct the respondent to appear at a specified date, time and place not less than three (3) business days later. The letter shall also describe briefly the alleged violation(s). If the respondent fails to respond to a notification and the required pre-hearing interview, the respondent forfeits the option to request whether the case is heard administratively or by the Student Academic Honor Board and the dean of students/designee will decide how to route the case. The student will be notified by email sent at least five (5) business days before a hearing before the dean of students/designee or, at the option of the dean of students, the Student Academic Honor Board.

At the hearing, a decision of responsible or not responsible will be made based on available information, with or without the respondent. If the respondent fails to attend the hearing, all allegations against the respondent shall be deemed to be denied. When appropriate, a sanction will be determined and the respondent will be notified by email.

I-5 PRE-HEARING MEETING and HEARING OPTIONS

All cases referred to the Office of the Dean of Students will result in an honor hearing. If the student has no prior Honor Code offenses, the student shall choose a hearing either before the dean of students (or designee) or before the Student Academic Honor Board. Based on the nature and scope of the alleged infraction, the dean of students (or designee) may elect not to hear a case and to forward it directly to the Student Academic Honor Board. If the student has one or more prior Honor Code infractions or a history of serious non-academic misconduct, the case shall be heard by the Student Academic Honor Board. During a pre-hearing interview, the Office of the Dean of Students will provide each student respondent the opportunity to accept responsibility for the alleged offense and to accept a penalty appropriate for the offense without proceeding to the Student Academic Honor Board. If the student accepts the sanction, authority to determine the course grade resides with the instructor; however, an assigned grade of "F" for the course is generally appropriate for an Honor Code offense. If the student disagrees with the sanction, the case shall be heard by the Student Academic Honor Board.

If the respondent is found responsible and sanctions are imposed, the respondent is responsible for completing sanctions regardless of their participation in the hearing process. Failure to complete assigned sanctions may result in further conduct action.

A. STANDARD OF PROOF

The standard of proof for all allegations of the academic honor code will be preponderance of evidence. This means that there is greater than a 50% chance, based on all reasonable evidence, that the respondent is responsible for the alleged violation.

B. STUDENT RESPONSIBILITIES & RIGHTS STUDENT RESPONSIBILITIES

Participants in the Student Academic Honor Code process have the following responsibilities:

1. To know and adhere to the *UNCW Student Academic Honor Code*.
2. To be honest and complete in all information they provide in the process.
3. To attend all meetings or hearings in a timely manner.
4. For respondents to complete any imposed sanctions on time and consistent with the decision in their case.
5. To participate in a manner that is civil and respectful.

STUDENT RIGHTS

All students are entitled to the following rights prior to a student academic honor board hearing:

1. To a pre-hearing meeting with a university hearing officer where rights, responsibilities and procedures are explained.
2. To written notice of the charge(s). In the event that additional charges are brought, additional written notice must be forwarded to the respondent. Notices are sent via e-mail to the student's UNCW e-mail address.
3. To review all available information, documents, and a list of witnesses that may testify against him/her. This is a continuing obligation of the complaining party and the dean of students/designee.
4. To choose an Administrative or Student Academic Honor Board hearing. (The dean of students/designee may elect not to hear the case. The case would then be heard by the Student Academic Honor Board.)
5. To appear in person, hear all testimony and present any relevant information on their behalf, call witnesses and ask questions of any witnesses at the hearing.
6. To elect not to appear at the hearing, in which case the hearing shall be conducted in absentia (in the respondent's absence). A respondent who elects not to appear at a hearing may not be represented by a university or non-university advisor.
7. To know the identity of witnesses testifying against them.
8. To a closed hearing. A closed hearing is closed to the general public.
9. To a university or non-university advisor.
10. To refuse to answer any questions or make a statement - however, the hearing body shall make its decision solely on the basis of information introduced at the hearing.
11. To have all statements, information or comments given during the hearing held in the strictest of confidence by the hearing body before, during and after deliberation.
12. To have the hearing conducted as outlined in the *UNCW Student Academic Honor Code*.
13. To have one level of institutional appeal as outlined in the UNC Policy Manual 700.4.1.

C. UNIVERSITY and NON-UNIVERSITY ADVISORS

A university or non-university advisor is permissible in an Administrative and Student Academic Honor Board hearing. Upon the request of the respondent, the Office of the Dean of Students will appoint a university advisor to help a student prepare for a hearing. The advisor may not speak on the respondent's behalf at the hearing. The university/non-university advisor's role is to:

a. advise the respondent concerning the preparation and presentation of his/her case.

b. accompany the respondent to all conduct proceedings as requested by the respondent.

c. have access to all materials relating to the case as provided by the respondent.

A respondent who elects not to appear at a hearing may not be represented by an advisor at the hearing.

I-7 ADMINISTRATIVE HEARING PROCEDURE

1. If a student requests an administrative hearing before the dean of students/designee, the dean of students/designee will forward the student written notice of the date, time and place of the hearing to the respondent at least five (5) business days prior to the hearing. The respondent may waive all or part of the five (5) business days written notice requirement. All waivers shall be executed in writing.

2. Prior to a hearing in cases which may involve suspension or expulsion the respondent is entitled to the following:

   a. A written notice of the charge including possible sanctions will be sent via email.

   b. Review of all available information, documents and exhibits.

   c. A list of witnesses that may testify against him/her.

   d. An outline of student rights.

   e. A formal hearing date scheduled no less than ten (10) business days after the respondent receives notice of the referral, unless the respondent waives the limit and agrees to an earlier hearing date. Waivers are voluntary and must be in writing and signed by the respondent and the dean/designee.

   f. In cases that may result in expulsion, the written notice will specify that expulsion precludes matriculation at any UNC constituent institution.

3. Reasonable extensions of time for either party to prepare for the hearing may be allowed.

4. The dean of students/designee shall:

   a. set the date, time and place for the hearing.

   b. summon university witnesses and prepare evidence for each hearing.

   c. notify the respondent in writing via e-mail of the following:

      i. the date, time and place for the hearing - the letter shall specify a hearing date not less than five (5) business days after the official notice is sent.

      ii. the names of witnesses who may testify against the respondent.

      iii. the charges against him/her.

      iv. the dean of students/designee may question a student testifying in the respondent's behalf or question the respondent if he/she testifies in his/her own behalf.

     v. if the student charged is a minor (under 18 years of age), a copy of the letter may be sent to his/her parent or guardian.

     vi. if a student chooses to present witness testimony at an administrative hearing it is the student's responsibility to notify their witness(es) of the day, time and location of the hearing.

5. Additionally, a list of witnesses and copies of any documentary evidence must be presented to the Office of the Dean of Students at least two business days prior to the hearing.

6. If a respondent fails, without good cause, to comply with the letter sent under this section, the dean of students/designee may proceed with the hearing in the respondent's absence, as has been outlined.

7. A final administrative decision will normally be determined immediately, but must be determined within ten (10) business days after the date of the hearing. The decision of hearing form will be presented to the respondent in writing within five (5) business days of the decision.

I-8 STUDENT ACADEMIC HONOR BOARD

The Student Academic Honor Board ("Board)" is activated when a student requests a hearing before the Board or if a case is referred automatically by the dean of students/designee. The associate vice chancellor for student affairs or designee serves as the advisor to the Board.

When hearing a case involving an undergraduate student, the Board shall be comprised of four (4) undergraduates and two (2) faculty members. One of the two faculty members must come from a different UNCW college or school than that in which the infraction occurred, as referred by the academic dean and appointed by the Office of the Dean of Students. A fully comprised board constitutes a quorum.

When hearing a case involving a graduate student, the Board shall be comprised of four (4) graduate students from the current Graduate Student Association or assigned by the Graduate School, one (1) faculty member from the Campus Conduct Board, and one (1) additional faculty member appointed by the Dean of the Graduate School. A fully comprised board constitutes a quorum.

The dean of students or designee will select and train Board members and those that will serve as chairs.

No member of the hearing body who has a personal interest in the particular case may sit in judgment during the proceeding. If a member refuses to recuse him/herself due to a conflict of interest, the dean of students/designee will make the excusal decision. The respondent will also be given the opportunity to challenge a committee member or official on these grounds.

In such cases in which a member cannot serve due to a conflict of interest, a temporary member may be appointed by the vice chancellor or designee to serve for the duration of the hearing.

A. JURISDICTION OF THE STUDENT ACADEMIC HONOR BOARD

The Board may have, at the request of a respondent or the dean of students/designee, original jurisdiction in student academic honor code cases.

B. PRELIMINARY INFORMATION FOR STUDENT ACADEMIC HONOR BOARD HEARING

1. If a student requests a Board hearing, the dean/designee will forward written notice of the date, time and place of the hearing to the respondent at least five (5) business days prior to the hearing. The respondent may waive all or part of the five (5) business days written notice requirement. All waivers shall be executed in writing.
2. Prior to a hearing in cases which may involve suspension or expulsion the respondent is entitled to the following:
   a. A written notice of the charge including possible sanctions.
   b. Review of all available information, documents, exhibits.
   c. A list of witnesses that may testify against him/her.
      i. An outline of student rights.
      ii. A formal hearing date scheduled no less than ten (10) business days after the respondent receives notice of the referral, unless the respondent waives the limit and agrees to an earlier hearing date. Waivers are voluntary and must be in writing and signed by the respondent and the dean/designee.
      iii. In cases that may result in expulsion, the written notice will specify that expulsion precludes matriculation at any UNC constituent institution.
      iv. Written notice will be sent via e-mail.
3. Reasonable extensions of time for either party to prepare for the hearing may be allowed.
4. The dean of students/designee shall:
   a. set the date, time and place for the hearing.
   b. summon university witnesses and prepare evidence for each hearing.
   c. notify the respondent in writing (pursuant to Section I-C-3) of the following:
      i. the date, time and place for the hearing - the letter shall specify a hearing date not less than five (5) business days after the official notice is sent.
      ii. the name of the person appointed to serve as chairperson of SAHB.
      iii. the names of witnesses who may testify against the respondent.
      iv. the charges against him/her.
      v. the dean of students/designee may question a student testifying in the
      vi. respondent's behalf or question the respondent if he/she testifies in his/her own behalf.
      vii. if the student charged is a minor (under 18 years of age), a copy of the letter may be sent to his/her parent or guardian.
      viii. A respondent may request in writing that an earlier date be set, if feasible. Reasonable extensions of time for either party to prepare for the hearing may be allowed. Board, with good cause, may postpone or continue the hearing and notify all interested persons of the new
      ix. hearing date, time and place.

If a student chooses to present witness testimony at a Board hearing it is the student's responsibility to notify their witness(es) of the date, time and location of the hearing. Additionally, a list of witnesses and copies of any documentary evidence must be presented to the Office of the Dean of Students at least two (2) business days prior to the hearing.

If a respondent fails, without good cause, to comply with the letter sent under this section, the dean of students/designee may proceed with the hearing in the respondent's absence, as has been outlined.

C. STUDENT ACADEMIC HONOR BOARD HEARING PROCEDURES

The Student Academic Honor Board shall proceed generally as follows during the hearing:

1. Board chairperson states the hearing is closed to the public.
2. The chairperson of informs the respondent of his/her rights as listed in Section I-5-B, and asks the respondent whether he/she agrees or disagrees to the charge(s).
3. The dean of students/designee presents the university's case and may call witnesses. The instructor alleging the violation will be asked to speak at this time.
4. The respondent and the Board may question the university, the instructor alleging the violation and/or each witness called.
5. The respondent presents his/her case and may call any witnesses they have present.
6. The university and the Board may question the respondent and/or each witness called.
7. The dean of students/designee and the respondent present rebuttal evidence and final statements. Both the dean of students/designee and the respondent may make closing statements.
8. The Board deliberates in a closed session and decides the issue of responsible or not responsible for each charge.
9. If the Board finds the respondent not responsible for all charges, the hearing is concluded.
10. If the Board finds the respondent responsible, the dean of students/designee will indicate whether the student has any prior findings of responsibility for academic or non-academic conduct violations.
11. If the Board finds the respondent responsible for one or more charges, the dean of students/designee and respondent may present evidence and argument on an appropriate sanction.
12. The Board deliberates in a closed session and determines an appropriate sanction.
13. The Board renders a written decision as to whether they find the respondent responsible or not responsible for the charge(s). The decision states the sanction, if any, and procedures for appeal. The respondent and dean of students/designee shall each be given a copy of the decision. A final Board decision will normally be determined immediately but must be determined within ten (10) business days after the date of the hearing. The final decision, containing a brief summary of the evidence, will be presented to the respondent in writing. This will generally occur immediately following the hearing, however may take up to five (5) business days.
14. The student conduct file is confidential and consists of:
    a. the original referral.
    b. all correspondence directed to the respondent.
    c. all material presented to, or considered by the Board.
    d. the official decision of hearing.
    e. appeal documentation submitted, if any.

Student Academic Honor Board records are maintained in the Office of the Dean of Students and are confidential. They may be released only with the consent of the student involved or as outlined in Family Educational Rights and Privacy Act. A written record of the proceedings and action taken will be filed in the Office of the Dean of Students.

I-9 APPEAL PROCEDURES

The respondent may request an appeal within two (2) business days after notification of the original decision. Notification is defined as the date the decision is given to the respondent in person, or the date stamp of the email sent to the respondent. Such petition shall be submitted to the Office of the Dean of Students and explain in detail the reason(s) for the student's appeal. Original sanctions are normally put into effect only after an appellate decision has been made or the timeline for appeal has expired.

The provost/designee shall serve as the designated appeal officer for all Student Academic Honor Board cases.

The function of the provost/designee in hearing an appeal is that of reviewing the action of the Student Academic Honor Board to determine if:

a. an alleged violation of the rights guaranteed the respondent has occurred;
b. the sanction is too severe for the violation; or
c. new evidence has developed which has bearing on the outcome.

Upon receiving a petition, the provost/designee shall obtain the record of the Student Academic Honor Board/administrative hearing officer. The record shall include relevant documents, the decision of hearing including a case summary and rationale for supporting the decision. With this information, the provost/designee shall decide whether an Appellate Review is warranted. This decision is based on one or more of the three options for an appeal outlined above. The respondent will be notified in writing of the decision within ten (10) business days after receipt of the petition. Reasonable extensions of time are permissible.

If the provost/designee determines that an Appellate Review shall be granted, that Review shall be held within ten (10) business days of such determination and notification shall be given in writing at least three (3) business days prior to the date set for the Review, specifying time and place of the Review and informing the respondent of his/her rights as outlined herein.

The provost/designee will review all written correspondence associated with the case, may request additional documents and information from the student hearing chair who presided over the student board that heard the case, and may invite the respondent, the chair, and such other persons as deemed appropriate to appear to make statements and respond to questions.

The provost/designee has the authority to approve, reject or modify the decision in question or to remand the case back to the Board. For cases that do not result in suspension or expulsion, the decision of the provost/designee is final.

Consistent with Section 502 D(3) of the UNC Policy Manual, where the sanction is suspension or expulsion, an appeal may be made to the Board of Trustees for an individual student conduct case (not campus organizations), provided the appeal is based on 1) violation of due process; or 2) a material deviation from Substantive and Procedural Standards adopted by the Board of Governors. For suspension level cases, the appeal to the Board of Trustees is final; for expulsion level cases, a final appeal may be filed with the Board of Governors.

I-10 EXPEDITED REVIEW

The provost or designee, at his/her sole discretion, shall have the right to order an expedited review of the student's case. In such circumstances, the provost or designee shall sit as a hearing officer in lieu of the Board or the dean of students. This expedited hearing procedure shall be used only in emergency circumstances as identified by the provost or designee at his/her sole discretion. The decision of the provost/designee in such expedited proceedings is final unless the outcome is suspension or expulsion. Consistent with Section 502 D(3) of the UNC Policy Manual, where the sanction is suspension or expulsion, an appeal may be made to the Board of Trustees for an individual conduct case, provided the appeal is based on 1) violation of due process; or 2) a material deviation from Substantive and Procedural Standards adopted by the Board of Governors. For suspension level cases, the appeal to the Board of Trustees is final; for expulsion level cases, a final appeal may be filed with the Board of Governors.

I-11 AUTHORIZED DISCIPLINARY SANCTIONS

The outcome of a Board hearing is either a "responsible" or "not responsible" decision. If the student is found "responsible" for the charge, penalties shall be imposed according to the severity of the offense and made in consideration of whether it is the student's first offense. The sanction of disciplinary probation is typical for a first Honor Code offense, although the sanction of suspension may be assigned. The appropriate sanction for any student proven to be a repeat offender is suspension from UNCW. Authority to determine the course grade resides with the instructor; however, an assigned grade of "F" for the course is generally appropriate for an Honor Code offense. The assigned grade of "F" to a graduate student will result in ineligibility to continue in the Graduate School.

If the Board or Office of the Dean of Students finds the student not responsible for the charge, the instructor will ensure fair treatment of the student.

A. LEVELS OF UNIVERSITY DISCIPLINARY SANCTIONS

Written Warning – is a status of warning through the end of the next full semester, which terminates automatically when the imposed period expires.

Disciplinary Probation – is a status of probation for up to one calendar year, which terminates automatically when the imposed period expires. A student who is placed on disciplinary probation is considered not to be in good standing with the university.

As part of disciplinary probation, the student may have restrictions placed on specific student privileges, as determined by the hearing body or administrative hearing officer, not to exceed the duration of the probationary period. In the event of a further violation of this Code or other applicable rules while on disciplinary probation, the university will seek the penalty of suspension or expulsion.

Suspension - Suspension is withdrawal of enrollment privileges and cancellation of registration, at a minimum, through the end of the next full semester, and carries with it conditions which must be met for re-enrollment. All suspended or expelled students must meet with the dean of students or designee to make clear the terms of their suspension or expulsion from the university. Re-enrollment after a suspension period requires that the student apply to the dean of students at the close of the imposed period, and the dean will determine whether the student has met the conditions imposed and is otherwise eligible for re-enrollment. A denial may be appealed to the Committee on Extraordinary Disciplinary Emergencies.

During the term of suspension, the student may not come onto campus. Failure to abide by this condition may result in arrest for criminal trespassing.

A student who is suspended after the deadline for withdrawal with a "W" shall be assigned a grade of "WF" or "W" by each instructor based upon the academic performance prior to the suspension.

A sanction of suspension requires that the student's name be added to the UNC Suspension/Expulsion Database.

Expulsion – is the permanent dismissal of a student from the university, and it precludes matriculation at any UNC constituent institution, unless and until the chancellor who imposed or approved the sanction or his/her successor concludes on the basis of the former student's petition and any supportive documentation that the individual should be given a new opportunity to pursue higher education within the UNC system. The student will be trespassed from university property for as long as the individual is considered a risk to others or to university property. Expulsion will result in a permanent transcript notation.

The chancellor or vice chancellor for student affairs may impose the sanction of expulsion. A sanction of expulsion requires that the student's name be added to the UNC Suspension/Expulsion Database.

I-12 DISCIPLINARY RECORDS

The hearing record, notice of appeal and each petition for review are confidential and may not be disclosed in whole or part except as provided in Section III-4. This disciplinary record shall be separate from the student's academic record but shall be considered a part of the student's educational record and maintained in the Office of the Dean of Students.

A student who is suspended or expelled will have a "hold" placed on their registration file by the dean of students/designee. The "hold" will be removed when the term of suspension expires and/or conditions for re-enrollment have been met.

A notation of suspension or expulsion will be placed on the transcript as "Honor Code Suspension" for Honor Code withdrawals. The student's name will also be permanently added to UNC suspension/expulsion database.

Records for cases not resulting in suspension or expulsion will be destroyed one year after graduation.

I-13 SPECIAL PROVISIONS STUDENTS WITH DISABILITIES

When a student with a documented disability is charged with an offense, and informs the Office of the Dean of Students of such status, the university will assure that all requirements of Section 504 of the Rehabilitation Act and the Americans with Disabilities Act are met.

WITHDRAWALS

Once a student is alleged to have violated the Student Academic Honor Code, the student will be prohibited from withdrawing from the course. Should a student withdraw from the class, the grade of "W" will be considered temporary pending the final resolution of the case, which may lead to the designation of a grade in place of the "W".

REPEATS

A failing grade posted as a penalty for an admitted or adjudicated Honor Code offense shall not be replaced if the course is repeated. Both the penalty grade and the new grade shall appear on the student's transcript and count in the student's grade point average.

BECOME A SKILL SEEKER

How to Develop Skills Sought By Employers

Year after year, regardless of job market conditions, employers have a similar wish list for candidates' skills and qualities. Below is a list distilled from employer surveys published by eminent national associations, universities and research groups.[1] Listed below each skill are some opportunities to explore and develop that particular skill or behavior. Use these suggestions to create your own powerful set of skills while at UNCW-- in and out of the classroom. These career readiness competencies will increase your marketability for internships, jobs and graduate school.

The number one way to develop any of these skills is through becoming a student leader or peer educator on campus![2]

1. *Communication Skills- oral & written*
- Write stories, advertisements, press releases or newsletters for Student Media, or a campus or community organization
- Enroll in an academic class that is writing intensive, or includes presentations or speeches
- Work in a campus office; i.e. at an information desk, or in an operations or program assistant position
- Improve the way you listen to others; use empathy and self-control when diffusing disagreements
- Refine your job search materials (resume, cover letter, interview preparation) at the Career Center
- Act with a theater group, film or broadcast production
- Do fundraising for charities or nonprofit events; volunteer to work on a political campaign
- Help in a literacy or conversational English program

2. *Interpersonal Skills- relates well to others, self-confident, tactful, friendly, outgoing, sense of humor*
- Engage in discussions with people different from you
- Participate as an active team member in class, a campus organization, or at a job
- Live in a group living environment (on or off campus)
- Conduct interviews with people to gather information for a class project, organization or personal goal
- Volunteer for a telephone hotline, women's shelter, after school program, hospital, nursing home, etc.

- Work as a tutor, coach, camp counselor, mentor, literacy or conversation partner, or teacher
- Work as wait staff, info desk assistant, office or retail staff, recreation assistant, customer service staff, etc.
- Become a personal assistant for an individual with disabilities
- Develop interpersonal skills in classes that emphasize human relationships or intercultural issues

3. *Teamwork Skills- works well with others, flexible, adaptable, collaborative*

- Lead a project team or committee in class, a student organization or job
- Use an internship, study group, class or research project to help turn a group of people into a team with common goals
- Help a new team develop through the stages of forming, storming, norming and performing
- Join a musical group or act in a play
- Participate on intramural team or sports club, coach Little League, become a summer camp counselor or recreational leader
- Contribute as a valuable member of a team focusing on team goals more than personal goals

4. *Initiative- strong work ethic, professional, risk-taker, work ethically and with integrity, entrepreneur*

- Identify a campus or community need and proactively find and implement solutions
- Select a skill which you would like to improve, and seek out experiences which help you achieve that goal
- Appropriately balance academics, co-curricular activities and employment
- Solicit strong instructor/supervisor references from academic, co-curricular or employment activity
- Take pride in your work
- Study abroad; interact with other cultures
- Start your own business while in college

5. *Critical Thinking Skills- analytical, problem-solver, detail-oriented, organized, creative, strategic planner*

- Participate in undergraduate research with a faculty member
- Work as a lab assistant with computers, science or language
- Organize a campus event, including volunteer staff, budget, publicity, etc.
- Seek opportunities to evaluate data to support decision making
- Manage your time well; meet deadlines
- Take a topic you are passionate about, and research the opposing view
- Read an article in an academic area different from your own and develop implications for your area
- Develop a decision tree for an upcoming purchase, researching all relevant information (brand, model, size, etc.)
- Develop a three-year strategic plan for a student organization
- When considering a difficult decision, appraise your choices realistically and seek professional advice when appropriate

6. *Leadership Skills- communicate vision, action orientated, influence/motivate others, enthusiastic*

- Gain leadership education and experience through the Office of Student Leadership & Engagement, the Cameron School of Business or a Leadership Studies minor
- Run a campaign for student government or campus issue; or get involved in local or state politics
- Be an active officer or committee chair of a campus organization
- Identify a campus or community need and proactively find and implement solutions
- Facilitate group discussions in class or in a campus organization
- Organize and manage an intramural sports team, camp or recreation group
- Lead children's programs, tutor kids in a local school, or coach a children's sports team
- Get an internship in an area of career interest; consult with the Career Center and your department's internship coordinator
- Train new campus organization members or employees at your job

7. *Technical Skills- utilize computer software & hardware, web and financial resources*

- Work as a student network or computer lab consultant with Residence Life or ITS
- Design or maintain web sites for a student or community organization, campus office or yourself
- Design a brochure, advertisement or newsletter using desktop publishing software
- Assist community agencies with databases, statistical analyses, financial or service reports
- Keep budgets or financial records for campus or community organizations, or work in a billing office
- Design PowerPoint presentation for class or a campus organization
- Work as a tech or projectionist in Campus Life
- Sell computer hardware or software, or start a web-based business
- Work in the studio or control room of a radio or TV station
- Learn computer and technical skills in classes and workshops that focus on software programs and applying technology

For More Information

Become a Skill Seeker ©	http://www.uncw.edu/career/documents/beaskillseeker.pdf
Student Organizations	http://uncw.edu/studentorgs/
Jobs & Internships	www.myseawork.com

UNCW CAREER CENTER	Career Center • Division of Student Affairs *Creating Experiences for Life* Fisher University Union 2035 * 910.962.3174 careercenter@uncw.edu • www.uncw.edu/career

Rev. Dec. 2015

UNIVERSITY STUDIES REQUIREMENTS

2017-2018

FOUNDATIONS

COMPOSITION	3-6 HR
LIFETIME WELLNESS	2 HR
MATHEMATICS & STATISTICS	3 HR
FOREIGN LANGUAGE	3-6 HR
FIRST YEAR SEMINAR	3 HR

BUILDING COMPETENCIES

WRITING INTENSIVE	9 HR
INFORMATION LITERACY	9 HR
CRITICAL REASONING	3 HR

EXPLORATIONS BEYOND THE CLASSROOM

1 APPROVED EXPERIENCE

APPROACHES & PERSPECTIVES

AESTHETIC, INTERPRETIVE, LITERARY	6 HR
HISTORICAL & PHILOSOPHICAL	6 HR
SCIENTIFIC APPROACHES	7 HR
HUMAN INSTITUTIONS & BEHAVIORS	6 HR
LIVING IN OUR DIVERSE NATION	3 HR
LIVING IN A GLOBAL SOCIETY	3 HR

RULES TO REMEMBER:

Foundations

Foreign Language proficiency through 201 level (102 level in language not previously studied)

Building Competencies

At least 3 hours at 300-400 hour level for WI

At least 3 hours in the major for WI and IL

Approaches & Perspectives

No more than 3 hours (4 for SANW) from any one discipline

Scientific Approaches requires one lab course

Only ONE course can double-count for LDN or LGS and another Approach & Perspective

Visit our website for further details:
www.uncw.edu/universitystudies

INFORMATION LITERACY VALUE RUBRIC

for more information, please contact value@aacu.org

Association of American Colleges and Universities

The VALUE rubrics were developed by teams of faculty experts representing colleges and universities across the United States through a process that examined many existing campus rubrics and related documents for each learning outcome and incorporated additional feedback from faculty. The rubrics articulate fundamental criteria for each learning outcome, with performance descriptors demonstrating progressively more sophisticated levels of attainment. The rubrics are intended for institutional-level use in evaluating and discussing student learning, not for grading. The core expectations articulated in all 15 of the VALUE rubrics can and should be translated into the language of individual campuses, disciplines, and even courses. The utility of the VALUE rubrics is to position learning at all undergraduate levels within a basic framework of expectations such that evidence of learning can by shared nationally through a common dialog and understanding of student success. In July 2013, there was a correction to Dimension 3: Evaluate Information and its Sources Critically.

Definition

The ability to know when there is a need for information, to be able to identify, locate, evaluate, and effectively and responsibly use and share that information for the problem at hand. -Adopted from the National Forum on Information Literacy

Framing Language

This rubric is recommended for use evaluating a collection of work, rather than a single work sample in order to fully gauge students' information skills. Ideally, a collection of work would contain a wide variety of different types of work and might include: research papers, editorials, speeches, grant proposals, marketing or business plans, PowerPoint presentations, posters, literature reviews, position papers, and argument critiques to name a few. In addition, a description of the assignments with the instructions that initiated the student work would be vital in providing the complete context for the work. Although a student's final work must stand on its own, evidence of a student's research and information gathering processes, such

	Capstone	Milestones		Benchmark
Use Information Effectively to Accomplish a Specific Purpose	Communicates, organizes and synthesizes information from sources to fully achieve a specific purpose, with clarity and depth	Communicates, organizes and synthesizes information from sources. Intended purpose is achieved.	Communicates and organizes information from sources. The information is not yet synthesized, so the intended purpose is not fully achieved.	Communicates information from sources. The information is fragmented and/or used inappropriately (misquoted, taken out of context, or incorrectly paraphrased, etc.), so the intended purpose is not achieved.
Access and Use Information Ethically and Legally	Students use correctly all of the following information use strategies (use of citations and references; choice of paraphrasing, summary, or quoting; using information in ways that are true to original context; distinguishing between common knowledge and ideas requiring attribution) and demonstrate a full understanding of the ethical and legal restrictions on the use of published, confidential, and/or proprietary information.	Students use correctly three of the following information use strategies (use of citations and references; choice of paraphrasing, summary, or quoting; using information in ways that are true to original context; distinguishing between common knowledge and ideas requiring attribution) and demonstrates a full understanding of the ethical and legal restrictions on the use of published, confidential, and/or proprietary information.	Students use correctly two of the following information use strategies (use of citations and references; choice of paraphrasing, summary, or quoting; using information in ways that are true to original context; distinguishing between common knowledge and ideas requiring attribution) and demonstrates a full understanding of the ethical and legal restrictions on the use of published, confidential, and/or proprietary information.	Students use correctly one of the following information use strategies (use of citations and references; choice of paraphrasing, summary, or quoting; using information in ways that are true to original context; distinguishing between common knowledge and ideas requiring attribution) and demonstrates a full understanding of the ethical and legal restrictions on the use of published, confidential, and/or proprietary information.

Corrected Dimension 3: Evaluate Information and its Sources Critically in July 2013

CRITICAL THINKING VALUE RUBRIC

for more information, please contact value@aacu.org

Association of American Colleges and Universities

The VALUE rubrics were developed by teams of faculty experts representing colleges and universities across the United States through a process that examined many existing campus rubrics and related documents for each learning outcome and incorporated additional feedback from faculty. The rubrics articulate fundamental criteria for each learning outcome, with performance descriptors demonstrating progressively more sophisticated levels of attainment. The rubrics are intended for institutional-level use in evaluating and discussing student learning, not for grading The core expectations articulated in all 15 of the VALUE rubrics can and should be translated into the language of individual campuses, disciplines, and even courses. The utility of the VALUE rubrics is to position learning at all undergraduate levels within a basic framework of expectations such that evidence of learning can by shared nationally through a common dialog and understanding of student success.

Definition

Critical thinking is a habit of mind characterized by the comprehensive exploration of issues, ideas, artifacts, and events before accepting or formulating an opinion or conclusion.

Framing Language

This rubric is designed to be transdisciplinary, reflecting the recognition that success in all disciplines requires habits of inquiry and analysis that share common attributes. Further, research suggests that successful critical thinkers from all disciplines increasingly need to be able to apply those habits in various and changing situations encountered in all walks of life.

This rubric is designed for use with many different types of assignments and the suggestions here are not an exhaustive list of possibilities. Critical thinking can be demonstrated in assignments that require students to complete analyses of text, data, or issues. Assignments that cut across presentation mode might be especially useful in some fields. If insight into the process components of critical thinking (e.g, how information sources were evaluated regardless of whether they were included in the product) is important, assignments focused on student reflection might be especially illuminating

---

Glossary

The definitions that follow were developed to clarify terms and concepts used in this rubric only.

- Ambiguity: Information that may be interpreted in more than one way.
- Assumptions: Ideas, conditions, or beliefs (often implicit or unstated) that are "taken for granted or accepted as true without proof." (quoted from www .dictionary.reference.com/browse/assumptions)
- Context: The historical, ethical, political, cultural, environmental, or circumstantial settings or conditions that influence and complicate the consideration of any issues, ideas, artifacts, and events.
- Literal meaning: Interpretation of information exactly as stated. For example, "she was green with envy" would be interpreted to mean that her skin was green.
- Metaphor: Information that is (intended to be) interpreted in a non-literal way. For example," she was green with envy" is intended to convey an intensity of emotion, not a skin color.

Definition

Critical thinking is a habit of mind characterized by the comprehensive exploration of issues, ideas, artifacts, and events before accepting or formulating an opinion or conclusion.

---

[1] The assigned grade of "F" to a graduate student will result in ineligibility to continue in the Graduate School.

[1] Sources include the National Association of Colleges & Employers (NACE), Michigan State University, University of Illinois at Urbana-Champaign, Hart Research Associates, Career-Builder, US News & World Report, World Future Society, American Society for Training & Development and the U.S. Department of Labor.

[2] Campus leadership and peer educator positions include Resident Assistant, Orientation Leader, Ambassador, Seahawk Link, ACE, Fraternity & Sorority Life, SGA/GSA, Office of Student Leadership & Engagement, CARE/Crossroads, Health Promotion and the University Learning Center.

Evaluators are encouraged to assign a zero to any work sample or collection of work that does not meet benchmark (cell one) level performance.

	Capstone	Milestones		Benchmark
	4	3	2	1
Explanation of issues	Issue/problem to be considered critically is stated clearly and described comprehensively, delivering all relevant information necessary for full understanding.	Issue/problem to be considered critically is stated, described, and clarified so that understanding is not seriously impeded by omissions.	Issue/problem to be considered critically is stated but description leaves some terms undefined, ambiguities unexplored, boundaries undetermined, and/or backgrounds unknown.	Issue/problem to be considered critically is stated without clarification or description.
Evidence *Selecting and using information to investigate a point of view or conclusion*	Information is taken from source(s) with enough interpretation/evaluation to develop a comprehensive analysis or synthesis.	Information is taken from source(s) with enough interpretation/evaluation to develop a coherent analysis or synthesis. Viewpoints of experts are subject to questioning.	Information is taken from source(s) with some interpretation/evaluation, but not enough to develop a coherent analysis or synthesis. Viewpoints of experts are taken as mostly fact, with little questioning.	Information is taken from source(s) without any interpretation/evaluation. Viewpoints of experts are taken as fact, without question.
Influence of context and assumptions	Thoroughly (systematically and methodically) analyzes own and others' assumptions and carefully evaluates the relevance of contexts when presenting a position.	Identifies own and others' assumptions and several relevant contexts when presenting a position.	Questions some assumptions. Identifies several relevant contexts when presenting a position. Maybe more aware of others' assumptions than one's own (or vice versa).	Shows an emerging awareness of present assumptions (sometimes labels assertions as assumptions). Begins to identify some contexts when presenting a position.

	Capstone	Milestones		Benchmark
Student's position (perspective, thesis/hypothesis)	Specific position (perspective, thesis/hypothesis) is imaginative, taking into account the complexities of an issue. Limits of position (perspective, thesis/hypothesis) are acknowledged. Others' points of view are synthesized within position (perspective, thesis/hypothesis).	Specific position (perspective, thesis/hypothesis) takes into account the complexities of an issue. Others' points of view are acknowledged within position (perspective, thesis/hypothesis).	Specific position (perspective, thesis/hypothesis) acknowledges different sides of an issue.	Specific position (perspective, thesis/hypothesis) is stated, but is simplistic and obvious.
Conclusions and related outcomes (implications and consequences)	Conclusions and related outcomes (consequences and implications) are logical and reflect student's informed evaluation and ability to place evidence and perspectives discussed in priority order.	Conclusion is logically tied to a range of information, including opposing viewpoints; related outcomes (consequences and implications) are identified clearly.	Conclusion is logically tied to information (because information is chosen to fit the desired conclusion); some related outcomes (consequences and implications) are identified clearly.	Conclusion is inconsistently tied to some of the information discussed; related outcomes (consequences and implications) are oversimplified.

CPSIA information can be obtained
at www.ICGtesting.com
Printed in the USA
LVHW01s2153100817
`44510LV00001B/1/P

9 781524 936761